Readiness Signs

- Stays dry for at least two hours.*
- Gets bummed by wet or messy diapers*
- Knows potty lingo*
- Likes to please*
- Imitates and follows simple instructions*
- Walks and runs
- Asks for diaper changes
- Tries to dress herself
- Likes things in the proper place

(*Musts for potty...

Potty-Training Steps in a Nutshell

1. Have your little doll teach her little doll how to use the potty.
2. Do hourly potty-sits throughout Potty Training Weekend.
3. Set up a Success Chart with gold stars or fun stickers for good tries and even minor successes.
4. Switch from diapers to training pants after your toilet-trainee has racked up a few successes.

Myth

Put your baby (12–1... on the potty, and sh... learn what's up.

You're the only pers... world who thinks th... potty training is a ba...

Your child's life is ru... mess up his potty tr...

Potty training is alwa... a time of conflict wit... a toddler.

Professional caregiv... experienced potty-tr... so let them train you...

DATE DUE

DEMCO, INC. 38-2931

For Dummie...   ...ginners

Potty Training For Dummies®

Cheat Sheet

Potty-Speak

Your child needs to know the meaning of:

- ✔ Wet
- ✔ Dry
- ✔ Pee
- ✔ Poop or BM
- ✔ Messy or Dirty
- ✔ Clean
- ✔ Bottom

Ways to Keep Potty Training Working

1. Take on a laid-back attitude. Your chickadee is the star, hitting his mark. You're the coach/director/teacher.

2. Back off when your child gets feisty or "no-no's" you.

3. Keep in mind that your toddler is new to the role but willing to be a winner. Just respect his learning curve.

4. Accept (and help your little miss accept) that she's not going to be perfect right off the bat. She'll drip and slip and miss — and that's okay.

5. Laugh together, clap your hands — cheer your kiddo's willingness to give it a try! Keep the praise coming, and don't scold or criticize.

Take Your Tot to the Doc When

- ✔ She hasn't had a BM in three days.
- ✔ He strains when trying to pee or poop.
- ✔ She complains that having a bowel movement hurts.
- ✔ He says peeing burns or hurts, or his pee stream is intermittent.
- ✔ She pees very seldom (every eight to nine hours).
- ✔ He has sudden urges to pee and pees frequently.
- ✔ She uses the potty regularly but has wet pants, too.
- ✔ He has blood stains on his underwear.
- ✔ She has frequent BM stains on her undies.
- ✔ He's five and still bedwetting.

Signs that S/He's Almost a Potty Pro

He tells you when he's gone in his undies.

OR

She goes to the potty chair, sits down, and tries.

OR

He has racked up a string of successful potty trips.

OR

She's proud of her superhero undies and likes them clean and dry.

Hungry Minds, the Hungry Minds logo, For Dummies, the Hungry Minds Bestselling Book Series logo and all related trade dress are registered trademarks or trademarks of Hungry Minds, Inc. All other trademarks are the property of their respective owners.

For Dummies: Bestselling Book Series for Beginners

Potty Training® FOR DUMMIES®

by Diane Stafford and Jennifer Shoquist, MD

Hungry Minds™

Best-Selling Books • Digital Downloads • e-Books • Answer Networks
e-Newsletters • Branded Web Sites • e-Learning

New York, NY ◆ Cleveland, OH ◆ Indianapolis, IN

Potty Training **For Dummies®**

Published by:
Hungry Minds, Inc.
909 Third Avenue
New York, NY 10022
www.hungryminds.com
www.dummies.com

Library of Congress Control Number: 2002103282

ISBN: 0-7645-5417-4

Printed in the United States of America

10 9 8 7 6 5 4 3 2 1

1B/QV/QW/QS/IN

Distributed in the United States by Hungry Minds, Inc.

Distributed by CDG Books Canada Inc. for Canada; by Transworld Publishers Limited in the United Kingdom; by IDG Norge Books for Norway; by IDG Sweden Books for Sweden; by IDG Books Australia Publishing Corporation Pty. Ltd. for Australia and New Zealand; by TransQuest Publishers Pte Ltd. for Singapore, Malaysia, Thailand, Indonesia, and Hong Kong; by Gotop Information Inc. for Taiwan; by ICG Muse, Inc. for Japan; by Intersoft for South Africa; by Eyrolles for France; by International Thomson Publishing for Germany, Austria and Switzerland; by Distribuidora Cuspide for Argentina; by LR International for Brazil; by Galileo Libros for Chile; by Ediciones ZETA S.C.R. Ltda. for Peru; by WS Computer Publishing Corporation, Inc., for the Philippines; by Contemporanea de Ediciones for Venezuela; by Express Computer Distributors for the Caribbean and West Indies; by Micronesia Media Distributor, Inc. for Micronesia; by Chips Computadoras S.A. de C.V. for Mexico; by Editorial Norma de Panama S.A. for Panama; by American Bookshops for Finland.

For general information on Hungry Minds' products and services please contact our Customer Care department; within the U.S. at 800-762-2974, outside the U.S. at 317-572-3993 or fax 317-572-4002.

For sales inquiries and resellers information, including discounts, premium and bulk quantity sales and foreign language translations please contact our Customer Care department at 800-434-3422, fax 317-572-4002 or write to Hungry Minds, Inc., Attn: Customer Care department, 10475 Crosspoint Boulevard, Indianapolis, IN 46256.

For information on licensing foreign or domestic rights, please contact our Sub-Rights Customer Care department at 212-884-5000.

For information on using Hungry Minds' products and services in the classroom or for ordering examination copies, please contact our Educational Sales department at 800-434-2086 or fax 317-572-4005.

Please contact our Public Relations department at 212-884-5163 for press review copies or 212-884-5000 for author interviews and other publicity information or fax 212-884-5400.

For authorization to photocopy items for corporate, personal, or educational use, please contact Copyright Clearance Center, 222 Rosewood Drive, Danvers, MA 01923, or fax 978-750-4470.

Hungry Minds is a trademark of Hungry Minds, Inc.

About the Author

Diane Stafford: Diane's writing career began when she snagged a great summer job as a speechwriter for the astronauts while she was attending college. After teaching high school journalism and English, she went on to her second career as a writer/editor, serving as editor-in-chief of *Health & Fitness Magazine, Texas Woman Magazine, Houston Home & Garden, Dallas–Fort Worth Home & Garden, Philanthropy in Texas,* and *Latin Music.* Also an entrepreneur, Stafford co-owned *Health & Fitness Magazine* and helped with startups of the magazine in New Orleans, Philadelphia, Miami, and Atlanta. She has won awards for health writing. Stafford has written hundreds of articles and now edits books for Arte Publico Press in Houston and writes books.

Diane Stafford lives with her husband, David Garrett, in Houston, where she is a well-known writer and a community volunteer for Casa de Esperanza de los Ninos and the Emergency Aid Coalition Clothes Center.

Stafford's book *Tilted Heart* comes out in 2002, as well as another book that she and Jennifer Shoquist co-authored — *No More Panic Attacks: A 30-Day Plan for Conquering Anxiety,* also slated for publication in 2002.

Jennifer Shoquist, MD: Jennifer is a family-practice physician whose interest in writing began when she was attending the High School for the Performing and Visual Arts, while also interning at *Health & Fitness Magazine* in Houston, Texas. Later, she completed her medical degree at the University of Texas Medical School at Houston, followed by family practice residency at Memorial Southwest Hospital. Today, she works in family-practice medicine and serves as a health-issues resource for journalists. She and her husband, Robert San Luis, live in Houston with two shih-tzus, Lucy and Sophie. Their family will soon expand with the birth of a child, due in September 2002, a baby destined for an over-the-top potty-training extravaganza. Jennifer and Robert are both avid fitness enthusiasts.

Dedication

We dedicate this to parents and caregivers who potty train with TLC because they know how important it is to show children that we love them every single day of their lives. And, we dedicate this book to all the kids who inspire us with their fresh way of looking at the world, and remind us to keep the child in each of us alive. Kudos to our family tykes and tots — Xanthe, Cameron, Lindsay, Jack, Sam, Sidney. And, to those we were once "little people" alongside: Allen, Camilla, Austin, Fletcher, Shari, Amber. Shih-tzus Lucy and Sophie also deserve their share of the credit.

Authors' Acknowledgments

This great project came our way thanks to the efforts of our incredible literary agent — Elizabeth Frost-Knappman of New England Publishing Associates, whose energy and optimism and warmth make everything more fun. She introduced us to Project Editor Kathleen Dobie and Acquisitions Editor Natasha Graf, both of Hungry Minds, who worked hard to bring the book to fruition. Kathleen proves that amazing things can be communicated via e-mail. She's such a gem to work with, and we thank her for being so patient and helpful; so gifted with super-word skills; and so generous with compassion. Natasha was always quick with answers, encouragement, and publishing expertise. Rob Annis also merits a pat on the back for his skillful copyediting.

Thanks to our wonderful friends and family who cheered and shared: David Nordin, Gina Bradley, Sarah Shoquist, Richard Pierce, Britt Pierce, Chris Fleming, Dot and Laurens Horstman, Eddi Lee, Christina Shirley, Joanne Goldstein, Cari LaGrange, Donna Pate, Jami Exner, Fred Aguilar, M.D., Dana Chandler, Wendy Corson, Shannon and John Mathis, Christy Waites, Liz Lemaster, Kristina Holt, Tweetie Garrett, Martha Steele, Michele Fisher. For helping us know what matters, we thank the folks at Emergency Aid Coalition Clothes Center, and the little children at Casa de Esperanza (and all the angels who work with them), and the big kids at South Houston High.

From Diane

Deep appreciation goes to my husband, David Garrett, who gives
me friendship and love. My loving thanks goes to my daughter,
Jenny, who has made my life wonderful. Her good heart and sweet-
ness are unparalleled. Also, my thanks to her husband, Robert,
who is always supportive. For everything I know about loving ways
to nurture kids, I thank my wonderful daddy, Clinton Shirley, and
my beloved mother, Belle Shirley, who parented so beautifully, and
gave all children — and all people — compassion and respect.

From Jennifer

I want to thank my amazing husband, Robert San Luis, for all of
his love and support, and my wonderful mom for her constant
love. I also thank my sweet dad Martin Shoquist, Dr. Leticia Carlos
San Luis, Dr. Tom and Gina Cartwright, and Lina Carlos. To my
friends and patients, I send love and best wishes for positive potty-
training days.

Publisher's Acknowledgments

We're proud of this book; please send us your comments through our Hungry Minds Online Registration Form located at www.dummies.com.

Some of the people who helped bring this book to market include the following:

Acquisitions, Editorial, and Media Development

Project Editor: Kathleen A. Dobie

Associate Acquisitions Editor: Natasha Graf

Copy Editor: Robert Annis

Technical Editor: Beth Ann Martin, MD

Senior Permissions Editor: Carmen Krikorian

Editorial Manager: Christine Meloy Beck

Media Development Manager: Laura VanWinkle

Editorial Assistant: Melissa Bennett

Production

Project Coordinator: Dale White

Layout and Graphics: Stephanie Jumper, Brent Savage, Jeremey Unger, Mary J. Virgin

Proofreaders: John Greenough, Angel Perez, Linda Quigley, TECHBOOKS Production Services

Indexer: TECHBOOKS Production Services

General and Administrative

Hungry Minds Consumer Reference Group

Business: Kathleen Nebenhaus, Vice President and Publisher; Kevin Thornton, Acquisitions Manager

Cooking/Gardening: Jennifer Feldman, Associate Vice President and Publisher; Anne Ficklen, Executive Editor; Kristi Hart, Managing Editor

Education/Reference: Diane Graves Steele, Vice President and Publisher

Lifestyles: Kathleen Nebenhaus, Vice President and Publisher; Tracy Boggier, Managing Editor

Pets: Kathleen Nebenhaus, Vice President and Publisher; Tracy Boggier, Managing Editor

Travel: Michael Spring, Vice President and Publisher; Brice Gosnell, Publishing Director; Suzanne Jannetta, Editorial Director

Hungry Minds Consumer Editorial Services: Kathleen Nebenhaus, Vice President and Publisher; Kristin A. Cocks, Editorial Director; Cindy Kitchel, Editorial Director

Hungry Minds Consumer Production: Debbie Stailey, Production Director

◆

Contents at a Glance

Cartoons at a Glance

By Rich Tennant

page 67

page 209

page 7

page 45

page 141

page 117

Cartoon Information:
Fax: 978-546-7747
E-Mail: richtennant@the5thwave.com
World Wide Web: www.the5thwave.com

Table of Contents

Introduction

• •

Sure, you can be a potty guru. Spend a little time with *Potty Training For Dummies,* and you'll be ready to handle anything in the Mad, Mad World of Potty Deeds — the absurd toilet-paper fiascos, the nudity-cult behavior, the tinkle terrors, the poo-poo bribes. Even getting prepped for the process can make you nervous.

That's why it's important to have terrific ideas — and psychic insight into what your kiddo's thinking right now. If he could talk like a big person, he'd say, "Learning how to do the potty stuff will be tough, but with your help, I can pull it off."

So, who cares if you're second-guessing yourself. That's natural — potty training can be intimidating. Truth is, most parents and caregivers are baffled by old wives' tales and conflicting potty advice and the endless chances to mess this up.

This book sets you straight about what's true and what's misinformation, what works and what may gum up the works, in an easy, breezy style you and your tiny tot can relate to.

About This Book

You can't help but look at that cute little biscuit and wonder how in the world you'll ever manage to fill his brain with toilet talking points and still stay super-close with him. You stare at his new potty chair and wonder if he'll use it for a toy box or a candy depository. You also wonder what he'll say when you tell him, "Hey, tiny tot, put your poop and pee right in there."

With this book, we make you a potty-training pro. We hand you knowledge and confidence and potty procedures. We share scads of tips and best-kept secrets for rookie parents and novice caregivers, as well as veterans in both categories. You also get helpful Web sites, potty-chair ratings, cool potty videos and books, as well as lots of reassuring stuff on what's normal in the way of accidents and kooky behavior. We encourage and prepare you. We think of everything — even surefire lines to motivate your youngster.

You'll be totally ready when training day comes, because you're packing *Potty Training For Dummies.* Don't worry your pretty head because we answer all the pressing questions that parents and caregivers want answers to:

✔ What's the secret to kicking off potty training on the right foot?

✔ How can you make sure your toddler is really ready?

✔ What gives better results — extreme structure or wild freeform?

✔ Should you include some fun parts along the way to snag his attention?

✔ Can you trust all the advice that relatives and friends give you?

✔ Is it possible to pull this off in a single day?

✔ What's the best response if your child says "no way!" when you tell him it's potty-training time?

Clearly, you need a plan. While we're not here to tell you to buy an amulet for good luck, or to sprinkle your home with Indian rattle-balls that get rid of evil spirits, we do know the truth — that your child's interpretation of this experience will be as uniquely his own as his eye color, skin type, and temperament.

Meanwhile, check out all of the things that *Potty Training For Dummies* can do for you:

✔ **Help you let your child "own" the potty experience:** This is her deal, not yours. Little Nicole will lead you; you won't steamroll her. You can lead your child to the toilet, but you can't make her use it!

✔ **Foster a team approach:** You rally the troops together for supporting toddler Juan's efforts. You're already being bombarded with advice, but you can use your potty savvy to extract the best from helper-bees.

✔ **Separate fact from fiction:** For example, it's fiction that your child is ruined if you show any signs of frustration during potty training. But it's fact that your actions during these formative first years of life absolutely impact your child's quality of life in a major way.

✔ **Keep you focused on the goal — helping your child feel good about himself:** It doesn't matter if he piddles on the bed. Or acts like a budding pervert. Or turns his poop-pushing dramatics into a comedy act. He's your doll-baby, and he's doing his best.

✔ **Show you how to potty train solo:** Thank goodness, to make this work, you don't need an entourage. Or a personal trainer. You won't need to ask "your people" to talk to "his people." You'll keep potty training simple and lighthearted and fanciful, and your child will learn to use the potty in his own sweet time.

✔ **Boost your enthusiasm and attitude:** Truly, a toddler's natural playfulness and curiosity are terrific building blocks. So, all you have to do is go with the aces a toddler brings to the table, and don't spend two seconds wringing your hands about what he can't do yet. As a famed Texas football coach once said, "Just dance with who brung ya."

> ✔ **Prepare you for anything:** We spotlight tons of techniques that will work for your child and make you feel like an able-bodied teaching pro. A million, trillion times all of us have heard that attitude is everything, and nowhere does that glitter in neon more brightly than in the Portals of Potty Training. You can't play this game with sweaty palms.

The *Potty Training For Dummies* Guarantee: Just to help you keep things in perspective, we promise that if your child is still in diapers when he makes the football team or gets her college degree, you can send him or her off to us for a weekend remedial course — *and* ask for a refund of the book cost.

Of course, we're kidding. Though it may seem like an eternity when you're cleaning up after yet another accident, your child is practically certain to be potty trained long before he or she begins elementary school.

Foolish Assumptions

We're guessing that you — mom, dad, babysitter, nanny, daycare worker — have a child in the two-three-four age range. Either you're in the throes of potty training already *(ouch)* — or you're getting ready to rumble.

You may be a little intimidated by the whole potty-training mystique and need reassurance; you may be looking for a method that works because training an older child became a battle of wills and egos that went on and on and on, and you sure don't want to go through that again; you may be completely baffled about the whole process — when to start, what to do, and not do.

Our biggest assumption is that you're looking forward to finding out how to potty train without too many tears for you or your tyke, so no matter what your perspective, you can find what you need in this book. We give you clear and comprehensive information about all aspects of potty training, along with tips and reassurances and encouragement.

How to Use This Book

A reference book for anyone who's helping a child transition from diapers to the big-people's toilet, *Potty Training For Dummies* is set up in a way that makes it easy to pick up, put down, pick up, put down — which is what busy folks who are taking care of small fry tend to do, anyway. Each part's a freestanding unit so that you can read every one separately — no need to read them in order, unless you want to.

One quick scan of the Table of Contents, and you can zip toward the parts you want to read first. Later, you may turn to the others.

How This Book Is Organized

Your potty-training book is split up into six parts, featuring 21 chapters. You can read the parts randomly — without having to read what came before. If a section does require prior knowledge, we'll refer you to the chapter number so you can flip there and brief yourself. Here's a rundown of each part and what's in store for you.

Part I: Setting Up for Success

First, you take a look at the big picture and all that's involved in seeing your child reach his goal. The program starts when you assemble your team: This means giving Junior the starring role and making sure he's ready (emotionally and physically). You — caregiver or parent — put on the captain's hat, and that gives you the privileges of coaching and motivating. You'll educate yourself and make the most of your talented supporting cast: family, friends, and outside caregivers. To ensure success in your upcoming potty adventure, you provide your child with the tools of the trade (potty chair, star chart, doll, training pants), and you suit him up for success.

Part II: It's All in the Timing

This part gives you the readiness signs (Chapter 4) — from physical clues to magic words to behavior upgrades. Noting your child's ready-set-go posture, you then proceed to the next step — pinpointing the very best time for potty-training startup, which we have named Potty-Training Weekend.

Part III: Surefire Steps for Ditching Diapers

In these chapters, we look at prepping for the big game, which includes big-people role modeling and potty-trip promotions. Then we go on to the Super Bowl of potty training — the weekend your child starts dancing the Potty Mambo.

After Potty-Training Weekend, you focus on keeping a good thing going (Chapter 8) and taking training on the road (Chapter 9).

Part IV: Using Psych-Up Skills

Want some super advice on getting your child excited about the potty? For the weeks/months of potty training, stay very much on message — and deal smartly with the do's and don'ts of the ups and downs. And, zip your lips before you compare your moppet with the potty wizard down the street. While you're doing all these neat tricks, you can "get by with a little help from your friends" and the rest of the posse who're all set to cheer on the toddler's success.

Part V: Coping with Special Cases

You need wiggle room. Things are never black and white in Pottyville, so you need to show considerable flexibility when dealing with special situations. You'll find out how to train kids with disabilities; handle major-league pee problems; and help your child stop soiling his undies. And, you'll even discover some good tricks for softening up those wild-and-wacky balkers. Be sure to find out when you should say, "Doctor, doctor, give me the news!"

Part VI: The Part of Tens

Here's a hodgepodge of cool tips and ideas, from ten reasons to let your child lead, to ten of the most-often-encountered quandaries that give parents and caregivers gray hair. We also share: ten ways to pump up potty prowess, and ten woulda-coulda-shouldas if you got do-overs in potty training.

Icons Used in This Book

The paragraphs with the icons next to them contain special information of one sort or another. We highlight this information according to how you can use it.

A mental sticky note, a Tip icon points to some fresh idea or a tried-and-true one that you'll want to sample at some point. Tuck these tidbits away for future reference — pearls that will come in handy when that little Jolly Charmer (or Challenging Personality) has you buffaloed.

Here's a heads-up for when your child's potty training takes a dicey detour. These signposts, usually of the medical variety, often recommend a trip to the doctor for tiny tyke — or tell you how to avoid one.

This alert is especially for you worker bees. People who parent and work outside the home have special concerns and sometimes confront different problems associated with being gone for long blocks of hours. This icon addresses the speed bumps professional folks face while potty training.

 If you could pull nothing but a handful of items from the entire text of *Potty Training For Dummies,* the Remember-tagged messages would be perfect ones to take with you to the potty room.

 Boost your morale by reading one of our real-life stories of parents and caregivers who have potty trained tots and want to share what they learned firsthand.

Another convention we use has to do with gender: The first and last chapters use female pronouns because they're odd-numbered chapters; even-numbered chapters have male pronouns.

Where to Go from Here

Now that the intros are out of the way, we hope you'll enjoy your adventure into the Never-Never Land of Potty Capers.

- ✔ If you're potty training a child for the first time, we suggest you start by reading Parts I and II — to get acquainted with the lingo, the tools of the trade, and the do's and don'ts. Then, skip to Part III, which explains how to prep your child for the showdown — learning how to potty, which is covered in Chapter 7. In your spare time, check out Parts IV and VI, chock full of sanity-maintenance tips for you and praise potions for small fry.

- ✔ If you have potty trained in the past, but hit heavy-duty snags, go straight to Part V, which deals with tough problems and how to handle them.

- ✔ If you're a true veteran — a grandparent or a longtime daycare worker or a nanny — you can use this book as reference, or to spiff up your rough spots. You'll find plenty of ways to curb problems you've encountered in the past. Flip to the Table of Contents and look for the info you need most.

By the way, Big Person, as you zero in on meaty parts and put them into action, be sure to accept the hearty pats on the back that are definitely due to someone like you who's taking the time to do the right thing. Your little one will thank you. Someday. When he learns about real, big-kid stuff like appreciating wonderful people who gave him a leg up in life by being understanding.

Dance on!

Part I
Setting Up for Success

The 5th Wave   By Rich Tennant

"Changing-station accessible or potty trained?"

In this part...

As a newcomer to Potty Planet, you may feel baffled about how to deal with pee and poop pranks. With your toddler all lined up for his brand-new challenge, you know you need plenty of prize nuggets on how to mold that little whippersnapper into a champion potty-user — and have fun doing it. So, you'll be happy to hear that this crash course features both laugh lines and life lines.

Where do you start? Part I gives you the big picture, along with the one-two-three on assembling your team, putting pumpkin out in front, and giving him the proper tools. You're bold. You're ready. And, you're okay with knowing that your toddler's potty learning will come in baby steps — tiny and tentative, but, with you around, right on target.

Chapter 1

Launching the Potty-Training Adventure

*Y*ou've toted that barge (diaper bag) and lifted that bale (evil poop) long enough! After changing thousands of diapers, you probably have major issues relating to small-fry output. Still, the fact remains that you can't send your child away to potty-training boot camp and get her back when all the work's done. What you can do, though, is pull off a truly bang-up job of helping her fine-tune her potty skills — without ever feeling as if you've moved into some kind of frightening, feces-filled parallel universe.

The problem is that when you start potty training, you throw open the door to confusing advice if you puzzle out loud about toddler training; and then you're knocked over by a rapid-fire barrage of answers: "I stuck my kid on the washing machine till she got the idea." "I waited to start training until my kids were real old!" "When your kid hands you a dirty diaper, she's ready." Ask and you will be given at least fifty million ideas on how to potty train. But, use the *Potty Training For Dummies* approach, and you won't have to ponder which tales are right and which ones are wrong. You'll have the snug comfort of a bona fide plan that works.

With *Potty Training For Dummies,* you'll enchant your child by tucking brass-tacks skills into a package wrapped with pretty bows (games) and cute paper (rewards). As chief dance-master, you will provide oodles of patience, soft-voiced tips, and readiness for quirky behaviors.

No matter what you encounter, you're good with it. Have no doubt —
you can teach your child how to use the potty with ease, as long as you
wait until your wee one shows she's geared up for the challenge.

Starting Potty-Mambo Dance Class

Imagine that you're going to take a mambo class, but you've never even
done a square-dance do-si-do, a tango swoop, or a tap dance shuffle-
ball-change combination. What would you need to start out? Who
would you bring along for help and comfort? You'd want warm supporters, and you'd want the right stuff. Don't ask me to do a cha-cha
with no castanets, please! (For those of you that don't know, castanets
are the little wooden cymbals you click together with your fingers in
beat to the music!)

Promising plenty of help

Your toddler will definitely need some cool people on her team for
moral support — the same ones who totally flipped out when she took
her first steps.

On her first day out, let your child know she's going to have lots of supporters cheering her on — to help her feel warm-and-fuzzy while she's
learning this brand-new potty dance. Mommy. Daddy. Teacher-at-day-
care Miss Allison. Nana. Gran and Gramps. Aunt Christina. And big
sister, Jenny.

Tell your tot that you'll be her main teacher in the Potty Mambo, but
she'll be the star. Early on — before you've even pinpointed the time
for Potty-Training Weekend, start some pre-potty-training pep talks.
Talk up how much everyone will applaud her success when she's a
full-fledged potty user.

Providing the right stuff

Get ready by buying the right stuff — from potty chair to hotsy-totsy
videos to pants that are easy to pull up and down. See Chapter 3 for
suggestions.

Your toddler will like the excitement of knowing she's equipped for this
new challenge. And the pleasure of those new things will carry her past
any nagging fears that may be flitting by.

A well-dressed potty trainee will need both training-pant pullups and
big-kid underwear (to look forward to). You have lots of options here —
so many, in fact, that you may need help in sorting what's what and
what works best in certain circumstances. (See info on training-pant
options in Chapter 3.)

Keeping an Eye Out for Your Window of Opportunity

The biggest key to success in potty training is: starting it at the right time! Get a good feel for when your child is really ready — both her mind and body are in gear — and you're halfway home.

Do it too soon, and you may end up staring at each other like a couple of zombies. If she's unready, she'll potty-sit in a trance just because she knows you want her to. As long as she's hanging out in that spot, you can't make her do stupid stuff like put up toys or go to bed. While she's working on potty deeds, she's queen-for-the-half-hour.

So work hard to leap on readiness signs (we put a list of them on the Cheat Sheet at the front of the book), and soon you'll be entering that twilight zone of tinkle talk, toilet-paper clogs, and mega-emphasis on making safe deposits in a small innocent bowl that's ready-and-waiting to be called to the front line for action.

Noting her approach to the dance floor

For potty training to work, your child must be at the point when bowel and bladder control are within her reach. Otherwise, if her body refuses to help, she'll only get frustrated. (Talk about feeling like a klutz with two left feet!)

So keep your eyes peeled for signs that your child is now peeing and pooping on a more regular schedule — less often, bigger amounts. Other things that signal all-clear-ahead are when she's acting like a neat freak and complains of wet/dirty pants. See Chapter 4 or the Cheat Sheet for these signs. If you're training a child with disabilities, read both Chapter 4 and Chapter 17 to check for potty-training startup signs.

No matter what the age, a child who's unfazed when she pees and poops is not going to be ready to cooperate with potty training or understand why it's necessary.

Knowing when the timing's cool

Try some high-drama thinking to conjure up what your tiny tot could be feeling right now. So far, in her two short years, she has found the world a whirlwind of color and smell and texture and sound. And you've been her right-hand guide in sorting through the maze of wonders.

But this time she's trying to learn something that goes against the grain of what she has done naturally since emerging into the world. Dumping her bodily goods in her diapers was so easy, so stress-free, and from what she can tell, it sounds like you're asking her to crank up her brain and body to some strange new sophistication level that doesn't yet make a lick of sense.

Be wise and avoid high-stress periods for your startup of potty training. Also, look for a time when she has passed the "terrible twos" and is moving on to a sweeter, gentler stage. (See Chapter 5 for timing tips.)

Giving the Potty Mambo a Good Beat

The caregiver or parent who's potty training for the first time can see clearly that this process can go bad in fifty-jillion ways. Why? Because completing potty deeds takes a whole bunch of skills: Your toddler must

✔ Be able to control her impulses

✔ Have motor skills that are really cooking

✔ Like the idea of being a tiny bit self-propelled

✔ "See me hold back my pee or poop till I reach the potty. See me walk, tug down clothes, wipe myself, pull up clothes, flush the toilet. See me even want to do these things alone." And, besides self-control, walking, undressing, and climbing onto the potty, she may need to run the hundred-yard dash in order to get to the bathroom on time!

Believe us, from your child's point of view, all of this probably seems freaky-scary, which is why you must pretty-up the whole dance with a friendly approach.

You, you world-wise pottyologist, must entice this sweet-and-sassy kiddo by chatting up the time set aside for her to learn the Potty Mambo. To engage your child fully, you'll stage a special launch weekend, when you declare an embargo on distractions and start writing a first-draft diaper-eulogy. The Potty Monologues are under way. Get her swaying to the beat!

Prepping for the real training time — Potty-Training Weekend — calls for some subtle and warm persuasion. (See Chapter 6 for more.)

Kids can really get moving when you get them in the right mood — so take time to flaunt the role models ("See your big sister Monique — how cool is that? She uses the potty — but I can remember years ago when she was in diapers and then had to learn to use the potty herself.") Notice that you're not saying, "Why can't you be more like her?" You're just pointing out that Monique uses the toilet in a big-person way.

You're in a partnership here, assisting your child in achieving success as a natural offshoot of the adventure. Your trainee has to forge ahead, but you can certainly give a lot of hands-on guidance.

As you nudge your little pip toward the weekend of her magical coup, help get her jazzed about what's coming up. Let her sit clothed on her potty chair and bask in the newness of her spiffy seat. Coach her on buzzwords that she'll use to dazzle when she Potty-Mambos.

Make the most of psych-up talks. You're letting bathroom words become commonplace to her — in a "by the way you'll soon be doing this" kind of way. Encourage her anticipation — this will be a special time with you, one of her favorite people. But don't create dread by outlining great expectations for Potty-Training Weekend. (See Chapter 6 on prepping.)

If she looks worried and says, "no go potty," that means one thing: She's afraid that when the time comes, she'll fail to deliver what you want. So reassure, reassure, reassure. "Whatever you do, Potty-Training Weekend will be fine — you're a beginner. You're just learning, little gal. We'll play and sing and have fun together. You'll learn how to use the potty, but if you have a little trouble remembering, no problem!" High-five — let her know that it's a joint enterprise, and you're her number-one supporter.

Making Sure Everyone Enjoys the Big Dance

Ah, the chaperone. That's you — the one with the power to make Potty-Training Weekend fun — or a big fat washout. So, go into it with your sense of humor tucked under one arm and a passel of patience under the other. Only good things can happen because the main outcome you're shooting for is this: Both of you should walk away with good feelings and memories of toddler/grown-up bonding at its best. You'll make sure that little potty trainee feels like she did something really good.

Hey, wait a minute, you say. She didn't pee or poop in the potty a single time! No matter. You still heap praise on her for the big T — Trying. In potty training, effort is good — very good — and gets rewarded. Enough little efforts, and she'll actually be using the potty on a regular basis. (See Chapter 7.)

Toting an emergency kit

Going into Potty-Training Weekend, you're excited. Plus, you're armed with an "emergency kit," so you're ready for accidents, surprises, and attitudes.

Just like getting ready for her first dance recital, do what you can to make things go smoothly. The more groundwork you lay, the better her potty training will go.

Make available all the props and supplies your child will need for potty training. (Get your child really into the idea by letting her be your shopping-trip sidekick.) See Chapter 3 for more ideas.

To be prepared, gather startup info on training problems, smart responses to relapses, guidelines on special-needs children, and savvy ways to handle sparring with a spouse or relative who may have a different philosophy on potty training. (See Chapters 12, 13, 14, 15, 16, and 17.)

Warming her up for the big time

As Potty-Training Weekend starts, you'll go through a whole lot of shenanigans to get your child cooking: You'll help her teach her doll to use the potty chair for peeing. You'll take your toddler to her potty chair every hour (and after meals) all Potty-Training Weekend (except during the night). Together, you'll set up an exciting Success Chart. And, finally, you'll switch her to training pants after a few successes during the weekend. (See Chapter 7 for details on dancing the Potty Mambo.)

Then, when the weekend is over, you'll help her mesh the new skills into the framework of everyday life: You'll give any outside caregivers the poop on her potty program. And, you'll spend time every day reinforcing her brand-new tricks.

Knowing Your Place as Mentor

You have to stifle all great expectations during potty days. Simply stay on message: Be calm and patient. Laugh often. Smile a lot.

Be prepared for taking your child's act on the road. You have to get ready for outings. And, ensure that outside caregivers are following your lead.

You can keep your child in step by staying enthusiastic about her progress, not overreacting to odd behavior, and handling speed bumps with ultimate cool.

Biting your tongue

During potty-training days, you may learn a lot about yourself. Maybe you never knew you were such a control freak. Or maybe you suddenly turned into one of the neatness police. All kinds of "I told you so" things seem to fly to your lips, uninvited.

So you must do absolutely anything (short of gagging yourself) to keep from nagging your little chum, who's probably chugging along about as ably as a two-year-old can be expected to. This just could be the perfect time to learn how to tie a knot in a cherry stem with the end of your tongue. (You know you've always wanted to do that.)

Covering the A B Cs of car trips

Help your child feel safe and secure by making sure she's got all sorts of situations covered.

Staying potty trained at home is one thing — out in a spooky bathroom at a sports arena is something entirely different. (See tips in Chapter 9.)

Keeping her in step

Do three things to keep your child in step while she's doing the Potty Mambo. Provide loads of theatrical enthusiasm. Use lots of motivating lines. And troubleshoot when funky snags show up — things like pee accidents, mondo-modesty, or freak-show moments (pooping in her toy box, streaking when friends visit, and so on). See Chapters 8 and 11 for more.

Benefiting from Others' Cool Moves

Don't get the feeling you're out there on the stage all by yourself — far from it. Lots of people like to get in on promoting Potty Mambo moves.

Just figure they're out to help. Invite them inside the loop. From doctors and Web sites, to ex-mates and relatives, you'll find support everywhere you turn. (If you're divorced, see the tips in Chapter 12 for snaring good potty-training results when your child goes from dad's house to mom's house.)

Becoming the Grand Poopbah of Potty Mambo (Trouble-Buster Supreme)

Well, no one ever learned anything valuable without a few mistakes, right? And, potty training's no different. Just when you think, "Wow, she's got it!" something happens that rewrites the entire script.

So, you're back to square one — older, more tired, but definitely not down and out. You're a fountain of ideas, a trouble-buster supreme. And while you're establishing yourself as the Grand Poopbah of the Potty Mambo, your twisting trail may have enough gnarly detours to hone the heart of a champion.

Watching the Backslider Twist

Your little tornado toddler gives a whole new meaning to the word "accidents." Frankly, your mind is blown. What the heck is she up to?

Truth is, she's probably not bummed by you or the potty. Many things can cause kids to lapse into backsliding, but thumbing her nose at you usually isn't one of them.

Nevertheless, these are indeed times that try men and women's souls — so brief yourself on how to do what during side trips to strange places in the Potty Zone. See Chapter 13 for more.

Wetting in the morning, wetting in the evening, wetting at suppertime

Daytime accidents. Nighttime bed-wetting. If you want to be the Grand Poopbah of the Potty Mambo, you need to do a real fancy-pants job of problem solving. The wet-pants department, as you may have guessed, is especially perplexing.

Here you may be dealing with a child who bed-wets long-term — and can't seem to shake it — or the kiddo who day-wets after being potty trained. For tips on when to see a doctor, read Chapter 14.

Teaching a balker a brand-new dance

If you like a challenge, you got it in a kid who just won't dance. The key to leaping past balking is figuring out what's going on. When you have some idea of your child's problem — what's making her dig in and declare war on the potty — you can take any one of several approaches. You'll find that the ideas we recommend in Chapter 15 cut to the chase and usually get quick results.

Knowing what to do about soil, soil, toil, and trouble

Some children just aren't good at the Potty Mambo. So, they have trouble with stool-soiling their pants even beyond toddler years.

Often, the solution's as simple as getting rid of your child's constipation. Other times, the kid needs tons of handholding and special handling because she has gotten attached to her "product" and has become possessive and a bit weird about holding onto it.

Jumpstarting a child who's soiling can be hard at times, but Chapter 16 is packed with great ideas for resolving this mysterious detour.

Giving Special Attention to Special Children (with Disabilities)

Kids with disabilities need extra-special treatment when they're learning the Potty Mambo. It's not that they lack rhythm or can't be potty trained; most children with disabilities and chronic diseases absolutely can learn to use the toilet. But they need plenty of consistency, potty opportunities, and patience. Plus, you'll need to clown around a bit — put on your jazz shoes and entertain like a mad person. Sing a happy tune or two — you'll get her attention.

All kids think potty training's a little bit hard, and children who have trouble just moving around — or have difficulty with the mind-body connection — are going to require lots of TLC to get the process clicked in place. See Chapter 17 for more on this.

Polishing off a Super-Slick Potty Babe

Bottom line: Listen up when your child clues you in as to what she needs from you. And respond with loving support and patience and a fantastic sense of humor. Do those things, and you're guaranteed a good outcome: *Potty Training For Dummies* will work for your child — and you'll avoid that disconnect that you worried about.

Basically, we just don't believe in drudgery when it comes to parenting, so you'll discover lots of fun ways to get through potty training's rough spots as you flip through the pages of this book. Take note of the parts that fit your situation — and use *Potty Training For Dummies* to make your days of teaching the Potty Mambo full of joy and whimsy.

Then when you're all finished and your child is showing off her Potty-Mambo medal and her frilly pants, give yourself a pat on the back for doing this thing right. You've made it through the potty adventures, and you've come out the other side with a smile on your face.

And, your child still likes you. In fact, she thinks you're kind of cool.

Potty-trained tykes rule!

Chapter 2

Assembling Your Team

• •

In This Chapter

▶ Casting the star of the show: Your child

▶ Knowing your role

▶ Enlisting other folks' help

• •

Potty training is a totally cooperative endeavor involving a variety of people interested in the outcome. This chapter identifies the players and their roles.

Your child, of course, is the star of the potty-training team. You (along with your mate or partner) serve as the coach for your toddler and as the manager for the whole team. The supporting players may include your toddler's siblings and any other family members who are in your home frequently, as well as regular babysitters, and professional caregivers.

To make potty training work, tackle it as a partnership — a positive developmental experience in which you are the coach, assisting your child in achieving success as a natural offshoot of the "adventure."

Starring Role for Junior

Potty training is your child's chance to shine. Think of yourself as the coach. Your job is to help your child attain a level of mastery, making him the star of your team.

Your child's toilet training is simply one developmental landmark. Don't consider this a status symbol for you or an I.Q. test for him. Getting the hang of potty training early or easily isn't even a sign of future success in life. It just means that a child is out of diapers and moving on to the next developmental stage.

Focusing on your star

Consider the mass of information you want your child to take in, all of it leading up to his doing potty deeds on his own. So, you focus on your star player and center your efforts on helping him master this elaborate new skill-set. The goal? By the time he reaches the goal line, he will feel like he has succeeded to a spectacular degree.

Meanwhile, the getting there will be tough for him. For a two-year-old, the demands are great, which means he will need all the handholding he can get.

Making sure he's ready

From your child's point of view, using the toilet constitutes multitasking taken to a whole new and scary level. He needs certain skills and a certain level of maturity to tackle the project successfully.

For successful potty training, a toddler should have impulse control, improved motor skills, and a desire for autonomy. Plus, he must be packing several key physical skills:

- ✔ **The ability to walk**
- ✔ **The ability to undress by himself**
- ✔ **The ability to get onto the potty**
- ✔ **The ability to control his sphincter**

And you must consider those pesky little follow-ups:

- ✔ **Pulling off the right amount of tissue**
- ✔ **Wiping properly**
- ✔ **Disposing of the TP**
- ✔ **Flushing**
- ✔ **Washing up**

Then, to make things even more complex, he needs that all-important, but sometimes elusive, willingness to cooperate. (The chapters in Part II let you know how to tell when he's ready.)

You need to be aware that your child's need-to-go sensation isn't fully developed when he starts potty training — it develops during the process. He's used to going in his diaper as a matter of course, so getting to the point where he can tell you that he needs to go potty before he does his business in his diaper takes some practice. And remember that the ability to inhibit muscle contractions following the first urge to urinate varies greatly from child to child.

Emotionally, your child must show readiness, too. You probably can already see your toddler beginning to enjoy mimicking, pleasing people, and showing off mini-me behaviors. But, you also want to make sure he is ready to rise above the natural sassiness of just being two. He must be able to grasp new knowledge.

Taking on the Coach's Job

As coach of the team, you're the one responsible for doing the research, devising and sharing the game plan, and keeping the team focused and up to speed. You're the one who determines when your star is ready to start the potty-training game, and you're the one who coordinates the overall game plan to make sure that everybody is with the program.

Important as your role is, remember that your child is the focus — not you. Just as potty training isn't a reflection of your child's intelligence or virtue, neither is it a reflection on you or your parenting abilities.

Starting for the right reason — he's ready

Keep in mind that a child's readiness for potty training can be as individual as blue eyes or brown hair. Wait until he's truly ready (not when you're ready), and potty training will be a speedy process. Rush things and you'll probably give yourself up a few new wrinkles.

The only right reason to launch the new regimen is because your child is ready — you see many favorable signs that kicking off potty training would probably work very well. (Chapter 4 tells you what to look for in the way of readiness signs.)

Of course, you may want to start potty training for any number of reasons:

- ✔ **Pressure from family or friends:** People keep hinting that your child is lagging behind in this developmental landmark, and finally, you get sick of their nagging and give in, going against your better instincts. What does it matter? Maybe they're right. Or maybe not.

- ✔ **Another baby on the way:** Many pediatricians have heard the familiar anthem "I'm going to have another baby soon, and I'll have two in diapers unless . . ."

  The wording alone tells you everything you need to know about whether this is a good idea; you're really saying that you're ready, not your child. But you aren't the one who needs to be trained to use the toilet. The truth is that you've been ready to get past the diaper phase for months. The question is, does your child send out signals that he is ready?

✔ **Daycare facility takes only potty-trained kids:** This is high-level peer pressure for sure! Problem is, if you get your toddler going with potty use for this reason — and not because you see the appropriate signs — you'll probably just prolong the process.

✔ **Diaper expenses:** This may sound good — but it's just another bad reason — unless your child is showing readiness signs. Instead of rushing matters, keep in mind that starting potty training too soon will only end up costing you more in the long run because the process will take longer — more accidents, more laundry, more diapers.

Don't let your time constraints influence you to push things. As a busy working parent, you naturally want to get your child out of diapers; your daycare provider definitely wants to have your child out of diapers — that's just normal. But having your toddler start the process just to ease your burden or that of a caregiver is not smart. Undertake toilet training only when your child is actually ready and success will follow.

Motivating your star

Here's the fun part. Getting your child generally jazzed about potty training can be super-sized fun. Think of the excitement you felt upon seeing his first steps and hearing his first words, then apply the same degree of rah-rah to this landmark moment. Chapter 8 has ideas on rewards and incentives that will stir up some interest for sure.

Warming up: Pre-potty-training training

Even before your child shows readiness signs, you can start some preliminary training when your baby is about 15 months old to prepare him for the adventure to come.

What can you do prior to 18 months? Chat up your child. And this means using the power of patter to help your baby develop his vocabulary, a skill vital in potty training and pretty much everything else he needs to do developmentally.

Sing to him, talk to him, read to him. Fill his life with words, including some of the key terms he needs for potty training. You can use the proper anatomical terms — such as urinate, defecate, buttocks, penis, testicles, and vagina — or the euphemisms your family or culture uses — pee, poop, and bottom, for example. Make sure that your child knows the names for relevant body parts and bodily functions, as well as the difference between "clean" and "messy" or "dirty."

Be careful not to give your toddler the impression that his bodily functions are yucky — that he produces liquids and solids that are foul or disgusting or shameful. As the title of Taro Gomi's great book for potty-training toddlers says, *Everyone Poops*: Along with every other member of the animal kingdom, human beings all urinate and defecate.

Spotting signs that he's not ready

If your child seems like he is in the "possibly ready" category, but still very iffy, review this list of not-so-fast-there indications. These point to a child who is clearly not ready to climb onto the potty chair:

✔ Lacks awareness that he is urinating or having a BM in his diaper.

✔ Shows no particular pattern to his bowel movements.

✔ Urinates more than once every two hours.

✔ Exhibits no interest in using the toilet.

✔ Shows overt resistance to your references to potty training.

✔ Has a generally negative attitude (there's a reason they call them the terrible twos).

✔ Is experiencing stress or turmoil, such as sleeping problems, a new baby in the home, a new caregiver, or parental conflict.

Motivating your star

The motivational stage calls for helping your child warm to the idea that potty training can be a gigantic window of opportunity. If you can get him to be a visionary — imagine himself an older, savvier version of his toddler self — then you can help him take a first step toward readiness that will make the whole process go more smoothly.

Remember, he may need to be convinced that being a big boy has advantages. So far, just lying back and being diapered has worked for him.

 One mom tells of having her toddler "visualize" himself as a fully potty-trained big boy, complete with superhero undies. He drew a picture of himself standing by the toilet as he modeled his new underpants and flexed his little biceps. The image was a bit Picasso-like, mind you, but the point is that he was seeing himself achieving this next skill — and liking it.

Your job is to cheer the pipsqueak toward pulling off the magical coup of using the potty. Simply forge ahead armed with full-blown awareness that setbacks, anomalies, and strange behavior are going to be parts of the process. All along the way, you and relatives and outside caregivers will be there to cheer him, prop him up, help him do new things.

You want him to put another big notch on his confidence belt as a result of his potty-trainer endeavors. And you can help to make that happen by revving him up for the challenge. To make sure that he knows this is an extra-special undertaking, dangle in front of him some enticing carrots: "Big boys get to go to movies, stay up later, and wear big-kid underwear."

Educating yourself

Because you're the point person in this process, you should know your stuff so that you know what to expect from your toddler and can explain your method and your reasoning to the other folks involved in the process.

Anticipating the process

Potty training takes place when your child is ready to start. (See Chapter 4 or the Cheat Sheet at the front of the book for a list of readiness signs.) Once you have noticed several readiness signs in place, seize the moment.

The training process features several steps: In the preliminaries outlined in Chapter 6, you set him up for success with clothed dry runs, role modeling, buzzwords, and diaper-drop demos. Then, in the actual Potty Mambo itself, explained in Chapter 7, you follow a multistep plan that gives him the keys to unlocking his skills. You are psyched up, and so are relatives and caregivers. Everyone knows there will be setbacks and surprises; you have them well briefed: Your toddler will be mostly trained, with allowances for slipups, and then will ultimately reach the stage of fully trained.

Before Potty-Training Weekend, devote a week to preliminaries — enough time to ensure that your child has the hang of the potty lingo and the role modeling has made him eager to imitate using the toilet. (Role modeling is covered in Chapter 6.)

You will take your child through all potty-training steps during a special weekend set aside for that purpose. (Check out Chapter 4 for an explanation of how this is done.) Your child will be getting in the groove by the end of the weekend, so after that, he will be moving, hopefully, on toward maintenance mode. Expect it to take several weeks or months from that memorable Potty-Training Weekend until accidents are once-a-week occurrences. Some kids can stay dry all day every day months before they can manage dry nights. The timetable for your child's bed-wetting ceasefire is especially hard to predict. (See Chapter 8 on keeping a good thing going by reinforcing success and dealing with accidents wisely.)

If he's back in daycare that Monday, be sure to give your toddler's caregiver his schedule for potty-sits. And, switch him to training pants now that he is settling into a routine. Along the way, keep handing out liberal praise for good tries and actual successes.

Knowing the timelines

Your little calf is going to act just like others of toddler ilk — he'll bolt at first, frisk around, meander a bit, and finally, get the hang of potty training.

Separating reality from rumor

What about all the people who swear their kids were potty trained in the space of one remarkable day? A few — maybe one or two — are telling the truth. The premise is that it will work in one day because you've pounced on perfect timing. But if your child has one of his cylinders still sputtering and you fail to detect it, he won't be able to pull this off.

And if you can't make it work after you've talked up the Great One-Day Feat, you may have trouble convincing your toddler that he's not some kind of loser for failing. Leave that level of backpedaling to Lance Armstrong.

Your toddler knew he was supposed to learn his potty skills in one day. Ah, but his body didn't get it. His bladder and bowels refused to get in sync that quickly, and he got shook up, and pretty soon, dissolved in tears. Big bummer. Any plan that gives your child a very big chance of failure is not a great idea.

Also, don't listen to the old wives' tales, the most popular of which is the one that claims you can put a youngish baby on the potty right after eating in the morning and the potty will receive the movement. But — and this is an important but — the child's awareness of what is going on is just not there. So, even if you are able to use the toilet as a poop catcher, you cannot truthfully proclaim that your one-year-old is potty trained.

Most important, kids whom parents try to "precondition" in this way are usually the very ones who balk madly when it comes to real toilet-training time. See "Handling Hardcore Balkers," Chapter 15, for more information on this topic.

The journey from dry during the day to dry during the night can range from a couple of months to a year or so, but typically

1. **Kids first get the hang of daytime and nighttime bowel control.**
2. **After that, they master daytime bladder control.**
3. **Lastly comes the night bladder control.**

Don't worry about having your toddler trained in one function and running behind in the other. You tutor for urine and bowel action simultaneously because the two things occur at roughly the same time but not at exactly the same time.

So, how long does it take, typically, to get a child completely trained? You wonder if we're talking weeks, months, or years. Because your friends and family and strangers are all offering a variety of tales intended to inspire potty-training kickoff, you need to know the real skinny.

If you're very consistent with your teaching efforts, you can look to complete toilet training in about eight months. This includes periods of inconsistency, some accidents, and maybe a few perplexing standoffs.

When girls finish up their potty training, they are about 2.5; boys, on the other hand, generally are three. By about 30 to 36 months, many kids can be declared potty-training graduates. By this time, for lots of children, it has become fairly automatic to use the bathroom regularly. At the same time, though, accidents are not unusual for the next year or two.

Remember that even though you did the prep work and your toddler is primed and excited about potty training, this is still a brave new world to him. That means that the act of negotiating the minefield probably won't go exactly the way you expect, and maybe, not even close. (See Chapter 8 for info on handling accidents.)

Checking out potty-training stats

One interesting observation from the American Academy of Pediatrics is that parents who started training their toddlers at age 2 were able to proclaim their kids totally trained by their third birthdays, while parents who began potty training their tots at 18 months or younger did not see the project come to fruition until after age 4 (*Caring for Your Baby and Young Child,* edited by Steven Shelov, M.D., and Robert E. Hannemann, M.D., for the American Academy of Pediatrics, published by Bantam). So, clearly, training is much easier with older kids, who are ready to get with the program.

Getting everyone with the program

For you, your mate, relatives, and caregivers, the best gift for your toddler's current challenge is a consistent message: "We're all on your side, rooting you on. We'll cheer your successes and hug you when you're disappointed. We love you."

You and your mate must present a united front on the potty-training issue so that your child has a clear set of expectations. If you indicate to your tot that a specific aspect of the potty-training routine is crucial, but your partner has a "no big deal" attitude, your toddler gets mixed messages. If your child gets confused at the start of the program, he pretty much stays that way throughout. The last thing your toddler needs right now is a hazy mind while he's trying to process a complicated set of new behaviors.

On the other hand, if his parents and lead caregivers are all running around sounding the same battle cry, your toddler is much better equipped emotionally to take in the information with a cool head.

Presenting the program

It's important to take a stand on two key points:

  ✓ **Potty-training startup must hinge on the child's physical/mental timetable.** (The Cheat Sheet and Chapter 4 list the readiness signs.)

> ✔ **Punishment cannot be a part of the game plan.**
>
> Be sure to huddle with other caregivers in order to underscore this very important point. Let everyone involved know how strongly you (and your partner) feel about the policy of no reprimands, no timeouts, no tsk-tsks. Don't lay guilt on a child just because his bladder is running behind schedule. He can't do too much about it.

Get these two key points right — no punishment and the right startup time — and you'll speed the potty-training process, facilitate the pace of adopting new skills, and promote compliance.

As team captain, you need to have all helpers heavily invested in the game plan. This may require a little tender persuasion, convincing your mate that even though the way her mom potty trained clearly worked, you're still convinced that the Potty Training For Dummies method is the way to go. At the same time, you really, truly want to have her on board in order to make the plan succeed. See Chapter 1 for information on the very toddler-friendly Dummies Potty Training plan. And Chapter 9 explains how to get outside caregivers to follow the same routine.

Working through conflicts

What should you do if a pushy aunt tries to initiate potty training when you're not around? Suppose one day she's babysitting for you and launches a surprise attack: She pounces on that glowing opportunity and puts little Alec on the toilet and lectures him about the merits of using the facilities.

When you hear what happened, tell auntie dearest that you appreciate her interest in your child, and that you truly are looking forward to getting Alec out of diapers — but you feel that timing is everything when it comes to potty training. So, please, no more urging the kid right now.

When you're dealing someone who is sabotaging your potty-training system, whether he or she is doing it intentionally or not, follow these steps:

1. **Keep your cool.**

   Draw on that endearing trait called patience. Don't sabotage family ties, but do hold on to your resolve.

2. **Express your appreciation for their interest.**

3. **Assure the saboteur that you have a potty-training plan.**

4. **Share the main points of your potty-training plan:**

   Timing is everything.

   No punishment.

If Alec asks you exactly what Aunt Debra was talking about, tell him that she was just trying to prepare him for the time when he will start using the potty. If he says he'd like to try it, and you see a few readiness indicators, let him give it a shot for a couple of days. Otherwise, just add a note of reassurance: "You will be learning to use the potty very soon. Then you won't have to wear diapers anymore, and I'm sure you'll like that."

When relatives overstep boundaries, don't get too bent out of shape. Children survive all manner of mixed cues, from secret cookie bribes (that Aunt Maggie was warned against giving) to ill-fated potty-starts. Making an older person, especially a relative, feel that she's interfering can be far worse than ruffling your child's routine. Kids are resilient; parents need to be, too.

Thankfully, you're surrounded by people who want to help. While your philosophies may differ, most people will find that their child's many supporters are just interested in seeing the toddler succeed. If you present your profound belief in the Dummies way of potty training, they will undoubtedly follow your lead.

Some situations and how to deal with them:

- ✔ **The mate who opts out of the program:** Explain your belief that your child will think potty training is important only if both of you share the same level of enthusiasm. "Sammy really needs your support on this. With our help, I'm sure he'll be out of diapers in no time."

- ✔ **The partner who tries whatever method strikes her fancy that day:** Emphasize the "kids need structure" theme that elementary school teachers swear by. Tell your mate that your toddler will do better if everyone who's taking part in potty training him is on the same page. You don't want to confuse the young lad.

- ✔ **The older sibling who's acting out because he feels the toddler is getting all the attention:** To get a jealous sibling on board, simply tell him that he's a role model. Let him know that this is only the first of many times the toddler will be looking up to him for an example of what big kids do. The older sibling could well be the younger kid's idol by birthday number five. "If you tell him using the potty is the thing to do, he'll definitely pay attention to you. He'll think he's being hip."

- ✔ **The daycare provider who makes a show of listening to your explanation of the plan and then does it her way after you're gone:** To solve this problem, write down your expectations, hand them over, and tell her you'll be checking from day to day to see how your toddler is doing. In your written plan, be sure to mention that the two key aspects of the Dummies potty-training plan are having all those involved follow the same steps, and not scolding or punishing the trainee. Tell her that you'd love for her to jot down a brief and informal progress report once a week.

Resisting parental and peer pressure

Inevitably, some helpful person will remind you that your neighbor Tiffany was fully trained by the time she was 2, and her child Brent by the time he was 18 months, and Lisa, 20 months. Your answer? "That tells me that those kids were ready, but my child doesn't seem to be, so I'll just have to wait until the time is right."

Smile and say thanks, and move on. Don't burn any bridges. You can't alienate relatives or friends just because they get overbearing and obnoxious with their nonstop advice. (You may need them to baby-sit sometime!)

Remember that in our society, dispensing child-rearing tips is considered a birthright. Most women who have raised children think mothers are a big sorority, whose business is all the kids in the world. They mean well, really.

So, what are some effective comebacks that you can use? Just tell friends and in-laws that this is not your training time — it's your child's. That means you should wait until you see specific signs that she is ready.

Making Use of the Supporting Cast

Friends who have trained kids. Relatives. Siblings. Caregivers. That "it takes a village" concept definitely comes to mind when you kick off potty training. It won't be a one-person show for a child who has relatives and caregivers aplenty. And all of those folks need to know the gist of what's going on in order to enhance the trainee's chances of success. You, as coach of the team, must take the initiative to draw others into the fold, sharing the mantra that this is your son's project, but that he will flourish best with the support of those he loves rallying around him.

Family members and friends

Get grandparents, aunts, uncles, and others to work with you. This is a great time to draw on their experiences to deal with tricky situations. Sometimes, you discover a wealth of information.

One single dad tells of asking his own mom for training tips, and she told him, "Give little Austin five shiny gold stars for good potty days, and never, ever push." The guy used those two guidelines, and in four months, his son was clean and dry, both days and nights.

You're really in luck if you can enlist the aid of an older sibling during potty-training days. In most families, a toddler looks with awe on the family's big kids, so a sibling's role modeling can be vital to helping your two-year-old become a success story. (Chapter 6 has the scoop on role modeling.)

Outside caregivers

"Let's start training him now!" As a working parent, you may hear that advice when you drop off your child at daycare. Of course, outside caregivers want to get your toddler trained in order to ease their own workload. But, typically, their readiness comes before your child has any notion of shedding his diapers, how to do it, or why he would even want to.

If you're a working parent, it's quite likely that your caregiver will be the one coping with the lion's share of daily training. Don't forget that you're still the one who decides when to kick off the proceedings in a success-oriented way.

By following the Dummies Potty Training program, you can do the important prep work and then lovingly lead your child through Potty-Training Weekend. The upshot? When the daytime caregiver gets him the following Monday, your toddler knows the drill and he's raring to go (in the potty).

Remember, at the daycare facility, the best way to communicate clear expectations is to hand over a written potty plan. Otherwise, you'll find yourself trying to explain what you want over the roar of children's voices.

The point you're trying to drive home to one and all is that gaining empowerment over BMs and urination is not a litmus test for good-kidness. It all comes down to a body-function thing — no more, no less. The only reason it gets so much attention is because everyone on the team gets tired of changing diapers.

Chapter 3

Using the Tools of the Trade and Dressing for Success

....

....

*Y*ou can set your child up for success by buying a few cool tools designed to help make potty training a breeze. Together, you choose the perfect potty chair, motivational aids, and training pants.

Does she fall for (and won't fall through) the potty seat that fits on top of the adult toilet? Is he motivated by having a target in the bottom of his potty chair to aim for? Is she dazzled by PowerPuff Girls underpants or glittery Barbie panties? Is he jazzed by Spider-Man jockeys or galaxy boxers? (Let your child choose undies for end-of-training goals, but buy plenty of pullups for early Potty Mambo days.)

Then, back at home — after that all-important, post-shopping nap — put your toddler on her new potty chair, and set in motion a genuine lovefest with her "new best friend." Show the potty-training video that gives her a look at other cute kids getting the hang of the process, and read her that cool new book about potty kids.

Picking a Potty Chair

You're going shopping. And when you do, you and your child are just two lovable kids coming together to celebrate potty-chair diversity and raging potty-readiness. Keep an open mind as you check out the choices: seats that attach to the big toilet, little potty chairs — and don't forget that you can always use that hand-me-down chair (from an older sibling or cousin), and let little sweetkins personalize it with stickers, making the throne hers alone.

Encourage your trainee to sit on different chairs to check out size. How well each one fits her tiny backside can be a big factor in her speed of adapting to potty training. Find a nice fit: In the store, let her road-test a few and see which ones are comfy and best fit her baby-buttocks. The right chair will be sized so that she can rest her feet on the floor and use her muscles to bear down when she wants to start a BM. Feet dangling in the air aren't conducive to making the process work.

Study the nitty-gritty: Check out potty chairs and toilet-toppers for basic practicalities, such as stability and easily removable catch bowls. Opt for a remove-from-the-top bowl over the type of bowl that you remove from the back, which isn't as user-friendly. Also, make sure the chair doesn't slide around.

Try to predict your reaction to wild gadgetry before you buy a chair that sings to your toddler as she sits, or rings a bell when pee hits the bottom of the bowl, or any number of other combinations. Otherwise, your child will get confused if you suddenly deactivate her bell in mid-stream. Parents who find repetitive sounds annoying should definitely bypass the talking-singing potty chairs.

Do you feel overwhelmed by sound and fury when you get home from work? If so, scurry past the aisle with the rootin'-tootin', singing-talking potty chairs. If your chief desire is to avoid the noise of your trainee's potty chair, the process is doomed from the start. So, don't feel guilty if you decide to steer clear of the one that's crooning show tunes.

Choosing the right potty chair

When it comes to potty chairs, you have two different styles to choose from: a stand-alone potty chair you put in the bathroom, or a special adapter seat you attach to the big people's toilet. We cover each type in the following sections.

Consider the smart-device factor: Some kids and parents like a chair with all the bells and whistles — one setup has a potty chair, an adapter seat for later, and a stepstool (see chair ratings below).

Foster a love connection between child and chair. If you get your toddler's thumbs up on a chair she likes, she'll feel more like the chair is her own.

Going with a toilet-topper

If your kid is turned on by the adults' toilet, she's already motivated, so get a special potty seat that hooks onto the toilet to make it fit a child. Figure 3-1 shows a toilet with a seat attached.

Figure 3-1:
A toilet-
topper
potty seat
on an adult
toilet.

Also, buy a little stepstool because she must be able to plant her feet firmly on a base (and push), for better bowel movements.

Get a no-nuisance toilet-top adapter: If you're buying an adapter seat for the adults' toilet, try to find one that won't drive the rest of the family nuts because removing it is such a bother.

Opting for a potty chair

Buy a private chair for an individualist: The child who's fond of the "mine" word will relate more easily to a potty-chair than to the big people's toilet. Typically, a kid likes having her own private little pee-pot, such as the one shown in Figure 3-2.

Figure 3-2:
An on-the-
floor potty
chair.

Plus, she won't need your help in getting on the potty like she may with the adults' toilet. The one downside: You have to clean out the bowl — and that gets old.

A potty chair stationed on each floor of a multiple-level home is a good idea. You want to do everything you can to help your tot succeed — so, make it ultra-easy for her to complete the race to the potty. (Expect trips to be at warp-speed at first.)

Accessorizing the potty chair

You can take a bare-bones approach to setting up the potty environment or you can jazz it up big time. If you want a fanciful backdrop for your child's potty chair, buy the Potty Surround. Offering a dollhouse feel, this scaled-down bathroom for the potty chair is an off-the-wall way to ignite interest. The 33" × 33" corrugated paperboard surround arrives all ready to set up. (Available on the Internet at www.ablebaby.com.)

Boy-directed splash guards, such as the one shown on the potty chair in Figure 3-3, can be troubling for boys and girls. Be sure you remove the urine guard from the potty seat or toilet ring because it can scrape your child as she moves on and off. This device is meant to keep urine from splashing, but don't take a chance. If your child gets hurt, she will think the toilet is scary, and that's a whole new set of problems. You don't want to go there.

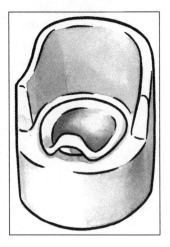

Figure 3-3:
A potty
chair with
splash
guard.

Some ultra-practical accessories are Jonny Glow strips that have a night-glow that helps your child use the potty in the middle of the night. Given a 15-minute charge from a normal bathroom light, the strips will glow for 10 hours, and they're easy to stick on any toilet surface ($6.95 at www.JonnyGlow.com).

If you want a little fluff in the bathroom, try a potty sticker chart or a bowl of tiny potty prizes displayed where your toddler can see it. She'll get the idea "If I get the hang of this potty thing, I can get stickers and a prize from that bowl — cool!" Or, hang up a hygiene chart, with pictures that take kids through the steps from wiping bottoms to cleaning hands (you can get one for $12.95 online at www.WeBehave.com).

For potty-team power, get your child a 'Go Potty' T-shirt (available for $7.99 at www.flipnflush.com), and some Sinkems, dissolving toilet targets that make it fun for both boys and girls to pee in the potty, available at www.sinkems.com.

Promoting chair-bonding

Give a tantalizing and spicy message when you first start promoting your child's new-best-friend attitude toward her potty chair: "You're going to be best buddies with your new little chair — you'll love it. It's going to help you move on up to being a big kid."

Make it a lovefest: Turn her first days of getting used to a cold, hard potty chair into fun and affection. Don't underestimate the power of a caregiver's or parent's enthusiasm. You can do a lot to trigger your child's sense of humor and imagination.

Let your trainee get acquainted with her equipment, whether she's chumming up to a new potty chair or the special seat that attaches to the toilet. Let her explore the new gadget — play with her chair, study it, handle it, stick her head in it. Don't cram the bonding idea down her throat, but, chances are, she'll enjoy the playful idea of buddying up.

Ways to help the bonding process along include

- ✔ **Go with the name game:** Let her use some letter-stickers to put her name on the potty chair. Encourage her to make it cuter with some stickers — flowers, stars, cartoon characters.

- ✔ **Start the doll demos:** Chapter 7 tells you how your child can teach her pee-doll to use the potty chair — as step one of the Potty Mambo. But, go ahead and get started right now, getting your child's mojo working, by doing potty-chair demos with a doll or stuffed animal.

- ✔ **Try baby steps:** Let your child sit on it with her clothes on. (Chapter 6 explains how this works.) Have her sit on it every day before you start the actual training so that she gets used to the feel of it.

Demonstrate how the potty chair works. Then take a soiled diaper and drop the stool from it into the potty-chair bowl. Ask your child to help you flush. Encourage her to watch the poop disappear. If she tries to put other things in the toilet, too, talk about what can be flushed — only poop, pee, and TP — and what can't be flushed — toys, silverware, fruit, siblings.

Potty-chair picks

Here are the authors' takes on some frontrunners in the Potty 500. These are available at baby stores nationwide, and on the Internet at www.babiesrus.com, www.babycenter.com, and www.babinski.com.

3-in-1s

🗸 Training Rewards Soft Seat Potty and Stepstool, by Graco: Soft Seat has a portable potty that also functions as a stepstool. The detachable seat can be used on an adult toilet. The closest look-alike to a big people's toilet, the Soft Seat Potty even has a cushioned seat to make your toddler extra-comfy. Also, parents like the large, easy-to-empty potty bowl — and the handles — your child feels safe and secure when she sits on it. $17.99

🗸 3-in-1 Potty Trainer Step Stool: A lot of bang for your buck, the 3-in-1 features a potty chair with easy-to-remove bowl, a seat that goes on the big toilet, and a base that doubles as a stepstool. $12.99

Standard chairs

🗸 Baby Bjorn Potty Chair: Comfy and fun to use, Baby Bjorn has one major advantage: The inner potty is really easy to take out for emptying and cleaning. Your child straddles this molded one-piece style. $21.99

🗸 Baby Bjorn Splash-Proof Potty: This one has a cute look and a wide base that lets your child plant her feet firmly during BM efforts. The high splashguard does its job of containing pee-splatter, and is shaped to prevent scrapes. Base stays put when the kid stands up. $14.99

Musical chairs

🗸 Hop On! Musical Potty: Sensors in the potty register moisture from pee and set off cheerful tunes. Kids like the feedback, but some parents tire of the songs. $22.95

🗸 Tinkle Toonz Musical Potty: Get ready to listen to lots of "Old McDonald Had a Farm" if your child chooses this one. The sensor sounds off when BM or urine hits the bowl. The potty is easy to clean, and naturally, kids like the instant gratification of music praising their efforts. But parents sometimes wish a dingo would steal it. $13.95

Toilet-toppers

🗸 Baby Bjorn Toilet Trainer: The best of the ones that fit atop the big people's toilet, the Baby Bjorn Toilet Trainer has an ergonomic soft shape that puts it head and shoulders above others of its genre. Thanks to a nifty adjustable-fit device, this trainer works on any toilet seat — not the case with others. No pinches when your child climbs off and on, and she can put it on and remove it herself (even has a handle to hang it up for off times). $29.99

🗸 Flip 'n Flush: This toilet seat adapter is easy to attach, and adults lift it up when they need to go — then, down it goes for toddler's turn. One big problem, though: Flip 'n Flush doesn't fit elongated toilet seats or ones made of plastic. $16

Using Other Cool Tools

In our smart-gadget-dominated world, bringing cool tools to the potty-training table can only pump up your pumpkin's excitement level. And, fortunately, parents and caregivers have amazing choices in role-model doll props, books, videos. Do some shopping, and when Potty-Mambo Weekend comes, you'll be ready!

Dolls

A totally cool (and pretty effective) way to get your child to focus on learning potty stuff is to have her teach a doll or stuffed animal how to use the potty. (It's so effective that it's Step 1 in the Potty Mambo covered in Chapter 7.) You can use an old teddy bear, but if you're buying your child a new doll, get the kind that just happens to — guess what? — pee.

Boys have just as much fun with dolls or stuffed animals — they're just a little rowdier/rougher in their handling of the potty-training props.

By the way, Potty Pee Wee Dolls are especially neat because they come in boy and girl styles. They're available for $12.95, from the Potty Store at www.thepottystore.com/pottyaids.html. Or, you can combine doll and book with *KoKo Doll Potty Book Package* by Vicki Lansky and Jane Prince: The story presents toilet training as a growing-up thing — and comes with a unisex doll.

The following explains how you use a doll or stuffed animal to micro-manage your child's potty training:

To get the ball rolling, you take the doll through its paces: put it on the potty chair, encourage it to pee, have it actually do so (if it can actually do so), praise the doll, and talk about how fun that was.

FOR WORKING PARENTS

It's always potty time!

A working mom in Houston, Texas — popular radio deejay Michele Fisher of 104 KRBE — likes to share parenting tips with her listeners, so she was quick to pass on the good news of a potty-training video that zoom-zoom-zoomed her daughter Emma to success. She gives a hearty endorsement to *It's Potty Time. $19.95.*

Fisher notes, "As soon as Emma heard the 'Super Duper Pooper' song (on the video), the idea of going in the potty became pretty neat. She also discovered reading while she sat on the potty, and that seemed to help as well. After watching *It's Potty Time* only a couple of times, she got over the training hurdle and out of training pants! She's 100-percent trained now, but still likes to watch 'Bobby's Birthday' just for fun."

You can get your toddler to help with dolly's cleanup. Smear the doll's bootie with jam and let your child practice wiping her baby-behind good and proper. Next, your trainee can wash the dolly's hands (if that's an option — soap and water may not be a good thing for a plush teddy bear). Then your toddler can help dump the doll's pee and poo into the big toilet.

Tell your child that when Potty-Training Weekend comes, you just know that she's going to do a super-cool job of teaching the doll. Cheer on every bit of doll tomfoolery, beginning to end. Show rollicking enthusiasm for the entire affair.

Wrap up with a comment that brings the whole thing bouncing back to her: "I'm sure you'll be using the potty very soon — you know so much about what to do! Look how happy your doll is — she likes the new potty!"

Kiddie books on potty training

Books on potty training today are so nifty. And, kids enjoy having parents and caregivers read to them — they love what they hear, and they love the undivided attention even more. Kids have such good memories, too, that they may want to "read" their often-heard potty-training book to you!

In any major bookstore, you'll find plenty of potty-training books. Make sure you go to the kids section — store personnel may try to send you to the parenting section, but the books you want are in the area marked "children's books."

Some good picks are

- *Uh Oh! Gotta Go!* (by Bob McGrath): This super book has clever artwork and a style that will excite your child. In one-liners, McGrath describes the experiences of 20 separate, individual kids, — from "Peter has perfect aim" to "Natalie waits and listens for the splash." Kids like the toddler-level humor.

- *The Princess and the Potty* (by Wendy Cheyette Lewison): Here, you read of a diaper-wearing princess who wouldn't use her potty, which upsets her parents — what to do? In this comic treatment, the solution comes from the princess herself.

- *The Potty Chronicles* (by Annie Reiner): Aimed at parents more than kids, this one goes into how a child reacts to this stressful time, so you'll find it helpful in that respect. Our take on The Potty Chronicles: The slant is super-frank.

- *What to Expect When You Use the Potty* (by Heidi Murkoff): This book has good specifics and is attractive enough to capture your child's attention.

✔ *It's Potty Time* (a Smart Kids Book): With simple info written clearly, *It's Potty Time* is a fun book that has a little button on the front that makes a flushing sound mixed with girl giggles. We liked this one.

✔ *I'm a Potty Champion* (by Kitty Higgins): Gives tips in storybook form and has a little trophy — plus, stickers to put your child's name on the award.

✔ *Where's Max's Potty?* (Hazel Songhurst and David Till): This one has a dad training his son, which makes it good role modeling for single parents.

✔ *What Do You Do With a Potty?* (Marianne Borgardt): An interactive book that tells toddlers what a potty is for, via tabs that make the kid's pants go down, TP roll out, and potty-contents go into the toilet.

✔ *The Rugrats' Potty Book* (Kathi Wagner): With schizophrenically fun illustrations, this book features lots of razzle-dazzle — a set of kids who are cheering on another child who's learning to use the potty — and the bonus of 106 potty-shaped gold stickers.

Kiddie videos on potty training

TV and videos? Kids get it. Potty-training videos have that wonderful visual/audio pop that snags attention and holds it. That makes potty videos great ways to show your child that lots of youngsters her age and size are jumping on the big-kid-underpants bandwagon.

Some popular potty-training videos (available in video stores and online) are

✔ *Once Upon a Potty for Her/Him:* One of the hottest videos available today, Once Upon a Potty delights kids, who watch and re-watch. Parents think the her/his versions are especially cool. This has pictures of real toddlers doing potty deeds. Plus, you'll like its Potty Song sing-along and a 13-minute doctor statement reassuring parents that it's quite okay if their children are potty-training slowpokes. Kids learn a lot from the animated tale of Joshua's potty progress. $13.99

✔ *Let's Go Potty!:* Here's a live-action video parental aid that even has a stamp of approval from the National Parenting Center. It has the advantage of featuring real kids in action, which makes it easy for your small fry to conjure up visions of herself duplicating the potty-stars' moves. $19.95

✔ *Now I Can Potty:* You get plenty of bathroom shots, kid testimonials, and six silly songs applauding the merits of growing-up, wearing underpants, and getting potty seats. $19.95

> ✔ **Bear in the Big Blue House — Potty Time with Bear:** Kids and parents praise this video for Bear's gentle, calm, upbeat approach as a super potty coach. The fun songs will send a toddler scurrying to try her talents as a Toileteer. Video characters deal with issues like bathroom etiquette and fear of the unknown. Downside: this video has two episodes that are unrelated to potty training. $9.95

Getting the Goods

Even if you have a hand-me-down potty chair and plenty of pullups for your current trainee, you can't get away from doing some shopping, even if only for stickers to put on a success chart. In these sections, we tell you what you need and where to get it.

Making a list

So many goodies, so little time. That means you need to make a list of items you'll want on hand for Potty-Mambo Weekend, which should be looming not too far in the future. Jot down: potty chair or adapter, special props (doll, video, book), cleanup stuff, training pants, and spiffy big-kid underwear. Totally optional items are: travel potty and all the things mentioned earlier in this chapter under "Accessorizing the Potty Chair." These are nice to have but not having them certainly won't be a deal-breaker.

✔ **Potty chair (or trainer seat and stepstool):** See "Potty-chair picks" at the beginning of this chapter.

✔ **Cleanup supplies:** Including wipes, paper towels, antibacterial spray, stain-removing wipes or spray).

✔ **A baby doll that pees:** For more on this, turn to the "Dolls" section earlier in this chapter.

✔ **A kiddie book that talks about a real child going through potty training:** See "Kiddie books on potty training" earlier in this chapter.

✔ **A potty-training video:** Check out the recommendations in "Kiddie videos on potty training" in the preceding section.

✔ **Training pants:** Explore the types in the following "Sorting out training-pants options" section.

✔ **Real underwear:** For "graduation" from potty training.

✔ **Fold-up potty seat (for travel):** If your family often takes to the road, you may want a collapsible potty chair that you can stick in your car trunk for potty emergencies.

Shopping together

Taking your toddler with you to buy potty-training supplies is a great way to invest her in the potty-training process, especially if you can make it a fun outing, complete with a stop for gobbling chili-cheese-fries and hot dogs. Enjoy a dandy parent-child day, when the two of you take to the mall for a supply run. You've already started talking up the whole potty-training thing (see Chapter 6), so your toddler is primed and excited and ready to be a half-pint consumer.

Getting your child dressed for potty success, you'll have fun, fun, fun — till your child gets her fill of shopping. (If she gets cranky and shopping gets unfun, just end the outing with good humor, and get the loose ends taken care of during a solo trip of your own.)

At the potty-supply emporium, ask for your kiddo's opinions in categories that feature choices. "Do you like training pants with Harry Potter figures or dinosaurs?" Having her make a selection gives her a greater emotional investment in the project.

Hype the excitement that's ahead during Potty-Mambo Weekend. "When kids are potty trained, they get to do more things, go more places, yada, yada, yada. We're going to have so much fun that weekend, getting you used to your little chair, and reading books. We'll have a ball!"

Being Clothes-Conscious

Being dressed to promote easy potty moves goes a long way toward making your kiddo hunker down and become a top cadet. Here, we look at the right kind of clothes and training pants for a toddler success story.

Your little one must be a wizard with her pants, and be able to pull them down easily and quickly. Oversized shorts and pants with elastic waistbands are perfect.

In warm weather, dress her only in loose training pants, with no extra set of pants over them. Think footloose and fancy-free.

Dressing your child for success

Dress your toddler for clothes-pulling and tugging. For potty training's early days, put her in saggy, loose clothing that can be easily pulled up and down. Tuggable duds are divine.

If she's just hanging around the house and the weather is warm, let her go bare or wear training pants only. Hopefully, this will help her keep her target mission at the front of her mind.

For going places, and colder days, some of the best toddler bets are plain, elastic-waisted, cotton-knit pull-on pants — long or short. Short dresses work well for your little miss. You can find a wide selection of toddler sweatpants and other pull-up pants anywhere you like to shop — online or in the mall.

Avoid jeans, overalls, and leggings — too tough for a potty-training novice's fledgling hand-eye coordination. And, forget about the kinds with crotch snaps and difficult ties. Later on, these will work fine, but not at the outset of the Potty 500.

If you need to buy clothes during potty-training days, super-size the pants. You want them as big and slouchy as hip-hop duds.

Sorting out training-pant options

Clearly, being clad in the right training pants is the A-number-one factor in dressing for success for Potty-Training Weekend. How can she be expected to show her flair for the Potty Mambo if she's feeling shaky about her casual chic wear? Unthinkable.

In studies of potty-training kids who went into the process with readiness signs in place, researchers found that the key to rapid progress boiled down to one thing — upward mobility from diapers into disposable training pants, cloth training pants, or underwear. That part is big. Huge.

Why do pants carry so much weight (forgive the pun)? They're messengers. Your child knows she is being informed that the show's on the road — that she's now a potty-work-in-progress. And, to her, this seems like very heavy stuff.

Don't worry, though. Very soon, your child will discover how nice it feels to be dry and clean. She'll get used to that feeling, and be ultra-motivated to tell you when she wants to potty.

Start potty training with your child in training pants that have a plastic exterior. You have to expect accidents early on, and any other option will result in urine trickling down her legs.

Your choices are:

> ✓ **Padded diapers shaped like underpants:** You child can pull this terrific design up and down. And, you'll find packs of them widely available in supermarkets. These "big kid" trainers with elasticized waistbands have the huge advantage of being disposable,

unlike plastic-type cover-ups and underwear. Another plus of pullable-upables: Your child won't get as embarrassed because her accidents aren't eyesores like they would be in pee-splattered training pants or undies, both of which show wetness and are droopier when soaked or loaded.

Most parents and caregivers give hearty thumbs-ups to padded diaper-pants. You'll see your child soon turn into a whiz at using these. They operate like underwear, absorb urine just like diapers, and have a cute little elasticized waistband. (Goodbye, adhesive diaper-flaps!)

✔ **Intermediate training pants:** You can skip padded diaper-pants and use training pants, which are underwear-like but made of thicker material than regular underpants. Plus, these offer some small degree of absorbency. Here we're talking regular-looking underwear with the added protection of slightly thicker material. This kind has definite pluses: They're reusable wash-and-wear, so you save money. And, they really, really bother a potty-training-ready kid when the material gets wet.

✔ **Regular underwear:** Kids love these because they're oh-so-grownup-looking. Parents don't love them, though — they're not made to absorb urine. Thus, regular undies are very iffy propositions on a half-trained kid.

Save the real-and-true underwear for the final phase of potty training, as a grand prize, when your child is in the home stretch, and has generally mastered potty use *most of the time*. Otherwise, you will be in for some extensive cleanup.

Training pants are a motivator only if your child is truly ready to potty train!

Part II
It's All in the Timing

The 5th Wave   By Rich Tennant

WENDY AND PETER PAN START A FAMILY

©RICHTENNANT

"Are you sure it isn't too early to start Peter Junior's potty training?"

In this part...

Part II tells you what you've probably already suspected — that potty success is all in the timing. So, you put out your antenna to pick up on the all-important readiness signs that clue you in to the right time for potty-training startup. You'll do some covert operations, James Bond style, and you'll begin some gentle brainwashing along the lines of: Wouldn't it be nice if you and your potty chair got friendly."

Soon, your child will be ready to multitask and primed for Potty-Training Weekend. You'll get his motor running. Head out on the highway. Looking for adventure. Or whatever comes your way.

Chapter 4

Recognizing Readiness Signs

● ●

In This Chapter

▶ Making note of patterns

▶ Spotting behavioral readiness

▶ Noting disgust with messy diapers

▶ Observing potty-related readiness

● ●

Several months before his second birthday, your child may say that he wants to use the toilet. You feel like popping a cork on a bottle of champagne — but not so fast. A declaration of interest in using the potty doesn't mean he's capable of doing it; it just means that he likes the idea. So, try to keep that favorable mindset going and wait until you see several other readiness signs glaring like neon.

If you can successfully pin down the time when your child is really ready — typically from 18 to 24 months old — you enhance your chances of helping him succeed by 75 percent. Between 18 months and 3 years, most children reach the point of muscle control that makes self-regulation possible. So, when that is apparent, along with an interest in using the potty and other strong indicators, go for it because after your child creeps up on his threesies, he will be much less jazzed by simple pleasures such as spiffy underwear and potty-training videos.

So, watch for the readiness factors, and zero in on prime time for training. Look for signs that your toddler can achieve control over his body — and that he's warming to the idea. Then, you fire the starting pistol to send your child sprinting from the potty-training starting mark with a burst of heady optimism. Set up a success-oriented mission by doing a little groundwork — your own careful observations of poop and pee timing and patterns.

Doing Covert Operations

You — number-one agent — are going on a covert operation: It involves monitoring your child's ready-to-use-the-potty signs, so that you can leap on the right timing. If you can get a good take on the elimination clock for his bowels and bladder, you will have a great launching pad for successful potty training.

How does it work? During daily scouting, you keep tabs on your child's regular habits of urinating and having bowel movements. You carefully take note of the frequency and timing of urination and the approximate amounts of fluid consumed prior to elimination. If you work out of the home, just ask your child's caregiver to do this for you for two or three days.

Keeping tabs on pee and poo patterns

After your child eats a meal, see how long it takes before he has a bowel movement. Is it 15 minutes, 30 minutes, or longer? When potty training actually begins, this knowledge cues you as to the perfect times to lead your toddler to his potty chair. You can expect far better results if you can time the bathroom moment when he is very likely to be feeling an urge to go — or at least an itty-bitty inclination.

Essentially, what you're trying to do is figure out when he will need to go so that you can sit him on the potty and he will do his deposit in the bowl, not the diaper. (Typically, he will first get the hang of doing a BM on the potty chair and then the peeing will come next.)

While you're in the keeping-tabs period, start prompting your child to tell you when he has a desire to pee and poop — and when he has peed or pooped in his diaper and wants you to change it.

Most kids have a bowel movement in the morning after eating breakfast. If your child's stomach is full, the inclination to defecate should come about 20 minutes after the meal is over.

If he gets up from breakfast and then goes in his diaper, have him go with you to dump the diaper contents into the toilet bowl. That underscores that this is the proper spot for depositing his body products. In other words, you are saying very gently: "Sweetie, take note. This is where your poop and pee will go once you start using the potty."

Because you're starting to put emphasis on potty products, your toddler may even want to feel the stuff he produced. Be patient. Steer him to put it in the toilet — without showing disgust on your face or in your voice. Your ongoing spirit: calmness in the face of all forms of normal curiosity. Your goal is, of course, keeping his hands off the poop. You should be firm, but don't make a big deal of it — otherwise, this may turn into a showdown issue (it's my poopie and I'll play with it if I want to). And remember that the family dog may be another Curious George, so keep him far away from the potty-chair bowl because pups have been known to scoop poop, too, and they don't use their paws.

Zeroing in on facial signs and noises

You eavesdrop and watch. You and your mate and caregivers take note of your toddler's unique set of facial signs and pacing and grunts and groans. If you are vigilant, you'll see patterns emerge — your child's very own individual precursors of bowel action and urination.

Some kids give you no indicators at all; others send out signals that are far too subtle to rely on. Still others give you a full-fledged Broadway production when they're doing their elimination work.

At any rate, when you're doing your fast-track spying, you'll discover whether or not your child is going to leave you clueless when it comes to special facial and sound expressions.

Don't beg for signs from a non-signal-giver. That's a waste of precious time that could be better spent dancing the Potty-Training Mambo with your child.

Fortunately, the fates make sure that most children are extremely generous with their foreshadowing: You will probably hear grunts and groans, see his face get red, watch him strain and emote, and finally, notice a greatly relieved look of "ah, that's better" relax his face.

Then you need to check out the specific timing of these signs; in other words, does he have a BM immediately after contorting his face and making grunting noises, or does that come several minutes before?

In some children, the only thing you can count on is that they stop whatever they're doing and stand still when they have a bowel movement. Most of the time, this is lost on a busy outside caregiver — so, if your child falls in the group of stealthy and quiet producers, you will have to rely exclusively on the timing of his BMs and urination.

Don't worry if your child's pottying expressions are bizarro-wild or nada-nonexistent. This part is just about studying his timing. All you need to take away from your observations are some concrete pieces of info on his elimination signs and signals.

Watching for Behavioral Changes

Toddlerhood is a time of growing independence and adaptations to the world. Behaviors are many and complex, as your child begins to understand delayed gratification, tolerating frustration, and enduring separation.

Normally, a toddler's displays of anger and frustration increase significantly during year two. The following year, however, these begin to mellow somewhat. Coping skills are ramping up a bit. You notice that the kid heading toward his third birthday is a kinder, gentler toddler, and that's the phase you are looking for.

He has begun to accept (to a very small and subtle degree) that maybe — just maybe — the entire universe was not created to suit his needs alone, and that other people around him may just have a few rights. From all indications, it appears that a more pliable kid lies right around the bend — an ideal candidate for potty training.

Before you declare him emotionally ready, be sure to add into the mix any kind of turmoil on the horizon. In the event of a move, divorce, new baby in the home, or any other major upheaval, most toddlers will show very babified reactions: thumb sucking, naughtiness, altered eating or sleeping patterns, and overall regression. In essence, home-front traumas make a child feel shaky and thus, he frets over the potential of lost love and attention.

Putting things in their proper places

Around age two, a child begins to show sparks of interest in self-reliance, and typically, that inspires mimicking of others' actions. Your child sees you putting things in specific places, and he decides that is really pretty neat. He suspects that his parents and relatives and caregivers know what they are doing, and thus, he figures, they are worthy of copycatting.

Some hallmarks of your child's new proclivity for pigeonholing things are

- ✔ **A fondness for putting things in proper places:** He shows an understanding that toys go in the toy box, canned goods go in the pantry, and body products leave the house via the toilet. Hmmm . . . this is looking very good indeed.

- ✔ **A love of lint:** A two-year-old often develops a habit of picking up pieces of lint off the carpet and looking at them, simply because of his growing sense of knowing what belongs where — and watching those who try to maintain cleanliness and order. Suddenly, his topsy-turvy way of approaching play and duties begins to get some fine-tuning as his mind expands beyond babyhood.

- ✔ **Liking lineups:** Some toddlers learn to line up blocks or little action figures, or like for a parent to stack up their blankets just so — or put the pillow in a certain place.

- ✔ **Enjoying the familiar:** Your child may want you to read a certain book over and over, and will ask you to repeat certain parts he loves. He may even get so fastidious about proper order that he can catch you when you try to skip a few pages when you're in a hurry.

When you notice your child's burgeoning order fetish, comment on it, and draw a parallel to other parts of his life. "I see you are beginning to put your toys and blankets in certain places. That's good. I really like to know where I can find things, too."

A good starting point for addressing the subject of where poop and pee go is to talk with your child about routines and proper places for things in the house. Ask: "See how I put food leftovers down the garbage disposal?" If he hasn't watched this before, give him a demonstration. Then, follow up with a trip to the bathroom, in which you use the toilet and show how the flushing mechanism disposes of urine or feces. Let him watch and talk about how he is going to learn very soon how to use the potty so that the poop and pee now going in his diaper will be going into the toilets (big and small).

Every chance you get, illustrate your point about where poop goes: Show him how you drop the discards from the diaper into the toilet because that's where they go when "big people" use the toilet.

Do not make him feel bad for having let his own body soil a diaper. No guilt trips whatsoever. You can't act as if his poop is disgusting or foul or smelly (even if it is). Body products are no-fault stuff.

Take his hand and let him help you flush, and praise his budding ability to do so. Play up to him how cool it can be to use the flushing mechanism.

Finding signs of growing independence

You are beginning to see a rather independent nature in your once-clingy child. Now, your job is to take this newfound pride-in-accomplishment and help him apply it to becoming toilet-proficient. The following are some signs of an independent lad who roams the world (and should, by all rights, be using proper bathroom facilities):

- ✔ **A good observer:** One sign of a newly independent nature is your toddler's fuller understanding of his surroundings and what is going on. In this vein, the child appears to be getting the hang of why people use the toilet, and this is starting to interest him.

- ✔ **Side-by-side play:** About this time, a two-year-old is usually happy playing alongside someone else or by himself. He doesn't really play *with* other kids at this age.

- ✔ **Follow the leader:** Your child is probably learning to love being a good mimic, and he likes people to follow his lead, too. If urged to do so, a two-year-old can lead family members in various kinds of hand jive, showing them how to put their hands over their heads, clap hands, touch their cheeks, and so on.

- ✔ **Finding his style:** During this period, many kids also demonstrate a marked preference for some degree of independence in dressing. You see your once-passive child now struggling to put on his own clothes and shoes, and apparently, liking the experience, however difficult it turns out to be.

Encourage your child's growing interest in dressing himself. Start learning how to back off and let things be somewhat disheveled. Resist your rush-rush attitude that makes you want to take over.

Building up buttercup

If you bow to the traditional parenting drive to fix things up, your child will cower in the shadow of your greater abilities. Why should he try anything when you're always hovering, eager to improve his pathetically deficient efforts?

On the other hand, if you can restrain yourself and just let him wear his pants crooked, he will feel a great deal of satisfaction at having accomplished a big person's activity. Better yet, he believes that his parent or number-one caregiver saw what he was doing and thought it was pretty cool. To parrot the unique words of Sally Field's Oscar acceptance speech, "You like me — you really like me!"

Try to convey that positive message to your child instead of the opposite one: "I like you, kid, but you're not very good at doing anything." What better way to foster anxiousness and insecurity than to show your child from early years that you think he screws up everything he tries?

Just when your toddler is acting ever so independent, be prepared for him to pull a schizophrenic switcheroo. One moment your child is saying, "I can do it — don't help me," and the next moment, he turns into a limp rag doll, hanging on your arm and whining to go home, screaming, "Me a baby." Some parents mistakenly interpret this as a willful mood change, when, in fact, it just happens to be part of the evolving personality of a two-year-old. Though you are strongly invested in having your child become less needy, you need to accept these wildly differing extremes in independence as what they are — indecisiveness, not stubbornness.

Waiting for a cooperative stage

As your child edges up to his third birthday, you'll see him pony up to some real big-boy attitudes and actions that make parents and care-givers beam with pride. Some good signs of an increasingly cooperative frame of mind:

- ✓ He can sit happily and play alone for five minutes or longer.
- ✓ He responds quickly to your requests.
- ✓ He's open to trying new things.

A cooperative spirit is one of the most important readiness factors. If you start potty training when your child still loves to defy you with radical, over-the-top rebellion, you are five steps behind the starting line from the get-go. Far better to postpone the launch of potty training until your child moves into a more easygoing mood.

Dealing with an uncooperative stage

If your child is fairly hard to handle most of the time, then just choose the week when you see any glimmer of sunniness, even a mere smidgen. If your outside caregiver meets you at the end of the day with "Kevin was really in a good mood today," that means you should go for it. With a tough-temperament kid, seize the day when you first glimpse cooperation — if several other readiness signs are already in place. That means you'll set up Potty-Training Weekend as soon as possible — and tell him about it while he's in that happy mood.

A positive mindset can open the door for you to tell him a story about how children get accustomed to using the potty, and how they like not having to wear diapers anymore. Explain to your child that when he starts potty training, you will let him teach his new pee-doll how to use the toilet. "You'll get to use your new potty chair and other things that big kids get to use." See Chapter 3 for info on the shopping trip for potty-training supplies.

The more you can make potty training sound like a fun adventure, the less likely he will be to make excuses or erect barriers to the process. Your announcements that "It's time to go to the potty" are not going to meet with a great deal of opposition if he already feels favorably inclined to get the thing going. Once again, you need the cooperative spirit.

If most of your child's responses are in opposition to the ideas you pose ("No, I don't want to!") consider this carefully when you're deciding whether to launch potty-training efforts. Having your child in the wrong frame of mind will be a huge drawback when you need his cooperation in learning an all-new and very tough skill.

You can expect a child with a dicey temperament to be harder to handle at stressful times, and potty-training prep work is one of those times. Just try to reduce his daily frustrations as much as possible. Arrange the environment so that his life flows smoothly and routinely. A high-strung child has more than his share of conflict in peer play, and thus, suffers lots of frustration outside the home. You can't be a total buffer from his getting roughed up emotionally, but you can do some small things to help. All of this tender loving care will make him a more cooperative potty trainee.

Using the power of suggestion and positive thinking

Every chance you get, chat briefly about how kids learn to use potty chairs and toilets, and no longer have to bother with diapers and skin cream and lying down to be diapered. They get to move up to pants that big kids wear because they no longer pee or poop in diapers. "Remember the big-boy underpants we bought last week? You picked them out, and soon you'll get to wear them."

Two to tango — and tangle

At this juncture in your child's life, remind yourself that his basic temperament will be a factor in all interactions. "Difficult" kids aren't very adaptable and are generally pretty negative. "Easy" children are regular in their habits (eating, sleeping), very adaptable, and mostly positive. A third group of children can be characterized as "slow to warm up." They are quiet, shy, and slower in adjusting to new situations.

All of these children are poised to thrive in life, but problems can arise when temperament clashes with a number-one caregiver. If the adult has a parenting style and a set of expectations that go against the grain of the child, all manner of conflict can result. For example, the mom who was a smiley Homecoming Queen may not show much empathy when her slow-to-warm-up toddler repeatedly disappoints her with his difficulty adjusting to strange situations, such as potty training.

On the other hand, when a good fit exists between parent and child, this compatible duo experiences less stress and conflict. A caregiver must understand that both temperament and behavioral style are inborn traits. So, instead of trying to "reinvent" your child to suit your temperament, you, as the adult in this equation, need to tweak your responses to bolster your toddler's development.

Rein in any desire to make your kid a clone of you or your partner or a sibling. Instead, work on developing the wonderful individual traits that set this child apart from all others in the world. It could be that the result of that amazing gene pool is a human being finer than anyone yet born, you or your mate included. Don't spoil the potential of that genuine one-of-a-kind snowflake by trying to mold him into someone different.

Consider it a good sign if he asks you what's going to happen to all the diapers you have left. Ah, he's accepting the plan. "We'll give them to Renee, who just had baby Sebastian, or Aunt Liz who is going to have a baby or donate them to a shelter that needs extra diapers." Add to that: "I'll let you decide who gets them. But I'm sure you won't need them anymore because you will be using your potty chair when you need to pee or poop. This is so exciting! You're growing up."

Take him with you when you go to the local agency to donate the diapers. That way, he sees that your family is helping people — and that the diapers are going to little babies now that he is growing up and no longer needs them. This also shows that he is accepting the idea of growing up as a good thing.

Detecting Physical Clues

Years two and three of a child's life are ones of challenges and skill building when children make noticeable strides in language development and motor skills. Consider the fact that between ages 2 and 3, the child has reached about 50 percent of his adult height. (Some think this is a myth, but it's actually true.) See for yourself: Multiply your child's height by two when he's 2, tuck the answer away and take it out when he reaches his adult height.

Keep in mind that a child has to develop in several ways in order to thrive in the toilet-training event.

> ✔ **He must be able to signal the need to go to the potty.**
>
> ✔ **He has to be able to walk, climb, and pull his clothes up and down.**
>
> ✔ **He needs to have a bladder that is developed enough for him to stay dry several hours during the day.**
>
> ✔ **He must have sufficient motor skills to make potty-training moves possible.**

If these conditions aren't met, he will just get frustrated and fall apart at the first signs of difficulty. Even though copying someone is lots of fun for a mobile toddler, it still may not be easy for him.

If your child is lagging behind his peers in gross or fine motor coordination — running, climbing, dressing, drawing — you shouldn't worry. He'll get there. But wait to start potty training until he shows the readiness to perform the tasks that are integral to using the toilet.

Potting cues

So, your child's body is in a maturing frenzy. You're very excited about that, as well you should be. He's leaving babyhood behind, signified by certain markers of toilet-training potential. Look for the following super-significant red flags:

> ✔ **Your child urinates a large amount at one time.**
>
> ✔ **His bowel movements are well formed and fairly regular.**
>
> ✔ **He notices the physical sensations that indicate needing to pee or poo, and sometimes tells you in advance.**
>
> ✔ **He stays dry for at least two hours.**

All of these things indicate that both bowel and bladder control are developing normally. No longer is a wet or soiled diaper a constant in his life. Readiness for toilet training is definitely on the horizon.

Start doing occasional diaper-checks at this time. You can tug open the back of the diaper and note that he is dry so that you can comment on it. "Hey, look — a dry diaper. Very good!" In a casual way, you are planting an association: Staying dry reaps praise from a parent or caregiver. So, your child thinks, "Hey, that must be a good thing. Maybe I should do more of that."

What if your child just has to try on his new big-boy underpants? If it seems to be important, let him model them. Then, in the absence of any readiness signs other than a good attitude, put him back in diapers and go about your business. On the other hand, if this seems like such a good omen that you believe it will take nothing but a small nudge for him to be ready, tell him that he will be choosing to use the potty chair for peeing and pooping — if he decides to stick with the big-boy underpants. "You want to do that?" Let him digest that idea, and see if it flies.

Walking, running, and following instructions

Your toddler is walking and running and following instructions. Mastering these competencies is a strong signal that the child is probably ready to work on bladder and bowel control. His motor development is such that the task of tugging pants down and then back up can be accomplished easily.

Before you go forward, though, check this readiness signal: If you ask your child to hand you a toy or deliver something to another room, is he able to understand what you want done and actually do it?

Being able to follow instructions is critical because you want your child to do several guidance-steered activities: tell you when he needs to go, pull his own clothes down for pottying purposes, wipe himself, flush the toilet, and wash his hands. If he simply isn't at the level of understanding these pointers and responding to them, he will have a tough time mastering the potty process.

Noting Changes Directly Related to Potty Training

Your child, once a very messy little thing, is showing signs of real humanity; he wipes his hands with glee sometimes. He doesn't like having a sticky face or dirty fingers. He even can get fairly excited about helping you wipe the table.

So, if you are lucky, around age two you'll see your toddler getting rather antsy over wet and soiled diapers. What once was quite all right aesthetically is becoming uncomfortable at least or maybe downright yucky.

Being annoyed with messy diapers

The dish from the diaper-kid is coming down the pike: No more messy-boy, shamelessly bowing to nature's call. This is a turning point developmentally, when the aesthetics of bebopping around the house in a messy diaper are suddenly bothersome to him. Having a low-slung diaper that is heavy with urine or poop is becoming a drag.

He may even pull at his pants or act restless when the need to urinate hits him. Sometimes, your child acts like he is extremely irked by the feeling of being cold and wet. This is a good thing.

When the aesthetics of being a diaper-kid begin to get on his nerves, quite possibly you will see, hear, and maybe even smell the signals. Your child may even take off his own diaper and bring it to you, simply because the feel of the wetness or poop seems gross to him. Here, you should capitalize on the fact that he has noticed a diaper that feels bad to him. A good response: "So, you don't like the way it feels when your diaper is wet or filled with poo." If he agrees, follow up with the logical transition: "That tells me that very soon you will want to start using your own potty chair to pee or poo in. Soon, we'll have our Potty-Training Weekend, and we're going to have a great time." Chapter 7 gives the specifics on Potty-Training Weekend.

Taking an interest in his body products

Increasingly, your child seems to be interested in his body products. This may even extend to the scary lengths of touching the poop he produced. Hopefully, your little charge will skip this phase, but if he does decide to get up close and personal with his products, humor him — and restrain yourself from eye-rolling or dry-heaving.

Explain calmly that his poop goes in the toilet, and then take it away and demonstrate where it goes and how it's flushed. "You don't want to play with it because germs are in our poop, and they can make us sick."

Switch the focus by using this as a hand-washing time. Show him how to wash his hands thoroughly, and tell him that you can tell that he will be a good hand-washer when he does that regularly during potty training. Any time that you must address something that's negative (poop-molding adventures, for example), try to end the conversation on a higher, better note: your faith in his awesome hand-washing talent, for example. Knowing that he is good at things translates to a child's mind in one way only: "I am worthwhile; I can learn how to do things. I am good."

If your attempts to curb poop-play result in temper tantrums (on your child's part, not yours), back off and defuse the moment. In two-year-olds, tantrums are common, and they are generally worsened by reinforcement by parents and taunting siblings.

If your child persists in showing he can be stubborn ("It's my party and I'll play with poop if I want to!"), do not give in. Be firm in diverting his efforts and turning him away from poop-play to another activity. But don't act overly concerned or agitated. See Chapter 8 for more tips on handling kids who persist in poop-play.

Prepping with potty-training bingo

When Potty-Training Weekend is about a week away, use your child's budding knowledge of bathroom words to set up a game to see how much he knows about the bathroom. Ask these questions in a game-show format.

Sit him on a chair, facing you, and use little cards to make the game look official. Don't worry if he doesn't do anything but laugh; the point is to have fun with it and establish a lighthearted feel to potty training. This is a great time for a few giggles.

Ask him things like:

What is the paper used for that comes in rolls and hangs next to the toilet? (a.) Washing faces; (b.) brushing teeth; (c.) wiping your bottom.

In our family, who uses the toilet for peeing? (a.) Goldfish; (b.) puppy; (c.) mommy; (d.) cat.

Why can't a cat use the toilet? (a.) It's too high up; (b.) she's not smart enough; (c.) she's too short; (d.) a litter box works better.

What do school kids wear? (a.) Diapers; (b.) training pants, (c.) regular underwear; (d.) sweat pants.

What does Nana use the big bathroom mirror for? (a.) To put on lipstick; (b.) to keep an eye on you; (c.) to watch TV.

What do family members do in the bathroom to take care of their teeth? (a.) Brush them; (b.) use wipes on them; (c.) take them out.

Why do two-year-olds like learning to use the potty? (a.) They don't have to wear diapers anymore; (b.) they feel taller; (c.) they get to go to school; (d.) the chair is for back-rubbing and hot-tubbing.

What do we do in the bathroom before we eat meals? (a.) Mop the floor; (b.) cook dinner; (c.) buy groceries; (d.) wash hands.

What kind of clothes do we wear to take baths? (a.) Swimsuits; (b.) shorts; (c.) dressy clothes; (d.) no clothes.

What do adults do with their pants when they use the toilet? (a.) Put them on the doorknob; (b.) put them on their heads; (c.) put them in the bathtub; (d.) pull them down.

Where does the pee and poop go after it falls in the toilet? (a.) It goes in the sink; (b.) it goes in the car; (c.) it goes in a wagon; (d.) it gets flushed away.

Why does it help small children to use potty chairs when they first learn to pee and poop in the potty? (a.) It's easier to climb on when you're little; (b.) it's a good place to eat your dinner; (c.) it flushes better than the big toilet.

Have a small prize for him when he wins the contest (which he will, of course). If he asks you if you can play this game again, tell him: "Sure, we're going to do lots of fun things during Potty-Training Weekend; we'll watch a video and read books, and you'll learn to use your brand-new potty chair. It's going to be so neat when you learn to pee and poop in your potty."

Hearing the magic words: Please change my diaper!

Even when your child starts being bothered by messy diapers, you can't predict when he will come to you to complain about it. But sooner or later, the moment will arrive: He will come up to you with a look of urgency in his eyes and deliver the great news, "I want my diaper changed," thus signaling a growing readiness for potty training.

Every time he tells you he has wet or soiled his diaper, praise the fact that he told you. "That's great! You remembered to tell me. Good!"

During diaper changes that he has asked for (and all the others), never use any drastic "your diaper's nasty" kind of talk. What your toddler has done is not repulsive; it's just normal. He's okay; you're okay. Dump all of your negativity in regard to urination, bowel movements, and potty training, so that you won't make judgmental comments on the products that come from your child's body. Instead, turn diapering moments into pep rallies: "Hey, won't it be nice when you do this in the potty and you won't have to lie down so I can change you? That's going to be so cool! Don't you think so? You're going to love it, I bet."

Noting when your child knows the lingo

There comes a wonderful time when you can tell that your child is definitely understanding the potty-training buzzwords. If you are fortunate, he will soon be using this new vocabulary in requests to use the bathroom.

What are the "right" words? As Chapter 2 mentioned, you can choose the lingo that you like. If your family chums up to very accurate terminology, such as urination and defecation, use those words, although most small fry will find these a bit heavy. In lots of families, "pee," "poop," and "BM" are standards. You just want to make sure that you and your child are speaking the same language.

One problem with precocious small fry is that they not only know potty lingo — they know some ghastly embellishments on it. If your child is exposed to outer forces in daycare, he may bring home some guttersnipe talk and shock your socks off. Stay cool, calm, and unshakable. Make it clear that this language is unacceptable, and hope that you've heard the last of it. Often, of course, that's not the case.

So, what if your child persists in naughty bathroom talk, no matter what you say? Rest assured, preschoolers are notorious for their noncompliance. The typical figure bandied about among developmental experts is that most kids prior to starting school refuse to follow adults' orders about half the time. So, because this is not a battle worth going to the mat over, try to switch your child's attention to something else. Dance a little sidestep, in other words. That way, you stop the nasty-babble, and you minimize the negativity of the moment, both in one fell swoop.

Chapter 5

Choosing the Right Time

· ·

In This Chapter

▶ Deciding on the best time for potty training

▶ Steering clear of stressful times

▶ Getting your trainee psyched up

▶ Working with your toddler's preferences

· ·

Starting potty training at just the right time is like tasting a tantalizing dessert — a chocolate soufflé, if you will. You could get along without it, no doubt — but choosing that perfect moment certainly makes life so much sweeter.

Like eating a chocolate soufflé, successful potty training is immensely satisfying. And, when you're able to lead your child past the landmines and safely to the target, you get a real sense of rightness — and a major-league charge.

So select an appropriate time for your toddler (low on stress and high on motivation), tout Potty-Training Weekend as an upcoming Fun Time — and get cracking on some super-toddler-brainwashing.

Finding the Best Times

The best of times. The worst of times. You're going for the first category, of course. And, you can make sure that happens by setting up your child for success so that the outcome is the "best of times." (Chapter 6 helps you prepare for the big weekend to ensure success.)

Slot in on your calendar a nice, calm weekend for potty training when you will have ample time to focus. At the outset, your child will need lots of attention and help, and you want to provide exactly that — in bucket loads. Besides, weekends are almost always the most ideal for free-form activities.

Choosing a weekend in spring or summer

Spring and summer are quintessential potty-training startup times simply because a child wears fewer clothes in warm weather. And, the ones she does have on will be light and scanty: Loose shorts. Tiny dresses. Not much to fool with.

Your child needs to be able to pull down her training pants with ease, an action that she must get the hang of so that she can be in control of her training. (See the dressing for success info in Chapter 3.)

Some parents find that vacations are perfect for launching potty training. The pace is less intense, and you — the caregiver — have time to supervise practice. You'll also be more inclined to sit and read a book to your child for the thirty minutes she's testing the potty chair. This leisurely approach lets the toddler check out how the potty chair feels to her tiny rear end, and grow accustomed to the strangeness.

In selecting the right startup period for potty training, just remember you have to make sure you'll have plenty of time to hover nearby and lavish your child in enthusiastic attention — foggy, distracted monosyllables won't get it. You can't be thinking about a corporate buyout or a Thanksgiving menu and successfully give your kid your undivided attention.

Also, think for the future. After the super-intense focus of Potty Weekend, you'll need to give your toddler some focused time every single day for about three to four months. And, during this follow-up time, you want to be at least in a semi-relaxed frame of mind so that you won't rush your child or show impatience with her progress or performance.

Making fall or winter work

Just like you'd do if you were starting potty training in the summer or springtime, choose an easygoing, laidback weekend for kicking off the process in fall or winter.

Make sure the spot you use for the potty chair is warm and comfy, and have on hand a good supply of cozy, loose clothes that your child won't mind pulling down, even though it's cold outside. (See Chapter 3 for more on clothes.)

If you want to let your child run around naked while sampling trips to her potty chair, set the temperature just right so she'll have a happy experience — not one that almost freezes off her privates.

For tasty treats in between potty-sits, serve soothing hot chocolate with some homemade marshmallows. (If you don't have time to whip those up, the store-bought versions work fine for even the most discriminating toddlers.)

Avoiding High-Stress Times

Just like other developmental landmarks, potty training is a time when you can stack the deck in favor of your cute little kid. Accomplish this by following two key rules:

1. **Do all you can to get her ready (see tips in Chapter 6).**

2. **Don't start potty training during times of chaos or stress.**

Certain kinds of moments stir up a kid too much for her to be able to learn new tricks. The following should probably be labeled "no-go" times for starting up potty training:

✔ **Enduring parents-in-chaos:** If you have just gotten a divorce or separated from your mate, or if the family is going through heavy-duty conflict, your child is probably reeling emotionally. Don't start her on potty training until things are back on an even keel.

✔ **Fielding new-home blues:** If you have just moved, expect your child to be more than a little bit discombobulated, as she tries to adapt to things like a new bedroom or new bathroom. So, let her settle in before trying to potty train.

✔ **Facing new-baby showdowns:** The month after the arrival of a new baby or the adoption of an older child is not a good time to kick off potty training. In both cases, your toddler may feel anxious or insecure, which does not bode well for potty-training success. Luckily, kids are adjustable — they forget their "grudges" in ten minutes — so you won't have to wait long, with most toddlers, to see a window of opportunity for kicking off potty training. Just watch for signs that your child has gotten comfy with the new kid on the block — curiosity and interest will replace her "get this interloper off my turf" attitude.

✔ **Avoiding sensory overload:** When your toddler moves from her baby bed to a twin bed, she will feel slightly off kilter. So, wait a few weeks before teaching her something new and hard to master. Same goes for the days when she's weaning from breast or bottle to the cup; she won't be in a good place for learning new tricks. Let a month go by before you look at a launch.

✔ **Getting used to a new face:** A change in caregivers can upset some little kids — in fact, most of them. Watch for your child's reaction to determine if this kink jolts her enough to postpone potty-training startup.

✔ **Adjusting to the Brady Bunch:** Happy times cause missteps, too. Maybe you're getting married and the new stepparent is bringing in a slew of stepsiblings, who are changing your child's routine. Even though your toddler may adore the new brood and all their noisy chaos, she will still have some stressful adjustment, and shouldn't be asked to get used to the potty at the same time.

✔ **Singing a Moody Blues tune:** Yet another time to avoid a potty-training startup is when your tot is in an overall moody frame of mind. If she's singing the blues, don't try singing "let's go potty" songs. Set aside the idea for a few weeks.

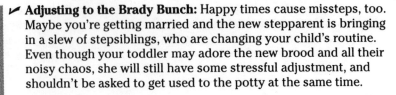

When your child is in a glum mode, be nice enough not to call attention to her moodiness. ("Look at Callie — she's in a funky mood!") Who needs that?

In fact, a good parenting rule for all 16 years ahead of you is this: Tell your child: "I'll let you have a bad mood now and then if you'll let me have one, too." No one — not even Mary Tyler Moore — feels cheerful all the time. Better to accept that fact than to insist that your child banish every low feeling.

Brainwashing Your Toddler (in a Nice Way)

For Potty Mambo Weekend, take along a fanciful mindset. Think of this two- or three-day stretch as a golden opportunity for bonding. You've set aside time — something many caregivers and parents have in scant supply. And, you're feeling happy about a weekend of lavishing emotion and energy and devotion and humor.

So, tug off that tie and pull out all your fun-stops. The first time she potty-sits, toss confetti. Later Saturday morning, have a tea party waiting for her right before it's time to potty — and pour her favorite beverage. Place an aluminum-foil (or real) tiara on her head and proclaim her Princess of the Potty.

When Big Person takes a let's-pretend carpet ride, Little Tyke gets caught up in the groundswell of excitement and becomes a willing pit crew for whatever the adult presents as a cool idea. Wait and see — she'll be ready to polish the potty chair, braid your hair, and deliver whatever she can into the potty bowl.

Afraid of looking silly? Forget about it. If you plan to be a parent or caregiver for the next 18 years, you'll look silly at least a trillion times — and really, who's counting? If looking foolish is tough for you, sometime prior to Potty Weekend, sit down and view the film *Scent of a Woman* just to get your hoo-hahs in place. Watching Al Pacino's blind man dip and dance and swoop just for fun can help you lose some of your starch. For one weekend, just leave behind all those very important responsibilities and entertain your child. Make her laugh. Sing her songs as you skip with her to the potty. Toss some glitter in her hair or flower petals in her path. You'll be glad you did.

Let potty-deeds (or the lack thereof) be side dishes to the main course — having fun together. That way, the weekend's a winner in two ways: You get the kiddo totally into the Potty Mambo (no matter how clumsy her dancing), and you tally up a few more bonding moments that will help your child blossom. At every growing-up stage, show her that you love her, that you think she's special, that you want her experiences to be good ones.

Try some of the following tips for helping your child get in the right frame of mind for potty-training success:

- ✔ Create a sense of game-player's anticipation. Start throwing around some potty-training buzzwords. "Hey, look — you're dry. You didn't pee or poop yet, did you? So, your pants are clean. How cool is that!" (See Chapter 6 for tips on how to teach potty lingo.)

- ✔ Point out that she has nothing to fear about the little potty chair or the big people's toilet that flushes. They're safe, and you will not let anything hurt or bother her. Give her lots of reassurance that nothing can come up and attack her backside from the water below. Don't wait until she tells you that she's creeped out by the possibility that trolls or sharks lurk below — she may never express her fears, but be hamstrung by them, nonetheless.

Don't turn away from training prep work just because your child shows a tiny bit of resistance at first. At the same time, don't hogtie her and force her listen to you.

Keeping Your Special Angel's Quirks in Mind

While you're brainwashing, stay acutely aware of the role that temperament and individual differences play in impacting the potty-training experience. While one child is easily excited about any upcoming new experience, another one will back away, fearful about anything that rocks her little world. Whatever your child's approach, work with it — not against it.

If your child's mind flits around wild and willy-nilly, getting her to focus on potty training will take plenty of patience and repetition. If your child is a whirlwind of activity, the idea of sitting on a potty chair may strike her as tedious. Sitting still all that time? That's just not me!

If your son likes instrumentation, play his cymbals as he aims into the potty. If throwing a ball is his idea of a divine interlude, tell him you're both heading for the backyard right after his next potty-sit.

The toddler who likes her routine — and tends to do things predictably (eat, sleep, have BMs) — will be an easy trainee, simply because she has an inborn affinity for orderliness.

Another key element in the training/psyche-up formula is how the personality of parent or chief caregiver blends with that of the tiny trainee. A tense caregiver makes toilet training nerve-wracking. A dramatic parent turns a small misstep into a fireworks spectacular, which revs up flamboyant kids and scares shy ones. An overbearing, controlling parent makes most children wary of trying at all, for fear of messing up. An easygoing parent takes potty-training ups and downs in stride, and brings out the best in a child of any temperament.

Bottom line: No matter how strange you find your child's reactions to potty training, be patient. No judging. Just stick to your cartwheels and back flips. Play up how well your child is learning, even if she goes at a snail's pace. Forget all speed expectations.

Time it right. And, watch for those all-important readiness signs (see the Cheat Sheet or Chapter 4). And she'll surely make you proud.

Part III
Surefire Steps for Ditching Diapers

The 5th Wave By Rich Tennant

"We covered the basics today — sitting on the potty chair, wiping, and flushing Daddy's whistle down the toilet."

In this part...

Part III lays out nitty-gritty steps for ditching diapers, including the lowdown on how to prep your toddler for the big game. You discover a great way to teach a fledgling potty prince or princess how to dance the Potty Mambo (steps in potty mastery). And, you get lots of tips on keeping a good thing going once the kid's two-stepping to the beat.

This section also features techniques you can use on days when slipups and puddles are as common as phone calls from telemarketers. Plus, you'll discover what you need to take the potty act on the road.

Chapter 6

Prepping for the Big Game

● ●

In This Chapter

▶ Encouraging him to learn by watching

▶ Previewing all the steps

● ●

*I*f you're slow and methodical in your approach to potty training, expect to see an amazing degree of cooperation. Go into it without planning, and you can look for things to erupt in chaos. The biggest predictor of success in potty training is timing it right, carefully deciding to launch the process only when a number of readiness factors are in place. (For readiness signs, see Chapter 4.) You can start instructing your child when he sends out several signals that say, in essence, "Yes!"

Crouch down, look your child in the eye, and talk about warming up for the Potty Mambo. Bounce around with him — maybe some "Rocky" moves. Get him loose, and watch for a sign that he thinks you're making sense, like a head-nod or a little look that says, "I get where you're going with this." Start by letting your potty-trainee watch you and other family members use the toilet so that he can check it out firsthand. In childcare settings, he'll see other kids using the potty, which will pique his interest; plus, the peer pressure helps get your child mentally ready. Start letting your little one practice clothed potty-sits, and invite him to observe how you dispose of diaper contents. Talk the potty patter.

For your mental prep work, brace your perfectionist streak for ups and downs. Take comfort in knowing that all college kids are toilet trained. Fact is, most toddlers who are ready to train do wonderfully well, as long as supporters provide a steady stream of praise for their efforts.

Modeling Big-People Behavior

Every child learns from observing those around him, and your toddler, in his fine new exploration of life, is fairly expert at taking in what is going on in his environment. He notices people's moods and activities, and picks up on everything from tone of voice to inflection.

So take advantage of your toddler's flourishing reporter-like ability, and be sure to tell him how good he is at it: "You notice so many things now; you're so good at that!" If making that statement sounds like much ado about nothing, welcome to the world of good parenting. Try to seize every opportunity to praise, and, by the same token, keep those no's to a minimum. "Hey, you can imitate your brother — that's good! You're learning."

Letting him watch you use the toilet

A terrific setup for potty training is letting your child watch you, your mate, and siblings use the toilet. If possible, have your child focus on same-sex folks (girls mimic grandmas, moms, and sisters, boys mimic grandpas, dads, and brothers). That way, he gets to see how people use the bathroom, and why they do what they do.

When you're phasing in big-people role-modeling, heap praise on your child for knowing the drill. And, with each effort he makes, respond with the kind of enthusiasm he'll love: "Hey, that's good — you washed your hands. You'll do great when you start using your potty chair soon. You always learn things so quickly!"

If this ultra-praise stuff sounds odd (and different from what you heard in childhood), just remember that praise is very, *very* important to successful potty training. Instead of recycling tired sayings — "you do it because I said so" and "you'll do what I say while you're under my roof" — take the enlightened approach of "expect good behavior and you'll get good behavior."

Avoid the biggest mistake parents make in role-modeling toilet use, which is rushing through it. We all lead such hurry-up lives, but your child will do much better if you're very methodical, allowing plenty of time for him to absorb all the moves.

Don't expect a toddler to connect the act of sitting on the potty with urinating in the potty. For you, it's a given; for a two-year-old, it's not. The connection comes when he does urinate there and gets praise from you for doing so.

The child has lots of things to put together and make some sense of: the sitting down, the feeling of needing to go, the actual act of urinating or having a bowel movement. For some children, making the connection comes quickly, while others are slower at the one-two-three. If your child takes longer connecting the dots, don't be concerned. Potty training is more a function of general temperament than intelligence. Remember, history shows that a number of geniuses were especially noteworthy for their full-tilt spaciness, which suggests that they probably weren't quick at toilet training, either. No doubt, they spent half their time on the potty pondering quantum physics or composing haikus.

Explaining the steps

Go snail-slow when you give verbal instructions. You have to allow time for your child to take in the information. Your child may be the tomorrow's mega-genius, but he still needs his potty steps outlined slowly and surely. Carefully explain each step, from sitting down to flushing.

Getting clothes off and climbing on the potty

You say, "Watch how I pull down my pants, and let's see you try it, too." That should get him rolling. "Now, let's see you climb onto the potty, just for fun." He's moving in that direction; he's trying; he's on it! Of course, his pants probably are bunched up under his behind, meaning they could get wet. But he's feeling like a self-starter, and that's a good thing.

Doing potty business

Tell him that when you or his sister sits on the potty, both of you expect some poop or pee to come out. "And when you start using the potty, that's where your poop or pee goes when you do your business."

Talk about how nice it is that babies can potty in their diapers. And then, enthuse about how toddlers move on up to using training pants so they can get used to using the potty.

Wiping

Next, demonstrate how to tear off some toilet paper and wipe clean. "You try to get just a small amount because too much clogs up the toilet. Not too big, not too small — but just right." Exactly like Goldilocks and the Three Bears. Talk about proper wiping, but don't overload him with info right now.

Flushing

The basics may seem simple to us, but that is not the case for small fry. Suddenly, in your toddler's life, the toilet that has been nothing but a bathroom backdrop is now looming large, a major player. Who would have thought it? And you can place some hefty wagers that your child is going to be pretty foggy as to why the toilet has become significant overnight.

And what if your toddler latches onto toilet flushing as his new best hobby? That's a normal response to a fun skill, but waste no time in pointing out that toilets aren't toys; they are types of bathroom equipment meant to be used correctly.

Washing up

Show how to wash up thoroughly afterward. Again, make it a methodical explanation. Using soap and warm water, show your child how he can gauge whether he is washing long enough: "You have to sing the 'Happy Birthday' song all the way through." When he's only two, you'll be the one singing the song, but later, he will be able to do this.

Helping with the whole process

So, the more you handhold and illustrate how easy it is for you, or his brother or sister, to use the toilet, the easier time your toddler will have adapting to this new equipment and fledgling skill.

- ✔ Encourage your child to get involved; let him help you flush and wash up with you.

- ✔ Make the process as game-like as possible. Keep a lighthearted attitude. If he's clumsy at it, giggle together. This is not rocket science.

- ✔ Forget about lengthy explanations on the mechanics. In two seconds, he'll get bored with details about plumbing and the germs-he-washes-away details.

- ✔ Tell him he won't fall in if that concerns him. Some kids will inquire about the hole in the bottom of the toilet, and if your child does ask that question, tell him that it's large enough for poop and toilet paper but not large enough for him to fall into. Explain that because the hole is small, he mustn't put too much paper in it or it will get stuffed up.

Kids who go bonkers over pulling off loads of toilet paper, or flush-flush-flushing like wild men, may make it necessary for you to take proactive measures. Store the TP up high, and attach a childproof attachment on the toilet lever. Fix the environment because you don't want him to associate potty going with you saying, "For heaven's sake, look at the mess you made! Now I have to clean this up."

Introducing All the Pieces

As you and your toddler powwow about Potty-Training Weekend coming up in the near future (see Chapter 4 on when to schedule potty training), keep in mind that the whole thing may sound a bit scary to him. A toddler must develop in several ways in order to thrive in the toilet-training event, and he may already be getting the feeling that this could be tough — and that diapers were really, really easy.

It's your job to break down the challenge into easy pieces so that he doesn't feel overwhelmed and back away. You want to make it easy for him to start signaling that he needs to go to the potty. You want to make sure he can walk to the potty, climb on it, and pull his clothes up and down.

If your child is Mr. Show Biz. . . .

Some children really love to bust a move. They'll perform at the slightest suggestion that someone may be willing to sit down and watch. For this kiddo, pull out the video camera. At the outset of this phase of potty prep work, videotape your child going through the entire process of using the potty so that he gets a chance to demonstrate his new skills up front. Talk about how special this is going to be — an exciting new game called "Goodbye, Diapers" or "Who Wants to Be a Potty-Trained Kid?" And, tell him the only pottying he needs to do for the video is just pretend.

You take the role of an announcer at a horse race: "The champion is moving up to the line, almost ready. Wow, there he goes! What a takeoff — he's sitting on the chair, focusing on poop and pee. Wait. I hear something! It sounds like success-tinkles! Look out! He did it! He's crossing the finish line! Hoorah for Nick the Natural."

Practicing clothed potty-sits

Letting your child sit on the potty while he is wearing clothes is key to getting him used to the feel of the potty chair, or the adapter atop the adult toilet.

During these clothed potty-sits, talk about Potty-Training Weekend that is coming up very soon, and explain that when that weekend arrives, he will start out by using the potty without his clothes on. Tell him that he'll be allowed to run around naked — and he will be getting used to the potty chair. Eventually, when he's pottying in it, he'll graduate to his big-boy underpants.

- ✔ **Get him comfy with the chair.** Later on, you will probably still hear complaints like "it's cold." Nevertheless, it will help that his clothing-clad rear end has already been introduced to the potty chair.

- ✔ **Encourage curiosity as he practices these clothed potty-sits.** If he studies how the chair is made, takes it apart, or picks it up and puts it on his head, that's all part of the process.

- ✔ **Don't press the issue if he gets bored with sitting, or resists.** Do not cajole or persuade. Be casual. Be jaunty. "Oh, you're not in the mood right now? Well, that's okay because you can try again later. Let's go find you something fun to play with."

- ✔ **Promote playfulness.** Some kids like to cart the potty chair around the house, and let their toys and animals try using it. The more familiar and comfortable he gets with his chair, the more likely he will adapt to using it with relative ease.

When one mom started her son's clothed potty sitting, she set a training goal for herself: "I wanted to see how well I could do at avoiding negativity. Every time the word 'no' would come to my lips, I would find a way to tell my son what I needed — but in a positive way. An example would be 'instead of dropping candy in the potty-chair bowl, tell me what you want to do when you leave the potty chair. Look for your blocks? Go outside?'" Distractions are always good, but especially during potty-training days.

Don't start handing out food treats to entice your child to sit on the potty. Lots of people get their kids to potty by doling out scads of candy, but it sets a bad precedent — candy for all good deeds. Remember, you want your child to associate eating with fueling his body, not with pleasing people. The only exception to the no-candy rule is the child who has special problems with potty training. See Chapters 13 and 17 for more on these exceptions.

If he seems reluctant to sit on the potty in his clothes, just accept that, and steer him toward another activity. (You can always try again later.)

Setting the scene

As you start touting the idea of using the potty, don't be surprised if your toddler wants to be the one to decide where the chair is placed. Remember that for your convenience positioning must be close to the big toilet, so give him just two or three choices: "We can place the potty chair over here by the bathtub. Or you may want it right next to the toilet that I use. Or do you want it over there by the cat's litter box? You get to choose."

To warm him to the idea of potty use, ask if he wants to line up his stuffed animals to watch his great new sitting act. Then tell him: "Later, when you start peeing and pooping here, you won't have time to get all of your animals, but it's fun for now, isn't it?"

While he's getting acclimated to the chair, read a book to him. And talk about why he is practicing sitting so that when potty training finally kicks off, he'll be ready to use it to pee or poop. Work the crowd, the boy, and his stuffed animals.

Using buzzwords

The buzzwords are your friends during potty-training boot camp. These help bridge the gap between your child's overall confusion about what's going on and your interest in getting him out of diapers.

Hopefully, by the time your child is ready to get started, he'll be comfy with using potty buzzwords. Your tot can remember and say "pee" or "pee-pee" and "poop" or "poo-poo" or "BM."

Keep it simple. Keep it matter-of-fact.

In this context, you and relatives and caregivers must remember that a child relies strongly on good recall in this new world of toilet use. Tell others that you usually refer to going to the bathroom as "let's go potty" or "we're going to the bathroom."

In these early days, provide frequent word wrap-ups of the way people use a toilet. And don't worry if your child shows a head-in-the-clouds attitude toward the potty lingo. When he has readiness going for him, he'll start getting an idea of what's expected, and recall some of the things you've told him. Then one day, in a zippy and unexpected twist, it will all gel. He will hop on the potty and strut his stuff like an old pro.

Dropping diaper contents

At this point in the prep game, you should make a point of having your child watch you empty his diaper contents into the bowl of his new potty chair. "Why?" he may ask. You say: "Because this is where poop is supposed to go." He'll probably ask why one more time after that. Your answer: "Remember how we've talked about things having places? You like to put your toys in the toy box, right? Well, we like to put poop and pee in the toilet because that's where they go. Then we flush it away." Tell him that this is what his siblings do with their pee and poop, and his aunt and uncle and you, and lots of grownup people and big kids.

Your child may react to this in a variety of ways. Some kids are fascinated by the flushing and the poop disappearing-act. Others show no interest at all. The worrywarts may be upset by seeing the poop get flushed away. If flushing makes your child anxious, wait to flush until he leaves the room — or leave the poop in the toilet for a while.

Take your cue from your child's reactions to this process. But whether he is enthusiastic, disinterested, or distressed is no indication of his smarts or potty potential. Some kids are curious and love to investigate and venture into new areas; others are cautious from the get-go, and those slow-but-sure types are always going to take longer adjusting to new developmental stages.

Avoid any hint that your child did something naughty: "You dirtied your diaper," sounds very much like you're saying that he made a creepy mistake. Instead, tell him "Oh, you pooped in your diaper."

Also, avoid "Your poop is really stinky today" — shaming him makes him feel like his body products are frightful. Anything you say that makes him feel funny about what he's dropping in the potty isn't going to help matters.

Chapter 7

Dancing the Potty Mambo

● ●

In This Chapter

▶ Showing your child the steps

▶ Doing the Potty-Training Mambo

▶ Stifling your fretting

● ●

*T*he big weekend has arrived. Your child is ready, and she's going to the "prom" of potty training. In one memorable weekend, your little star will learn the steps of potty use.

She's going to mambo her way through the steps of helping a doll use the potty, sitting on the potty every hour and managing the tissue-pull, the wipe, and the wash-up, setting up her progress chart, and moving up to training pants.

During Potty Weekend, you, the coach, will lead your player to the potty often, praise her efforts and successes, breeze through accidents, and keep her needs first. You'll also make sure that the kid is supercharged. Tell her: "We'll have a great Potty-Training Weekend, and you'll be leaving diapers behind after you learn how big kids pee and poop in the toilet."

You, too, are primed and ready for anything. You're also equipped with the info in this chapter, which gives you a surefire method to get your child off to a strong start. Before you're through, she'll need a warning label that says "Look out! High as a Kite Superstar Pooper Pee Girl."

Kicking Off Mambo Weekend

Start the fiesta on a playful note — that snags a child's attention faster than anything. Jump into it with let's-pretend games, and sweep her away for a weekend of song, dance, laughter, and potty-wins.

You set the tone — fun and upbeat. You steer the trainee. She goes to the potty, sits, grins, and has no idea what in the world she's doing there. And that's okay. She will have her hands full just doing the basics at the beginning — stuff like listening to her body tell her when she needs to potty, pulling clothes up and down, pulling off tissue and wiping up, and washing her hands.

You don't expect a beginner to swoop and dip around the dance floor from the get-go, and you can't expect your Potty-Mamboing preschooler to catch on to all the steps on the first day. But emphasize the fact that your tiny dancer only needs to master a few small skills and let your mambo partner know that you're confident she'll be dancing up a storm in no time.

Why weekends work best

You start potty training on a weekend because you have more time to give your child, and you're more likely to be patient and supportive and informative. (Chapter 5 has more information on getting the timing down.) The day you begin, approach your teaching as if the two of you are starting a real adventure.

You may want to travel to a retreat, or simply set up a potty weekend at home. Either way, you kick off training first thing Saturday morning, right after breakfast, with as much fanfare as possible.

Both Saturday and Sunday will feature lots of potty emphasis, along with good times spent in other ways, too — playing outside, singing songs, tossing a ball, having fun with pets, and more. Create a memorable weekend in which your child enjoys the riches of having an important adult lavishing time and attention on her. Keep things light and enjoy decompressing with your little one — albeit with a purpose.

A little planning goes a long way

Careful planning helps kick off your Potty-Training Weekend in fine style. You want your trainee to understand fully what's going on and what you're asking of her. To help improve her chances of being successful, feed her foods that keep her elimination processes flowing freely, and prep her mentally for enjoying the potty experience.

To drive home the notion that the bathroom equals potty stuff, move her changing area into that space, if possible. Forge a link between bathroom functions and the actual bathroom itself. You also get the chance to drop her discards in the toilet to illustrate directly and graphically where they go.

Feeding for success

Fix her the right foods: Beef up the likelihood of your child being in an eliminating frame of mind and body by increasing water and fiber. Peach or pear nectar by Kearn's can help keep stools soft because they contain *sorbitol,* a natural laxative. To help make sure that your girl drinks a lot, you may want to hand out some tasty salty snacks, and feed her stool-softening foods, such as

- ✔ Brown rice
- ✔ Dried fruits
- ✔ Fiber breakfast bars
- ✔ Fresh fruits, such as
  - • Apricots
  - • Berries
  - • Grapes
  - • Plums
- ✔ Prune juice
- ✔ Veggies
- ✔ Whole-grain breads and cereals

Keep the water and juice flowing and try to avoid foods that tend to constipate, such as

- ✔ Cheese
- ✔ Excessive milk
- ✔ Pasta
- ✔ White bread

You can use the food gambit to keep your trainee happy with the program: "I even fixed some of your favorite foods."

Explain the elimination process: Tell your child about the digestive process — she eats food and drink, and it travels down to her tummy where most of it fuels her body so she's able to run and dance and climb. The rest of the food and drink — the part that she doesn't need — leaves her body and goes into her diapers, and now, she's learning to put it directly into the potty. Poop represents the leftovers from food, and pee, leftovers from things she drank.

Let her know that she's in control of this: "Sweetie, you're the one making your poop and the pee. And you're the one who can decide where it goes and what to do with it."

Getting her prepped

Point out where the potty chair is and explain that you will help her get situated when it's time to get on it. Put her in her birthday suit. That way, she can let it all hang out — feeling good, feeling pumped. "Send me in, coach." Your goal is to do everything you can to simplify her sprint from the urge to pee or poop, to going in the potty.

Ask her to let you know when she feels like she needs to go. Then, when she does just that, walk her to the bathroom and praise her. (Put her in a room that has wipeable floors because you can expect some mishaps.)

Helping a Doll Use the Potty: Step 1

A totally cool (and pretty effective) way to get your child to focus on learning potty stuff is to have her teach a doll or stuffed animal how to use the potty.

Whether male or female, your trainee will enjoy potty teaching a doll or stuffed animal, and it puts your child in a good place mentally and emotionally. She can imagine the doll or teddy bear learning how to use the potty chair correctly, and she'll even get a chance to use her brand-new, two-year-old bossiness to steer the process.

You can be sure that no little boy will suffer gender confusion from a one-time encounter with a doll — but if you're still nervous, you can always use an action figure.

Any kind of doll, even an old teddy bear, will work, of course, but one that wets is best. So, if you're buying your child a new doll, get the kind that pees.

To make sure that everyone is excited about dolly's big adventure, use these tips:

- **Plant the idea:** You want to let the doll hang out with the potty chair. Tell your toddler: "Let the dolly sit on your potty and get used to the way it feels, just like you're been getting used to how it feels."

- **Create a fun little scenario:** "How do you think your doll likes her new potty? I bet she has loved it ever since we brought her home from the store."

  If you're using a teddy bear, the same kind of talk works: "Teddy has been wanting her very own potty chair for a long time — I bet she loves it."

The first thing you do when you're ready to model potty-training practices with the doll is to ask your trainee to go get a pair of her brand-new training pants and put them on the baby doll. Then you help her take the doll through its paces:

1. Pull the doll's pants down.

2. Put the doll on the potty chair.

3. Encourage the doll to pee and have it actually do so (if it can actually do so).

4. Praise the doll, and talk about how fun that was.

   Show your excitement when the doll does its deeds (even if you're both just pretending she peed)! Tell your child to applaud her doll's neat trick. "Oh, clap your hands for her! We're so proud of you, Dolly! You're learning to use the potty, just like Sarah's doing this weekend."

5. Get your toddler to help with dolly's cleanup.

   1. Smear the doll's bootie with jam and let your child practice wiping her behind good and proper.

   2. Let your toddler help dump the doll's pee and poo into the big toilet.

   3. Have her wash the dolly's hands (if that's an option — soap and water may not be a good thing for a plush teddy bear).

Using a doll can really get your child's attention and make this feel like mostly a fun game. That makes the fact that she's having to change her messy-diaper ways just a side issue. Also, when your toddler teaches her doll how to use the potty, she gets familiar with the process in a nonthreatening, hands-on way — this reassures her that she can do the steps herself. After all, if she can teach it, she can do it!

Sitting on the Potty Every Hour: Step 2

After the pee-doll drama of Step 1, it's your child's turn. Getting her to sit on potty is the next step after training the doll.

Be sure to ask your child to cue you when she needs to go potty, and sometimes she may let you know when she needs to go, but more often, you'll be escorting her to the potty for her hourly potty-sit.

So, put the dolly aside and ask your child to take the doll's place on the potty. Encourage the whole routine: pulling down the hot new training undies, sitting on the potty, and waiting.

Tell her what you want her to do: When she's doing her potty-sitting once an hour, be sure to say slowly, "Pull down your pants and sit on the potty. See if you need to pee or poop, or both. Wait a few minutes to find out. After you go potty, you pull off some tissue, wipe your behind, and pull up your pants. Wash your hands carefully." If she says no, despite all your prep work, don't insist. Just lead her away and try again later.

If she actually pees or poos, bowl her over with zippity-do-dah compliments! Don't restrain your excitement.

No pee or poo? That's okay — still enthuse over what happened: "Hey, you're learning how to sit on the chair. Won't it be neat when you do what your doll did! This is all such fun!"

Ritualize potty-sits: "You'll be doing this all the time very soon, without me around. You'll get so good at it you won't even need my help."

She may want assurance that you will be nearby to help until she is used to the potty. So, tell her: "I'll help you or your grandma will or Mrs. Miller at daycare. We're all on your team, and we want you to learn to use the potty. We know you can do it!"

Too many parents stick a kid on the chair and run away to do other things; during Potty Weekend, you absolutely have to make a big impression, and that takes ample time and friendly hovering.

Saying the right things the right way

Use smart sentences during potty training. Don't ask leading questions that give her a way to refuse , but do be firm, direct, and stress the rewards that will come with good results.

> Do say: "Tell me when you want me to take you to the potty chair."
>
> Don't say: "Would you like to go to the potty?"

Take the bull by the horns if your child doesn't ask to be led to the potty. "Honey, I think this is a good time for you to sit on the potty." Make sure you don't end your statement with "don't you?" because you'll be giving her an out.

Give her no option other than dancing the Potty Mambo: If you offer her a choice about participation, she may say, "No, I don't wanna." A battle of wills over pottying is a battle you don't want to engage in!

As your child gets the drift of using the potty, reinforce her new skills by laying on the praise — thick.

Here are some good lines that send the message "I believe you can do this alone!"

- ✔ "You got to the potty on time — good for you!"
- ✔ "You're so good at getting your pants down all by yourself."

> ✔ "I bet it feels great when you remember to go potty without having anyone reminding you."
>
> ✔ "You're doing better and better at this potty stuff — pretty soon, you won't need any help at all."
>
> ✔ "I like the way you tear off just the right amount of toilet paper."
>
> ✔ "What a good job of flushing all by yourself!"
>
> ✔ "You're a super child, and I love you!"

Using her name

When you're giving your child potty info (or any other tidbits), use her name at the front to get her attention. (The same trick works for puppy training.) Don't bury her name in the middle of a sentence, or at the end.

Adding the personal touch shows you're focusing on your child. You'll get her attention — even though she may not be exactly clear on why, or what's going on.

Here's how you put your child's name at the front of each request or instruction; "Rhiannon, I think this is a good time for you to sit on the potty." Take her hand and lead her to the potty chair. If she resists, smile and say, "Okay, sweetie, you just let me know when you feel like you need to go."

Telling you about her needs and her deeds

You may think of yourself as the card dealer, or the casino boss, or at least a worthy participant in the game — but the truth is, without your child tossing in her cooperation, you're nowhere. You can give her the tips for a win; you can demonstrate the appropriate places for discarding body products; but you can't score for her — she's the only one who can win the game.

So, make her feel like she's a huge player in the process (because she is!) — and try to drive home the following pertinent points: "Listen for your body to let you know when it's potty time."

Your goal is to help her learn to listen to her body. Explain the signs: Tell her that when she squats or makes straining noises, that means a BM is coming, so she should let those signals send her to the toilet.

If your child feels a poop moment coming, she may yell for a diaper. Assuming she's naked (acceptable Potty-Weekend garb), give her a diaper to hold to herself and drop the poop into. Then, help her take what she produced and dump it in the potty bowl. When she has a bowel movement somewhere other than the potty, take the poop and plop it in the toilet, and have her watch what you're doing. "See what the potty is for — that's where we put our poop and pee. See how it works? Soon, it will be easy for you."

When your child is beginning to sense the sensation or sense of pressure that she will feel when she needs to pee or poop, ask her for a little favor: "Emily, would you try to remember to tell me when you feel like you need to go potty?" She may well ask why. "Because, sweetie, that way, I can take you to the potty." Let that sink in. Then, add: "Whenever you feel like you need to use the potty chair to pee or poo, come get me . . . and I'll lead you to the bathroom and keep you company."

Ask her to let you know when it's too late: "Tell me when you've already gone in your diaper, and then we'll put the poop in the potty. Then, next time maybe you can tell me before you go in your diaper and we'll rush you to the potty."

Any time that she tells you "I peed" or "I pooped," even though she did it in her diaper or underpants, praise her like crazy for telling you. Often, that leads to a fabulous next step — she'll tell you before something happens. Ah, yes! So, take her hand and fast-step her into the bathroom.

Getting the mood right

Some kids like it hot and wild and frenzied when they're potty-training — the bigger carnival you can create, the more they'll like it. Others are shy and retiring — they like things more sedate, so they will probably respond to a potty scene that's serene. Still others just don't care — they're up for anything you suggest.

Keep potty-sitting sessions quiet if your child is one who responds best when all distractions are removed.

Entertain the child who gets fidgety easily — while she sits, chat a bit or sing or read. If you read her a kid's book on potty training, ask if she has any questions as you go along. If she looks sleepy or bored or cranky or tired of being taught, don't press. Put the potty book aside and tell her, "No problem. We'll read some more of it another time when you want to."

For the child who has an easy temperament, you can go for ambiance anywhere between a Mardi Gras atmosphere and a church service, and your tot will try to cooperate — to the best of her bodily ability, remember. Keep her smiling.

Keep potty-sits brief. If she hops up after a minute or so, that's okay. Offer a toy to hold if she gets antsy or dreamy-eyed, or starts playing with her genitals. Then give a gentle reminder: "You know what? I bet you probably need to pee or poo."

Stay cool. Don't force her to go to the potty area. If she protests, accept that idea for the moment, and say, "Okay, you can do it an hour from now. That's fine."

Dealing with the logistics

You've probably forgotten the logistics of the potty-training process — after all, you've had the hang of using the potty for years. But, the small things are often what cause problems for two-year-olds, so take these matters into account and have them covered. For example, change her pants often so she won't become lackadaisical about her state of wetness. Show the proper foot-press thing for getting BMs going. Let a little boy pee sitting down at first.

Frequent pants changes help you stave off the possibility of letting "wetness complacency" set in. You want your child to grow super-uncomfortable with walking around in wet or soiled training pants. But, you don't want to make her feel bad, so keep your reactions low-key.

Also, remember that a child has to be able to push down with her feet in order to start a bowel movement — at least, most kids need leverage. So, get your child settled and comfortable, feet on the floor. If she's on her potty chair, show her how to push her feet down on the floor in order to help the BM come out. Sitting atop the adult toilet, have her plant her small feet on a rung of the stepstool and have her push down on that. Ask her to practice the move and praise how well she does. "Good pushing!"

Of course, you want her to sit on the potty fairly bare (pants and diapers off) at about the time she typically urinates or has a bowel movement — or for her hourly potty-visit. If she happens to urinate or have a bowel movement, raise the roof with extravagant praise. "Cool! You did it! Let's put a star on your chart for pooping!"

Most little boys pee sitting down first, with their penises pointed downward. Later, they learn to pee standing up. But, if he does the standup thing first, that's okay, too.

Giving potty-ops all weekend

You — the potty-trainer — are in charge of making sure you're using the info you picked up when you were stalking her potty patterns (see Chapter 4 for more on this). So, not only are you going to provide frequent potty opportunities, you're going to make sure she's "there" at key moments.

Take her to the potty often. Do a potty-sit every hour. Keep your child on a routine. Just as you do when you housetrain a puppy, take your potty-training candidate to the bathroom shortly after meals.

Chat cheerfully about what big kids do after they eat their meals. Tell your child: "Big girls go to the bathroom and do their poop and pee, and after that, they play with a special toy."

Encourage many potty-sits — but with no pressure. Keep showing her how to wipe carefully (front to back), and help your child learn how to do a thorough hand wash-up. But, don't put too much focus on getting this part perfect at the get-go because she's undoubtedly having enough trouble remembering to key into the feel of needing to poop and pee and making it to the chair in time.

The reason you want a girl to wipe front to back is because the reverse action can transmit bacteria from the child's stool (poop) toward the vagina, where the *urethra* is — that's the opening to the bladder. The result of wrong-way wiping can be a urinary tract infection, which isn't unusual in novice potty-goers. Suspect a urinary tract infection if you notice any of these signs: sudden need to go, frequent peeing, foul-smelling urine, fever, blood in the urine, complaints that it hurts to pee or that her tummy hurts. A urinary tract infection can be a serious problem if it goes untreated — so be sure your child gets medical attention.

If she's a messy wiper, don't worry about it. You need to forget about neatness — that will come with practice, when you have time for that to matter.

When you take your child to the potty after sleeping, napping, and eating meals, and before bedtime, really play up the potty potential. "I bet you can do it right now. Let's see if you can try to poop or pee. I think you probably can!"

Often, when starting out, a child will stun you by doing her business right after she gets up off the potty and walks away. Don't take this personally — she's learning to relax the bowel-bladder muscles, and she doesn't have her timing down.

Your child will master using the potty as soon as her fledgling body and mind can get together about it. Rest assured, that toddler of yours isn't screwing up because she likes to make you miserable.

Setting Up a Success Chart: Step 3

Help her set up her star or sticker success chart. And, follow up any instance of successful peeing or pooping in the potty — or good tries — with a reward — a sticker on her chart. Of course, continue to give lots of verbal praise, too.

Make a big deal of how neat it will be when she gets sticker or star rewards that she can put on her success chart. Tots love stickers and stars, and this kind of reward setup can be very motivating.

Houston mom Cari La Grange found that a star-studded system produced great results: "I created a poster board that I made into a colorful calendar separating days and weeks, each board containing a one-month period. I hung it up on Taylor's bathroom door. Each morning that her training pants were dry, I would let her go through a box of stickers and choose the one she wanted to place on the day of the week it happened to be. If she could make it through a whole week and post a sticker every day, I'd give her a small toy. It worked really well because if she needed to pee during the night, she'd come and get me, so she would still get her sticker!"

Praising efforts and successes with stars

Stay sweet and cheery and laidback: Make her early trips to the potty totally pressure free, but do make casual mention of the possibility of putting a star or sticker on her chart.

Hand out kudos: She gets praise if she urinates or has a bowel movement, and she gets praise for her effort if the trip's a bust. If nothing happens in the potty bowl, tell her cheerfully, "Honey, you'll probably do it the next time. I'm sure of it. Your attitude is so good!"

After each potty-sit, give out kisses and hugs. Finish off with something like "It's really cool watching you learn to use the toilet like grown-ups do it. You're growing up, and that's very neat."

Use positive messaging: Say: "After you've gone to the potty, we'll go to the park." Waiting to leave the house until she "takes care of business" lets your wee one know that you're in no rush — you have all the time in the world while she's on an important potty mission. Most kids are mover-shakers — can't wait to get out the door and go places — so, this can be a real motivator.

Search for opportunities to give stars and stickers. Inspecting her pants frequently will really help. Then you can say: "Ah, you have dry pants — that's good."

Working through success-chart backlash

Stay positive no matter how grumpy she gets. "I don't want a star chart! I hate this!" If you hear those words, turn her attention away from the potty to some fun game. Don't get into a lecture on why she has to learn the potty, like it or not. Remember, a toddler will forget her stubborn stand against almost anything in 30 minutes or less. Little-kid grudges evaporate quickly.

If your child goes into combat mode — "No! I don't want to use potty" — take the high road. Smile at her, and dance a little sidestep. "Hey, I just thought of something fun we could do — let's go outside and swing."

Allow no detours for escapees: Even if your child says something disappointing — "I'm not ever gonna use the potty!" — remember, she just wants to see how serious you are about this toilet stuff. She's testing for backlash. So, you just smile and say, "Well, we'll see how you feel about it when you get good at it. You may think it's pretty cool to have your own potty — and to put stickers on your chart when you pee or poop. Later, you can tell me what you think about it, compared to diapers."

With little ones, it often works to act as if you didn't even notice the fury of their fiery outbursts, because that saves embarrassment and gives them some room to change their minds.

The child who doesn't seem interested when you lead her to sit on the potty may need the incentive of a special activity for potty time. Give her a fun little toy. "Missy, this is only for potty-sits. You can play with it when you're sitting here, trying to go potty." See Chapter 8 for more on rewards.

Switching to Training Pants: Step 4

Lots of children will make fast progress during Potty Weekend, especially when you've set it up carefully and provided your child with plenty of attention and time. If your toddler does seem to get the general idea of how to use the potty chair for peeing and pooping, move her into training pants during Potty Weekend. Do so for sure if you see your child showing good control of urination and bowel movements. Move her straight into underwear or training pants.

If you need a specific number, look for a string of ten or so potty successes to tell you she's ready for pullups. Then you can safely discontinue diapers. You want her to wear these training pants every day, even though three months may pass before she gets the merit badge that says "accident-free."

If your child puts on training pants by the end of Potty Weekend, she may well be potty trained for daytime in six or seven weeks. Nights take longer. But do be ready for plenty of setbacks and accidents — just normal parts of the process.

If you're nervous about whether she's really ready to put in training pants, give her the benefit of the doubt. With many readiness signs in place, the right pants-wear could be the little push she needs for success.

Pulling up pullups

Pullups kind of look like underwear, they're easy to pull up and down, but — they have one big advantage. The thick, absorbent material keeps your child from having a stream of urine running down her leg when she has a little accident. (See Chapter 3 for training-pant options.)

Watch for any sign that your child is simply using her pullups as great big diapers. If you think she's confusing them with diapers, sit down with her and define the difference, and explain exactly what you'd like to see her do.

You hope that she'll have a string of successes behind her by the end of potty-launch week. Then, after three to four weeks of zero accidents in her little pullups, you can transition that cutie into big-kid underwear.

Wearing underwear

How quickly your child graduates from training pants to the next level of real underwear depends on how well she adapts to potty training. If the mastery is well under way and practically done, go on and take her to the next logical step: putting on those cute big-kid underpants.

Your signal to switch your child into regular underwear is her showing that she can use the potty chair regularly. Her reward: She gets to wear the "graduation" undies and saves training pants for sleepy time. Also, she will interpret this as a sign of your trust in her — she's a big kid now!

Another plus of wearing big-kid underpants is that it makes your child less likely to fall back into her old pee-wherever ways. A certain responsibility comes with putting on pretty pink panties or superhero briefs.

Do make a major ceremony of moving up into underwear when it does happen. Announce that she is now wearing grownup underpants and praise her for this accomplishment — "what a big kid you are!" Enjoy and applaud her giant step toward self-reliance. She'll be feeling a huge sense of pride — you can count on it.

Great expectations

You can make a magical waltz out of the Potty Mambo. Go into the process of potty training with some very positive expectations, such as the ones that follow:

- ✔ Expect potty training to be a bonding experience for caregiver and child.
- ✔ Expect your child to be successful, and get ready to applaud her efforts.
- ✔ Expect accidents and forgetfulness.
- ✔ Expect to celebrate potty-training graduation with special underwear.

Making changes for night and day

Daytime dryness is easier for toddlers than staying dry all night, chiefly because the mind-body connection is more in gear during the day, and a child is less likely to be plagued by heavy sleeping, dark halls, or other drawbacks like having to get out of bed and trek to the bathroom.

Making it through the night dry is usually a major hurdle for potty greenhorns. So, continue to use the pullups at night since that extra absorbency will make bedwetting much less embarrassing.

Sticking with pants

If you get so frustrated by accidents that you stick your child back in diapers, she's going to be bummed. There she was, gliding along, not always smoothly, but fairly proud of herself, wearing big-kid underpants and looking pretty fine, when bam! You jerk her progress symbols right off of her, and send her packing. Sure, you mumble some comfort-talk; she *hears* you saying "that's okay — you're doing just fine," but if that were true, why are you taking her cute new pants away?

If your child were more verbal, she would say to you: "Tell me what's going on here. Am I bad because I have accidents that I can't really help? I feel like you're telling me I'm a naughty girl when you take my new pants away from me. But I'm doing my best." She's confused, and this is no time for mixed messages.

Bottom line (literally): Stick with the upgrade pants. Keep the rah-rah team committed to helping her succeed, and, even with a few slips, you have an excellent recipe for speedy results.

Minding Your Own Steps

Think slow, steady progress: Most important, make the weekend feel upbeat and positive for both of you.

Keep the word *patience* posted in neon in your mind: You want it flashing there like a computer screensaver. If you can push the mute button on preachiness, you'll make the whole potty process less stressful.

Keeping the kid's needs first

Potty training is unfamiliar territory that's more than a little bit scary for her. If she's a cautious type, she figures the landscape is filled with unseen frights. A bolder kid will be more likely to take her chances and not fret so much about what's upcoming.

Learning to use the potty can seem complicated to your child. Or, she may not even understand why it's important, or even necessary. So, give her a break. Laugh with her.

Bright, capable professionals sometimes have trouble understanding that learning to use the potty is tough stuff for a two-year-old. Imagine training a mini-version of Madonna or Bill Gates. Can you say the word *willful?*

Body-maturation rates are a huge part of this. Just because you're an organized, anal attorney or bright, mega-credentialed doctor doesn't mean that your two-year-old's bladder is ready to deliver dry pants, 24-7. In fact, no amount of obsessiveness on the part of parent or caregiver — can make it happen. That's sure to keep you humble.

Breezing through accidents

Even though you're just starting potty training, go ahead and plant a reminder clearly in your brain: Your child will have accidents, and most of these don't mean your child is acting out or being bad or even being stubborn. Even a smirk after an accident doesn't mean she screwed up on purpose. At this stage in development, your toddler is just getting the hang of defense mechanisms — and defiant expressions are one of the first pieces of ammo she'll toss into her arsenal of goodies. Truthfully, she has little notion what she's doing.

Be casual about accidents — not over-concerned. If your child has an accident because she was distracted by toys or playmates, say, "Oh, I bet you were busy playing and forgot — you'll remember next time, I'm sure."

Don't point out little mistakes — that she dribbled on her underwear or missed some poop when she was wiping. Your tot will feel like a failure if she has to face looks of disappointment or irritation.

You wouldn't get bent — or rant and rave — if you were watching your kid take a long time learning to read.

Rerun a mind video of watching your child take her first steps. And, use the same jolly, jaunty encouragement you used back then. You didn't say "bad girl" to speed the walking process. You just figured she'd do it when her legs and feet and muscles got jiving. And soon afterwards, you saw her toddling across the floor. You knew that was going to happen — and it did — and she'll also get good at using potty.

Sooner or later, she'll get in the groove — unless you mess things up by pushing too hard. And even then, she'll still polish off her skills, but probably at a much later date.

Each time you teach a potty-training move, remember that this isn't like other things you do in child-rearing. The complex tasks your toddler needs in order to get her mind and body in sync are many, and that's why she must be an active and enthusiastic participant. Nothing else will work.

But, you can expect your child to drag her feet if you take up that tired old "Mother/Father-knows-best" banner. You hated that when you were a kid, so why give it another run and hope that it flies this time around? Spare yourself the disappointment. She won't get trained by being browbeaten.

You guide and lead, not punish and scold. Don't forget, the best cheerleaders slather on praise like molasses on pancakes.

Don't crowd 'em

A woman who sells boots in Houston, Texas, talks about the perfect way to sell tough customers — a good analogy for handling potty-training toddlers.

"You want to fill them in on all the facts, but you don't want to crowd 'em. If they start to wander away, rein them back in. You have to know when to stay close to someone. You act like a border collie — don't let the kid bolt the flock. You stick with her, but don't crowd her."

Then, when your toddler gets the hang of the potty, expect her to be full of bluster. "Hey, I got it — I'm good, I'm good." All she needs is a pair of underpants with arrows and fringe and glow-in-the-dark bulls, which shouts "this kid is a real knockout!"

Keep the pep squad cheering: Have your child call her grandmother to tell her she used the potty chair. "I did it, Nana! I peeped in my potty. Are you proud of me?"

Don't give her an ounce of negativity in regard to smell, consistency, or appearance of her bowel movements, pee, or potty tries. Stick with words that are forward-thinking and upbeat: "Won't it be nice when you do this in the potty and you won't have to lie down so I can change your diaper. I know you're getting tired of that."

Giving kudos 'til it hurts

Potty training is one time when you'll be praising your child so much and so often that you may forget what you're praising her for — but keep the good stuff coming.

Praise her potty-sitting effort even if she gets up and then promptly goes in her diaper. Clap your hands. "I'm so proud that you're trying — you keep sitting there and trying so many times. Yay for you!"

Give your child a hug and clap your hands, and let her post stars on her success chart. You can define success however you want — dry pants, sitting on the potty with a cooperative attitude, or the real thing — being a top producer in the potty chair.

Make it clear that getting fully potty trained is what's expected of super-cool kids. Frame it right, and soon she'll be right in step with the program. Not immediately, but soon.

Staying away from saying the wrong things

The whole time you're teaching your child to dance the Potty Mambo, keep in mind that this is not a life-or-death matter. To make sure your sense of humor stays intact, here's a short list of do's and don'ts:

- Don't get too intense or serious. (On most people's list of regrets about silly things they did while potty training their children, this is usually number one.)
- Do promote the idea that everybody's pulling for the trainee.
- Don't act like "me boss, you little kid." Treat her the way you'd like to be treated if you were two years old and learning the potty and finding it pretty rough.

Behaving after the Dance: Post-Weekend Protocols

After Potty Weekend, you'll want to set up a nice, calm routine that centers around your child's pee-poop schedule. (See Chapter 4 for information on pinpointing your child's elimination patterns.)

On the Monday following Potty Weekend, after your workday — or if you don't work outside the home, anytime — set aside a 30-minute block of time when you can let your child run around with no diaper or pants. Be careful where you let her wander because you should expect accidents. The purpose of the 30-minute slot is to provide some carryover from Potty Weekend, when your child was making some progress, partly due to the nude policy that prevailed then. Again, you'll give hands-on attention and interest in what's she's doing and address any questions or concerns she has. Make lots of mentions of "you know what you did last weekend."

Meanwhile, when you're both coming down from the high adrenaline of Potty-Training Weekend, attack the next challenge: joining forces with other caregivers in using a real-world approach. This calls for fewer potty-sits and decreased drumrolls and sirens — but the same level of patience and support.

If you work, see the tips in Chapter 9, which tell how to keep all caregivers on the same page. It's very important to let the caregiver know what took place during Potty Weekend, and ask for her assistance in giving your toddler frequent potty opportunities.

You want to pursue a simple goal of keeping your child in the groove she found during Potty Weekend. She is getting the gist of potty deeds, and you'll keep reinforcing that over and over, until it becomes an engrained habit. For several weeks, you'll give her refresher comments, just to make sure she understands what's going on. Some kids find it easy to remember — other kids get forgetful very easily, and need lots of wakeup calls and hints.

Be sure you avoid having a "how did she do today" session every time you pick up your child — she has ears. Believe us, she'll understand if her accidents become hugely important, and that will probably scare her into malfunction. (If your caregiver wants to chat, ask her to give you a call at home.)

When your child has mastered the potty chair, graduate to a stepstool and a seat attached to the big toilet. (In Chapter 8, see tips on how to know when your child has mastered the chair and is ready for the switch to the big toilet.) That setup will be better for you and other caregivers (less cleanup) and helps move your child on up to another plateau.

How cool is this?

One day she hits pay dirt.

That darling toddler of yours walks over to her little potty, sits down, and uses it, without any urging from you or anyone. (You break out in song, "I believe in miracles!")

Does it get any better than this?

Each evening in the week or two following Potty Weekend, refresh her memory about the things she learned over the weekend. And, continue cheerleading: "Hey, you're learning these things! That's great! This is so exciting, watching you growing up. You are such a good girl." You're trying to keep her momentum going — she's interested, getting it right some of the time — so, work with this.

 If you're gone much of the day working and your child stays in daycare or with a nanny, tell her: "Lola, if I'm not here, just let Mrs. Marianna know if you want to use the potty chair and she'll help you. You can tell her when you feel like you need to go potty." But, don't question your child about the day's potty successes/failures the minute you pick her up in the evening.

Later, at home, you might casually ask your child if she remembered to tell Miss Carol when she felt like she needed to go potty. "She'll be happy to help you — don't worry about that."

Chapter 8

Keeping a Good Thing Going

- -

- -

*Y*our child is really making you smile these days: lots of successes in potty use, ample cooperation, fewer slip-ups. But stay vigilant. Keeping your focus goes a long way toward preventing potty training from becoming an extended, on-again-off-again ordeal, the way it does with some potty paratroopers.

When your toddler has shown some success and is regularly sitting on the potty several times a day, you can chalk it up as a trend. Now he is more likely to go in the potty than his diaper. How cool is that? But don't alert the media just yet. Move on to primetime reinforcement.

Reinforcing Success

Reinforcing success is an upbeat enterprise; one that lets you know that working with your child should be interactive.

When you heap affection on your child even though he is still having potty "accidents," that's very reassuring to him — it's not like you're giving him license to do the wrong thing. And finally (happy day!), he'll get so good at it he'll show you he's ready to switch over the big toilet.

Emphasizing his output

Make sure to have your child check out what he has done in the potty. "See, you pooped in there — that's good!" If he looks and notices what he has done, and gets the product-praise connection, this cements the feeling that potty training isn't all that hard.

It may be hard for a two-year-old to understand why this stuff (poop and pee) comes from his body and why you're making a big deal of talking about it — yet you want to get rid of it, just flush it away never to be seen again. Nonsensical, he thinks. So, you have to keep harking back to: "This is what your brother does and Grandpa, too. They have to poop and pee, and they use the toilet as a place for that poop and pee. But we don't keep it. Poop isn't like one of your pretty pictures that you color or a bird you shaped out of modeling clay. It's different; it's not meant to be kept, even though I am proud that you're noticing when your body needs to do it so that you can use the toilet like a big boy."

When your child uses the potty to poop or pee, be very open and enthusiastic in your praise. And make sure he sees you admire his output in the potty.

If you're a working parent, you don't witness all of his daytime successes, so try to underscore your pride and interest in his progress, on weekends and weekday mornings and evenings.

If your child does fine at home when you praise his potty products but seems to be having lots of accidents at school, tell his outside caregiver that you think it helps to admire his potty products.

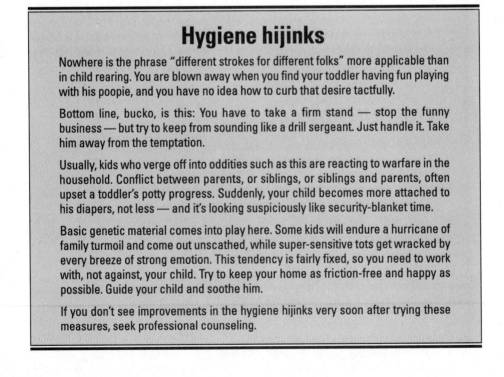

Hygiene hijinks

Nowhere is the phrase "different strokes for different folks" more applicable than in child rearing. You are blown away when you find your toddler having fun playing with his poopie, and you have no idea how to curb that desire tactfully.

Bottom line, bucko, is this: You have to take a firm stand — stop the funny business — but try to keep from sounding like a drill sergeant. Just handle it. Take him away from the temptation.

Usually, kids who verge off into oddities such as this are reacting to warfare in the household. Conflict between parents, or siblings, or siblings and parents, often upset a toddler's potty progress. Suddenly, your child becomes more attached to his diapers, not less — and it's looking suspiciously like security-blanket time.

Basic genetic material comes into play here. Some kids will endure a hurricane of family turmoil and come out unscathed, while super-sensitive tots get wracked by every breeze of strong emotion. This tendency is fairly fixed, so you need to work with, not against, your child. Try to keep your home as friction-free and happy as possible. Guide your child and soothe him.

If you don't see improvements in the hygiene hijinks very soon after trying these measures, seek professional counseling.

Using charts and other enticements

Ah, the glory days. You get to shower your kid with glitter-dumplings. And, if the kid has been experiencing a little turbulence, that gives you even more reason to set up a ride to remember.

Probably best to steer clear of food-treats altogether, though. You want your child to develop healthy attitudes toward food, and using candy and cookies for crime and punishment and cool stuff is usually a mistake.

Guaranteed to titillate toddlers are the following nonedible enticements:

- ✔ **Set him on fire with star or sticker success charts:** Buy one of these on the Internet or make your own. Just mark off days of the week, buy some cute stickers, and you're set to go. This works wonders because toddlers love game playing; they adore stickers; and they can be total little Thumper-bunnies for pleasing.

- ✔ **Tantalize with toilet targets:** Traditionally, most people think of these as cool training devices for boys, simply because they have better anatomies for pee aiming, but girls like targets, too. This pumps up the let's-have-fun-with-it game to heights that jazz up toddlers sky-high.

- ✔ **Excite the underwear prince:** Give your kid one look at some really pretty or fun or adventuresome underwear, and you may pick up a distinct hum of excitement. Kiddo's eyes sparkle; he's turned on. Ah, so easy to take a trainee from the state of flustered, wet, and worried to the Joyful Pottyer, just by the promise that he will soon be wearing big-boy duds under his jeans.

- ✔ **Bowl him over:** Tuck tiny wrapped gifts in a candy bowl, so he can draw one each time he has a potty success. You can use trinkets — the goodies just need to be things that make him smile and feel successful.

- ✔ **Hype up hygiene charts:** You can set up a chart that lets your child sticker-reward himself each time he performs one of the cleanup steps involved in potty training. Wily wiping. Wonderful washing up. Fine flushing. Savvy pants-straightening.

If you haven't already set up a game in which he wins stars or stickers to put on a success chart, the time is now to kick off this idea, which is the best of the list above.

"You know what, Bryan? I think you deserve to give yourself some stickers on this chart every time you remember to go in the potty." This usually works wonders — a truly fun game for as long as you can milk it. Of course, soon you'll probably have to up the ante — if your child is getting bored with all the pulling up and down of pants, going to the potty chair, and so on, pull him back into the game by letting him pick out some new stickers or some other chart item that he thinks is fun. Maybe he'd like to draw a picture with a giant-sized, neon-ink marker, each time he potties. Or put a doodlebug in a bottle. Something he thinks is neat and nifty will help you keep him on board until pottying becomes second nature.

So, hatch a plan: "I think if you concentrate on how it feels when you need to go, you'll start using the potty all the time. And to help you remember, I'll let you buy a small toy if you are successful all week long. On Saturday, we'll go to the toy store to celebrate your one whole week of using the potty consistently."

Yes, go ahead. Seal the deal with just a little tiny bribe. The only rule here is you need to make sure it's something small, not Christmastime-large. A tiny gift for compliance is worth it, believe us. Just think of it as an incentive for your toddler to work hard to stick with the program. Remember, he's just a little kid. His mind wanders, and so do his potty products unless you help him.

In healthy parent-child relationships, this milestone period is handled so that the child feels a sense of pride, not fear. You want him to polish bladder and bowel control carefully and slowly, because halfway mastery will leave a toddler unsure of himself. Then his shakiness will make him regress any time he's under stress.

Oops, He Did It Again: Dealing with Accidents

Just when you thought it was safe to go back to the little chest of drawers and pull out those big-boy underpants, an accident occurs. You see that look of chagrin on your child's face, and you know what has happened before a word is uttered. You're bummed. He's bummed. Talk about a no-fun moment.

Backsliding or waffling is the most common complaint among parents who are leading their offspring through potty training. So what happened? Your child was taking to the whole production with gusto. You thought he liked it, understood it, and then one day, boom — brain freeze. Walking into the room in wet underwear, your child looks confused. Is he wondering if he's going to get in trouble?

But no matter how many times your toddler screws up, you can't allow stress to make you act like you approve of him mainly when he's doing well. That would be passing your stress on to your toddler. Making him feel guilty about accidents is counterproductive. Here's how disapproval from Big People may translate to a toddler's impressionable mind: "When that little mutt starts controlling his bladder, I'll lavish him with hugs and kisses — but not until then!"

Handling an accident in the moment

After an accident occurs, get your child cleaned up and then put him on the potty chair to sit. Tell him you understand if he doesn't need to go right now, but you want him to practice sitting there. "I'm sure the next time your body tells you that you need to go, you'll let me know, and I can help you get to the potty in time." Keep mentioning how much he seems to like doing things on his own, and you know that he'll soon be that way about using the potty.

Very carefully, reiterate what you want him to do — and what you don't want him to do. Speak slowly and deal in specifics. "I want you to try to listen to your body, and try to know when you need to pee or poop. Then I want you to go to the potty chair, pull down your pants, and go there." Ask: "Do you understand what I'm asking you to do?" If your child nods or says yes, then proceed with the flip side: "What I don't want you to do is go in your pants. You're working to get out of diapers. I know it's not easy to remember all these things, so all I'm asking is that you try."

Hug. Kiss. "You are the best little kid in the universe, and I love talking to you and teaching you new things and watching you grow up."

One day if he's busy playing and actually halts in mid-pee or mid-poop and tells you, praise what he did do, not what he didn't do. Jump all over the good news: "Hey, that's great. You almost made it, and you even stopped when you started going in your pants. You're getting there!"

Looking for reasons

What you need to do after an accident is try to figure out what went wrong with a plan that was humming along so beautifully. To get a good take on what your child is feeling, hark back to your own early experiences in learning how to use a computer: Did you have lapses? Setbacks? Times when you had no idea why you were even attempting to learn something so tough? Ah-hah. There you have it. Your toddler is equally mind-boggled, and that's probably the likeliest explanation for his current backsliding. A few neurons sputtered.

Review the previous day or two to see if the plan died of natural causes. Is your child making some stressful adjustment right now? If the family just moved into a new home, or you're getting a divorce, or a new baby is in the house, backsliding is probably your child's way of saying, "enough already." He is feeling a little off-kilter — perhaps, a bit insecure — and is not in the mood for taking on a scary challenge.

Problem solving can help. If your efforts at potty training just aren't going very well, sit yourself down and ask a few questions: Did he really show those all-important readiness signs at the outset of toilet training? If the answer is yes, then can you pinpoint anything that caused ripples — a stressor, perhaps a sibling rivalry? Try to figure out if your child has any specific issue that could be interfering with his potty training: child or parent illness, parental disharmony or addiction, lack of structure in his routine, discord with a caregiver, strange behaviors, or something else entirely.

One mom realized that her child's daytime caregiver was making her son feel guilty about accidents, because when she picked Cooper up — on three separate occasions — the first thing he said was, "No pee-pee in pants." He looked upset and scared. Hmmm. And he was wearing his "extra clothes" that the daycare center kept in his cubby in case of accidents — a dead giveaway that he had, indeed, had an accident. But for some reason, young Cooper felt compelled to tell a lie to cover up his mistake. This gave the mother a good opening to talk to the caregiver. "Please make sure that no one here at the daycare is making Cooper feel guilty when he has accidents. Making him feel bad will be a setback."

The bottom line is that helping your child gain mastery over two orifices eventually will instill self-confidence. He will be pleasing you and himself. It's a toddler moment to be remembered, and it can definitely be something that makes parent and child closer.

Completion of toilet training usually signals the beginning of a newer, cleaner stage in the toddler's life. He has little tolerance for sticky fingers or a messy face. Basically, from potty training, a child gets his first inkling that there are right ways of doing certain things. The bulletin comes in loud and clear: Not all of life is simply flying by the seat of his pants, as it was in the past.

Modifying Your Own Behavior

Believe it or not, there will be a few times when you, excellent caregiver that you are, will probably need to step back and take a deep breath. Rein yourself in. You must remember not to drive your child wacko.

Hard as it is to remember, keep chanting that learning to use the potty is his challenge, not yours. His, not yours. You already know how.

You can assist, cheer on, and support. But only he can make it happen, and turn it into a habit. This learning curve is just like helping him adjust to other developmental phases, even something as big-league as academics. The goal is to instill self-discipline in your child so that his grades will matter to him, because you can't follow him to college and keep tabs on his homework. Similarly, you can lead your toddler to the potty, but you can't make him go.

The best lessons are ones that your child chooses to incorporate, and sees the sense of having learned — not ones that are crammed down his throat, or absorbed just because he fears loss of life or limb.

Parents who push too hard during potty training can cause physical problems. Believe it or not a correlation exists between hard-driving toilet training and chronic constipation. Chapter 16 has more on poop problems.

As for your own disappointment when the process is slow and erratic, just admit to yourself that you're disappointed. One accident after another can be disheartening. But don't reveal your displeasure, or he'll feel like a failure. And don't chat about it with your mate or friends in front of your child, as if he doesn't have ears. He will pick up on every nuance of disappointment, and your dismay will not make him feel motivated or successful.

Don't forget that your toddler wants to cooperate, but his body isn't fully on board with the idea. He has to be patient with himself, and he needs to know that your attitude is unflinchingly supportive, as if you have all the time in the world to wait for him to get this skill mastered.

Be sure to avoid water works. Don't turn on the water faucet for the power-of-suggestion thing — unless you don't mind creating a Pavlovian response. Thereafter, your child may always need to hear water running in order to pee.

Resisting the urge to tidy up

After he has racked up six weeks of successful potty prowess, you need to handcuff yourself: You have to relinquish your power. Let your child do all potty deeds by himself, no matter how unpolished his efforts. Many parents and caregivers send a negative message (accidentally) by letting the child know — through actions — that the things he's doing aren't being done quite right.

Your child is slow at getting his pants down, so you jump in there and help. You give him lots of little hurry-up looks and big sighs. When he finishes and his pants are crooked, you reach over and fix them. Even his method of tearing off the toilet paper prompts you to fix it.

All of these things are innocent enough on the surface — and well intended, no doubt, but you're basically telling your child that you have serious doubts about his abilities. You, superstar parent or caregiver, always want to spiff up his loose ends.

This makes your toddler nostalgic. Immediately, he is reminded that things were much easier and certainly less stressful back when he did all of his bodily deposits in diapers. There was no bad feedback. Life was simple and laidback. Thus, logic tells your child: Take cover. Go back to square one, to the Good Old Baby Days. Obviously, being a "big kid" is highly overrated and fraught with anxiety. Who needs this kind of grief?

Handling the young and restless

So, what if you had your child's interest at the outset, but something has gone wrong. You talk about the potty chair, and his eyes glaze over. He has a vacant look, and then glances away into space. Clearly, potty training has ceased to be a priority for him.

If your child were highly verbal at this age, here's what he would like to tell you: "This potty-training stuff makes me anxious. I liked the way it was before; we had settled into a perfectly good routine, and that is now being thrown off by a part that I don't understand yet. I don't like the question-mark part. I wish we could just forget about making changes. Listen, diapers work for me. Really."

Time to hunker down. Use your enthusiasm to lift him back up. When you lead him to the potty chair, ask your child to give you a heads-up as to when the urinating or bowel movement starts so that you can spout some quick and noisy praise. If he goes mute on you, and fails to share this information, you should nonchalantly check between his legs for a progress alert. When you spot the urine starting, offer instant affirmation. "Hey, look. You're peeing in the potty. Good deal!"

Sometimes a child seems like he is engaged, but you are surprised to find that most of his potty-sits are nonproductive. Instead, your toddler seems to be sitting there all day but doing little more than fidgeting and daydreaming.

This is when you want to jump in with incentives "Think how cool it will be when you can wear your neat new underpants all day." And cheerleading: "You're the sweetest little kid in the world! You make me so proud of you."

A little of this banter is okay, but don't overdo it if he seems like he's retreating. Try to cool your jets and quit pushing. The pace of adaptation is your child's, not yours, and your urgings may make him slow down. Even worse, it could result in his balking at the whole idea of using the potty chair. (See Chapter 15 for more.)

Putting a lid on the sermons

Parents have a natural bent for preachiness. It comes in handy for keeping kids out of traffic, away from fires, and safe from bad-tempered dogs.

But potty training is no time for sermonizing. You will undoubtedly be tempted — all sorts of great parables will spring to your lips. But no matter what kind of beautiful package you wrap them in, these will come out sounding negative. So, resist the temptation.

Instead of calling up an important piece of worldly wisdom when your child pees in his pants, just find some encouraging words. Take the same approach you would if he were a teenager struggling with algebra: "You can do it. I realize it's tough for you, but I'm here to support you."

Don't make your child clean up his "accident." That introduces a punitive element to the process. Liken it to making your child eat strained beets. Think how well that has worked for you.

Do give reminders. Just don't turn into some awful, repetitious nag. Simply harping on the idea won't make him feel like sprinting to the toilet; it will teach him to cultivate the skill of tuning you out when you get boring and overbearing.

Take a soft-sell approach. Don't force your child to get on the potty. Don't spank or berate or punish for failure to produce or cooperate. Don't even do the mildly obnoxious power-of-suggestion thing of running water while your child is sitting on the toilet. This ushers in the Pavlov's dog problem — yes, this works, but do you want your child to 'need' to hear running water to pee eight years from now?

Sideswiping snags

Sometimes you can see your child sailing along with potty training, and then a snag arises. Here are some of the common ones and what to do if you encounter them:

- ✔ **Linking pottying with just one parent:** Your child agreeably goes to the potty for you — but refuses when anyone else takes him. The problem here is that you have become a key part of the project, so it's time to detach yourself from his potty efforts. Tell him this is his "deal," and walk him to the door of the bathroom. Let him go inside and do the deed on his own.

- ✔ **Having trouble breaking away:** Kids get busy playing and have accidents even when they are a full year or two past completion of potty training. It's a very common snag. You can help by reminding your child to go to the bathroom when he's preoccupied with playing and you haven't seen him go to the bathroom in a while.

- ✔ **Experiencing fright-in-the-night:** Turn on a nightlight in the bathroom so that your child won't dodge going to his potty chair because he can't reach the light, or the hall's shadows look like ghosts. Little things such as this can easily turn out to be hitches that sabotage the whole project.

✔ **Avoiding the potty for physical reasons:** Bowel dysfunction can put a crimp in the program for sure. If he seems to be resisting having a BM, make sure that he's drinking plenty of liquids and eating lots of fruit and veggies so that he doesn't get constipated. If he has complaints of pain or other problems with bowel movements or urinating, check with your doctor. Diarrhea — another troublemaker — is usually short-lived, but if your child has the runs for more than two days, or if it's very severe and/or you see a significant amount of blood in the stool, call your doctor immediately. (Check out Chapter 16 for tips on handling constipation and soiling problems.)

✔ **Giving funky attitude (yours):** Certain kinds of parents and caregivers actually create their own slippery slopes in potty training. They mistakenly start the process when they themselves are in the wrong states of mind: demanding, impatient, stressed-out, or disinterested. If you sense that your own attitude is behind your child's difficulties in learning to use the potty, postpone the whole idea until you are in a better frame of mind and are able to be a real help.

✔ **Pooping in the wrong places:** Sometimes you may get the feeling that your child is getting skilled at pushing all the buttons that set you off — and that he knows it. You're tired at the end of the workday, so what does he do but find a place in the corner to poop. He has been trained for months, so what's that about? Typically, this kind of thing happens once or twice, and that's the end of it. More than that and you could be looking at a real problem. (See Chapter 16 for more on this situation.) But if it's just an off-the-wall moment he is having, stay cool. Don't get angry and don't take his prank personally. Chances are, he just didn't get to the toilet in time, so he decided to try to hide his mistake. And even if he is trying to get a rise out of you, consider it a tiny-voiced message: "Please give me some attention." So help him get cleaned up and take some time out for just the two of you — read him a book, talk about his day, play a game with him. Kids whose parents work usually adore spending time with them, but they don't know how to ask for it.

✔ **Not wanting to go there:** One day your child suddenly freaks when you try to lead him to the bathroom. So, put the plan away for a couple of weeks, and then pick it up anew. This breaks the chain of refusal, and gives the project a do-over. Then choose a day when you sense a good mood and a generally cooperative attitude in your child. Also, make sure things are calm and routine — not when you have guests staying in the house, or something new and different is in the air. Your child needs a predictable, fairly structured routine to resume potty training.

When it comes to accidents, don't make your child admit that he messed up. He is not a flight risk, and the last thing he needs is to be flogged with reminders of mistakes. You can rest assured that all children have pee and poop "accidents," not just your toddler. "Why do you keep messing up?" will mean to your child "Why are you such a loser?"

Switching to the Big Toilet

When you have steered your child past the snafus and it appears he has the potty-chair process mastered, encourage the idea of switching to using the adult toilet. And, soon after, make an effort to transfer all responsibility for toilet functions to your child, no matter how messy he is.

The child must be responsible for pushing his pants and underwear down, getting on the toilet, pulling off some toilet paper, wiping himself (if you have a girl, teach the important directional "front to back"), putting the toilet paper in the toilet, getting up off the toilet, pulling up the underwear and pants, and flushing the toilet. Then he will need to wash and dry his hands. (See Chapter 7 for an explanation of the front-to-back caution.)

Whew! That's a lot. So, be sure that you send him up from the farm team to the majors only when he has shown that he can do all of these things with some consistency. Graduating to using the family toilet is a milestone, and not one to be taken lightly.

You can nudge him in that direction, but be careful not to push. If he doesn't like the whole idea of changing to the big toilet — maybe the size or noise of it scares him, then just accept his reluctance and let him continue to use the potty chair. As he grows taller, the size of the toilet will become less intimidating, and he'll take less urging to make the upgrade. He will probably need a little stepstool and some support as he learns to balance and hold on.

What if he still wants the old potty standing by, like an old friend? That is just fine, and even if he still uses it occasionally, don't make a big deal of his flashbacks to baby days. You were the one who encouraged him to bond with his potty chair, remember, so he probably won't abandon it easily. It will be a reminder of the comforting feel of something that really fits his small behind, and temporarily, he just might want you to leave it close by.

When you're really tired of having the potty chair take up floor space in the bathroom, you can try moving it to his bedroom and putting a stuffed animal in the seat. Or you can ask how he would feel about giving it to a children's shelter, where the little kids need potty chairs and there's not much money to buy them. Or, you may decide to keep the potty chair around, just in case your toddler needs it at a holiday celebration, when the house is filled with guests and the bathrooms are staying occupied most of the time.

Chapter 9

Training Outside the Home

*S*ome kids are super-duper potty-goers at home, but when they leave the home front, they falter. They are fond of things familiar, so potties that look or feel different and caregivers who use a different approach or different buzzwords may throw them off stride.

In fact, for most small fries, potty training away from home requires special handling. So, if you leave your child in the care of others every day or only every once in a while, tell everyone involved the basics of your child's potty routine. Prepare well for day trips and sleepovers so that you and your child can feel secure. And, for the car, take along a potty for the road.

Don't make your toddler feel as if she's done something wrong or she's an oddball when she experiences that familiar need-to-go urge away from home.

Dealing with Daycare Issues

Some kiddos' potty programs get thrown off track by outside caregivers who really, truly mean well — but they just don't get why you think consistency from home to daycare is such a big deal.

But whether caregivers understand or not, most are willing to listen to your comments. Tell them that you believe that changing approaches will mix up your tiny tyke who is barely used to using the toilet, anyway.

So summon the troops and do what you can to get everyone involved on the same page.

Getting all caregivers on the same page

Go ahead and assume that most outside caregivers have their own ideas on potty training, so inform yours — right after Potty-Training Weekend — that you have a potty plan for your child.

Telling the caregiver, "Here's what we do," at the very beginning is so much easier than trying to back track. (Think how much you've liked bosses who made their expectations clear upfront, versus those who told you what they wanted after you'd screwed up.)

Daycare workers tend to use a one-size-fits-all method that works well with kids who are totally ready to cooperate. And your tot may not fit in that category.

A center's method is usually based on the owner/director's potty-training beliefs, so the approach can range from as rigid as Nurse Ratchett of *One Flew Over the Cuckoo's Nest,* to as touchy-feely-easy as *Mr. Rogers' Neighborhood.* Basically, though, you can bet that few daycare centers do much personalizing of potty training. On the other hand, their method probably won't be counter to the *Potty Training For Dummies* way, except for being a bit less flexible and a bit more blame shifting. Most daycare personnel simply don't have the time for one-on-one teaching.

Instead of asking a daytime caregiver what approach she takes with kids in potty training, just give her your handout and ask her to follow it. Otherwise, you'll have to say, "Your way doesn't suit me." Yuck. Ouch.

So clearly, emphatically, and tactfully state your desires: "Please, during the day while I'm at work, follow this plan for helping potty train Monica. She needs help, of course, but no forcing or punishing. She's going to make mistakes, and pressure just won't help — I'm sure of it."

Youngsters can get confused easily. So, the best way to handle the possibilities for divergent ideas is to jot down the one-two-three of your child's potty regimen and hand it to caregivers. Leave no room for improvisation. Hopefully, that will stave off the dicey situation of discovering that someone's doing things differently at daycare, and your kid is getting terribly confused. That forces you into a corner where you must ask for their cooperation and a switcheroo back to your way.

If relatives or friends also care for your child from time to time, make them copies while you're at it. Let your child know what you're doing and why. "This way, Aunt Camilla and cousin Gina and Mrs. Fritz at daycare all will know what you like to do when it's time to go potty."

Giving all caregivers the page

Make a big point of giving your lead caregiver a page of instructions. You may want to set up an appointment so you'll really have her attention.

Explain that you think you've found the best way to potty train your child, and you'll appreciate her compliance with the plan. Even go so far as to point out that you don't want anyone who takes care of Ava to meet you with a negative report at pickup time: "Your child was a total pee-renegade today — she wet her pants!" None of that stuff, thank you very much.

But do ask your caregiver to jot down an end-of-week progress report so that the wee lassie's potty deeds won't be discussed in front of her — unless, of course, we're talking rave reviews. Request four weeks' worth of progress reports, and be sure she knows you mean simply a quick rundown — nothing elaborate or typewritten.

Tell your caregiver, nanny, or relative: "I'd appreciate it very much if you'd follow this plan because we started it over the weekend, and Ally is doing just great. Otherwise, I'm afraid she'll get confused. Thanks so much, in advance, for your help."

Emphasize that you know this person (relative, nanny, caregiver) will be a major player in helping your child succeed. "I really appreciate you being up for this."

Here's the written plan that you can hand out:

1. **Take the toddler to the potty every two hours if possible.** (If she refuses, don't push it.) Be sure she potty-sits shortly after eating and drinking. Gentle prompting is fine.

2. **Ask the child to tell you when she feels like she needs to go.**

3. **Give praise, even if nothing happens during the potty-sit.** Don't apply any pressure. If she goes, she goes; otherwise, just say you're glad she tried.

4. **Please don't make the child feel guilty if she messes up her pants.** Just change them, and put on fresh clothing (if necessary). And, please say that you bet she will get it right the next time.

5. **Let her pull up underpants and clothes, even when these efforts are sloppy and awkward.** Don't jump in and straighten up. She needs to feel as if she's succeeding, so right now, tidiness doesn't count.

6. **Tell the toddler that she has done something very good when she actually pees or poops in the potty.**

When you hand over the poo-and-pee-plan for your child's day, make sure the caregiver understands that you have faith in her attitude of teamwork. Word this in a way that shows your faith in her: "Of course, I never doubted for one minute that you wouldn't be on board for this, but I just thought I'd write it down, for your convenience. I know you have a million things on your mind every day."

Savvy Planning for Day Trips and Sleepovers

At home, your child may be gleefully adapting to peeing and pooping in her friendly little potty chair, but she may turn into an uncooperative alien when you ask her to do her business in an unfamiliar place, such as a truck stop or grandma's house. All manner of ogres come to mind for kids in public places, and they may show you some of their oddest behaviors when out on the town.

If your child is going on a trip, or sleeping away from home, building a getting-ready-to-go hour into your time frame can be invaluable.

In the prep hour, talk about her potty routine — and how good she is at it — and get her to walk you through it. "Show me what you do, Conchita, when you go potty." Then, role-play possible scenarios like using a big toilet at Nana's house, for example, or put your trainee in actual situations so that you address and defuse potty fears. Have your child try a toilet at a restaurant or a friend's house so that you can talk it up and make the connection to your toddler's upcoming special event: "Sometimes it's fun to see what another person's potty is like, isn't it? When we're on our trip to Las Vegas, you may get to try a lot of different toilets in restrooms we visit."

Warm Water solves daycare pee problem

A South Carolina mom tells of her daughter's odd pattern of pee refusal at daycare. "Tasha would poop at daycare, but that was it. We were stumped. Then, one of the workers asked if she could try a method she'd used with her own kids. When Tasha was sitting on the potty chair, and mostly yawning and wiggling, Mrs. Jones slowly trickled a half cup of lukewarm water between Tasha's legs and suddenly, she began to pee! A few more times and Tasha was peeing in the potty at daycare like a champ, just like she did at home."

Proof once again that truth is, indeed, stranger than fiction.

Traveling with a potty trainee

During potty-training months — and sometimes for years thereafter — your child may get antsy and say she has to pee, although the urgency comes mainly from knowing she's in a car and far from a toilet. The upshot is that the family starts teasing — "we should take a potty in the car for Lana" — a form of ribbing that usually makes things worse, and certainly doesn't enhance her self-image.

Instead, be practical about your child's needs, and cart along an extra potty seat that's portable, or a toilet-seat adapter. You may be dealing with her smallish bladder for years.

Little kids have accidents, and the motion of cars can cause both queasy stomachs and hyper bladders. You have to be nonchalant about it.

Don't play up the child's itty-bitty bladder the size of a mockingbird's, or you'll launch a habit. Self-consciousness tends to make a problem bigger and more entrenched.

Tell her what she may see in public facilities, including the fact that some may not be as spiffy-clean as the one she's used to. In a restroom that's unhygienic and lacks paper toilet-seat covers, overlap pieces of toilet paper on the seat before you have your child sit down to do her stuff. (Of course, if you're using her porta-potty, you won't need to drape the public one.)

Always carry a roll of toilet paper — one that's small because it only has a few feet of tissue left on it. This comes in handy for your child (or you) when you run across that menacing trip-demon — the paper-less toilet stall.

Cruising through car trips

Your car trips with a semi-potty-trained tot will go smoothly if you get her to practice taking her action on the road, and pack items that will cover the comprehensive scope of potty freakiness. Psyche her up with a you-can-do-it theme. Tell her she may be peeing and pooping in her porta-potty, or a public restroom that seems different, or a clump of clover and wildflowers. Emphasize the adventurer aspect. Say, "You go, girl" and mean it.

Getting ready

Ingraining the last-chance concept is a good idea. When you take her to the mall with you, encourage her to use the bathroom "one last time" before leaving home. Put her on the potty-chair and cross your fingers. If nothing happens, accept that outcome. And if she refuses, don't push.

Before leaving home, let her practice on the porta-potty. That way, your child can get used to the feel of the foldable potty. Acclimating her in advance can make a world of difference.

Day or evening outings offer fewer problems than long car trips, but some problems still can arise when you drive a semi-potty-trained child around town.

Packing the essentials

Always leave home prepared, even when you're just dashing out to the grocery. Try to keep extra supplies in your glove compartment. The goal is to make her feel snug and secure.

And, having essentials on hand takes on even greater significance during the family's annual cross-country jaunt, when aromatic potty smells won't be a welcome part of the ambiance. Just to be safe, you may want to include some or all of the following:

- ✔ Extra undies, pants, shoes, and socks

- ✔ Cleanup materials for the kid and the car (Remember that a newly trained or semi-trained tiny tot in your car may put your upholstery in jeopardy. Little kids have the dribbles sometimes.)

- ✔ Porta-potty

- ✔ End of a TP roll

If you're prepared and your tot has a mondo-big accident, you can chill, calmed by the knowledge that you're equipped to clean it up.

To make long car trips more pleasant for you and your child, take a foldable potty along: Or, put your child's potty adapter seat in the trunk of your car. That way, you don't have to search for a restroom for pit stops.

One potty-to-go winner is the Graco folding potty seat — it's so small (condenses to 5 x 7 inches), you can stuff it in a diaper bag. And, you can put it atop any toilet. Rubber pads keep your child steady.

Making pit stops

Teach her to seize the moment: Pull over occasionally, get out the potty chair, and let her climb on it and try to go. Don't wait for her to tell you, because being new at the potty game, she's not going to ask for a potty opportunity until matters get urgent. Then you'll have to hazard life and limb to come to a screeching halt for a potty break.

Demonstrate back-to-nature style: Boys can be shown how to pee outdoors if that ever becomes necessary. Finesse a girl through this skill — kind of tricky because she must crouch carefully and keep from getting her clothes sprayed.

Slow potty production is usually the operative word when you have a toddler on the road. She may well get onto the potty and smile at you and look just as if she's interested in being a productive citizen. But, the action may be very slow in coming. Defuse the awkward moment by talking to her about some of the fun things you're going to do on the trip — that will help her relax and get the job done. "Soon, when you're finished using the potty, we'll start driving again on our way to Wally World."

Some kids are charmed and fascinated by investigating the looks and feel of assorted toilets. Cap the ambitions of your adventuresome kid by having her use the foldable potty from home. The excitement of foreign facilities will dry up when she sees that no matter where you go, she's still using the same potty. (The last thing you need on a trip is a half-pint toilet connoisseur.)

Stick with the wary-of-strangers policy: *Don't ever let a child go into a public bathroom alone, even if she insists she can do it!* A dad can take his daughter into the men's room, or ask a woman-friend to escort her to the women's restroom. Mainly, you want to do what your child is comfortable doing — except going into a restroom on her own.

Sailing through sleepovers

You can make sleepovers groovy gigs for all involved. Just have some backup plans in case being out of pocket upsets your child's flow. The right bed-cover gear and toddler pant options are important for peace of mind (yours). And to help the training program stay on track, stay consistent. When your little minx is out of her comfort zone, remembering to escort her to the bathroom regularly is even more important than it is at home.

When you get to your vacation spot or the relatives' home, try these tips for keeping your potty-training child stress-free and motivated:

- ✔ **Stick with the game plan:** Even during free-flowing vacation time, remember to put your child on the potty after meals, when she wakes up in the morning, after naps, and before bed.

  If you're in a holiday frame of mind, you may have trouble sticking with a regimen — especially when you're absolutely yearning for days without structure. But giving up some freedom now will reward you during vacations to come.

- ✔ **Protect the mattress:** A waterproof sheet or heavy plastic trash bag can be used to cover the mattress your child will sleep on (at hotels or homes you're visiting). With some backup, you and your child will snooze more soundly.

✔ **Keep her in big-kid wear:** Unless you're going to a place like a children's museum, equipped with special kid-style bathrooms, you probably should take extra underpants and clothing, just in case, as well as tissues and wipes. Expect to find most bathrooms totally ill-equipped for your needs, and take along all of the things that matter to you.

Some parents like to switch back to diapers or training pullables for outings, but that poses two major risks: confusing your child about what she's supposed to do, and defusing the full effect of the fact that she has now moved up to big-kid undies. Far better to prepare for accidents, and deal with them matter-of-factly, than to send the message, "I'm pretty sure you'll make a mistake today."

On the proper-pants issue, there are always exceptions. If you're on a trip, and your child acts like she has forgotten every shred of potty-training info she ever knew, it's okay to put her back in padded training pants if you need to. When things get a little tense, that's a far better option than getting into a tug-of-war over her brain block. Wrap it in a simple comment: "I can see you're having a little bit of trouble, so let's just have you try using the potty again when we get back home. I want you to have fun on this vacation, and I think you're kind of stressing."

Whatever you do, don't turn a fun outing or holiday into a why-can't-you-remember-to-use-the-potty? kind of thing. In your child's book of memories, you want this vacation to stand out for all the fabulous fanciful fun — not for the time you made her cry because you yelled at her when she dribbled pee-pee in her hot-pink shorts. Working parents have trouble winding down when they go on vacation. Taking off that CEO hat or laying down that teacher's ruler isn't always as easy as getting packed and hopping on a plane, so you may need to remind yourself of the reason behind taking a family trip — and the goal isn't teaching or carping or punishing.

Part IV
Using Psych-Up Skills

The 5th Wave — By Rich Tennant

"Don't forget to say please and thank you, don't grab anyone's hair, and don't announce that you just made a big poopie in the potty."

In this part...

Fun and games for chatting up your child are the foundation of the Part IV package, complete with ideas for staying on message, fielding odd behaviors, and schmoozing busy toddlers.

You get a boost of one-liners that you can use to jazz up your kiddo. Plus, we offer smarty-pants tips to get the whole team of relatives to pitch in and help make this happen. Pizzazz aplenty comes with working the relevant crowd — doctors, ex-mates, and outside caregivers.

Chapter 10

Staying on Message

Keep your eye on the goal — helping your child achieve success in the bathroom. He will use the potty. He will develop a flair for wiping, washing up, flushing. He will feel like a very big boy who can do many things well. Becoming an accomplished potty-user is just the first of many fine deeds that he will tuck under his belt along the way to big-boy-hood.

For you, the coach, one element critical to your tyke's success is staying on message. In your frenzied daily lives, it can be far too easy to grow impatient and blurt out inappropriate comments that may ultimately sabotage your toddler's success. Instead, strive for a cool head and try to stick with the *For Dummies* potty-training philosophy — easy does it.

Keeping the Game Upbeat and Pleasant

Put on a happy game face for potty training. Tell yourself: "If using smiles and games to train a toddler is wrong, I don't want to be right." Say it once a day, and keep moving forward with an awesome attitude that shows you're brimming over with positive vibes. You have to make it easy for him because the way your kid sees it, what you're trying to get him to do is basically all that and a bag of hogwash. Remember, once you've experienced the feel of soft diapers against your bare bottom, that's something no one can take away from you. Not willingly, anyway.

So instead of introducing your child to the scary world of rejection and provocation ("Do this or else!"), keep him feeling groovy by exposure to your serious case of the sweets. You've got all the time in the world, and all the love in the world, and you're just standing by until his body and mind are perky enough to use the potty regularly. That's your story and you're sticking to it.

Always be ready to walk a mile in his toddler-size sneakers.

Motivating with drama-queen enthusiasm and delight

Clearly, good motivation matters. And by using your rah-rahs to your toddler's advantage, the training process is sure to go more smoothly. With you — potty-trainee's parent or caregiver — as a uniter (not a divider, per the oft-quoted President George W. Bush slogan), things will move forward hummingly.

Call up your psych-up tools and apply them extravagantly: Lots of explanations of the proper moves. Lots of encouragement. Lots of reassurance: "I know you can do this — I'm sure of it."

Mommy see, Mommy do

Philly mom Jami Exner — a woman who is known for being super-positive at all times — tells how she used that trait when potty training her two sons. By keeping the game low-stress and upbeat, she was able to steer clear of the usual potty-training hitches, backsliding and bedwetting.

"At one-and-a-half, I'd have my son sit on his little potty chair next to me when I would go. I would take his diaper off and sit him there. Eventually, he would leak out a little by accident, just being on the potty chair, and then I would get really excited and act like he did it on purpose. Of course, he knew very well that he didn't plan the leak, but my reaction was enough to make him think the next sitting just might be fun.

"Then, when it was really time to train (second birthday), I simply got rid of the diapers and spent the entire next week working on it — every hour, sitting him on the potty. Derek trained in just one weekend, and Darion finished up in one week. We simply never put diapers back on. We always had extra underwear and wipes with us when we went places, but we put up with the accidents rather than resorting to a return to diapers.

"Once diapers were gone, we never looked back. Training them was easy as pie because I got them ready beforehand. If you get your child all psyched up, he's lots easier to train."

Get the kid on board, and you're halfway home. And if that means you must put on your drama-queen hat, do it and have a little fun. Send a loud-and-clear message, "I'm your biggest supporter!" Knowing that, he will see that many good things are possible.

Exude excitement about your toddler's' attempts. Show great pride in his eagerness to please and his displays of enthusiasm. Let that babe in the woods know that you have nothing but full-blown love for him — on days he actually succeeds, as well as those when he doesn't.

Making lots of affection part of the process

At first blush, you may wonder how you can possibly build into that oh-so-important training process things as joyful as kisses, hugs, and smiles. But you'll find that it's easier that way.

Here's how: Toss aside all your big-person seriousness, and set your sights on making your child a success — on his time frame. You want your little-big-boy to learn to use the potty, but you also want him to learn that he can accomplish things — pull off tough challenges.

If he sets his mind to it, he can do it. So, he walks away from the months or weeks of potty training with a vivid memory: With your love and support cheering him on, he can do terrific things.

Helping your child learn to use the potty isn't a somber duty. Both of you can have major-league fun with it: Kiss your child. Hug him. Smile a lot. Let him know that you love him all the time, whether he puts any pee or poop in the potty or not. Joke with him — tickle his tiny tummy.

Keeping your positive mindset wired

Think of all this positive stuff as good parenting and care-giving training (for you) for the rest of your child's life. No one can be a better helper to him in all endeavors than a totally positive cheerleader who is always on his side, even when he's stumbling and bumbling and mumbling.

Show your child respect in this awesome discovery process, and he will return the favor tenfold. Also, your positive approach will rub off on him. The next thing you know, you'll hear him telling another child, "You can do that — I know you can."

Establish early on that you're a total believer in him. And you can't imagine anything hobbling such a smart, adorable kid. Constantly send the mantra: "You are good. You are smart. You matter to me. I'm happy for you that you're able to do things so well."

Think of the absolute craziness of actually getting bent out of shape over your child's potty production, or lack thereof. Hey, aren't you glad no one rides herd over your daily output?

You will have dicey moments during potty-training days, no doubt about that. Sometimes you'll forget everything smart that you were going to do, and you'll want to corner him and just make him do it. Something inside you takes hold and says, "Sit that little thing flat down on the potty and make him stay there till he goes. No more foolishness."

But, don't let performance-on-demand demons mess things up. Life is all about choices, so keep your mindset above the fray during the sometimes-trying times of potty training.

Avoid stress overflow: Sometimes kids freeze up in all kinds of behavior if they feel like parents or caregivers are in a bad place emotionally. So, if you've had a fight with your mate, or you're pregnant and reeling from morning sickness, keep your parenting on an even keel. That's hard, all right — but better than burdening a set of small, young shoulders with heavy-duty problems that will only make him falter in his development.

Putting a lid on comparing

Certain words seem to spring to your lips when you see you see the occasional loose-cannon antics of your potty-trainee. You're dying to say, "Why can't you be more like your sister? She was so easy to train!" or "Gosh, your friend Benjy took to the toilet like a duck to water."

Unfortunately, comparing words are killers. They destroy confidence and make your little toddler want to tell you (if only he were more verbal), "Hey! Just when I thought you were on my team, you turn on me!"

One mom tells of getting so frustrated during potty training that she totally lost it one night when her son Fletcher refused to sit on the potty. She flew into "Gosh, why can't you be more like Cocoa — she was so easy to train!" Then, for good measure, mom gave Fletcher's behind a sound pop. He looked up with big tears in his eyes and said, "I thought you liked me." After that comeback, Mom didn't make that mistake again.

Comparing your child to a cousin or sibling or parent or kid-next-door will only frustrate him, not motivate him. You can point to a role model, of course, with something like, "See your brother peeing so nicely!" because you're not saying, "He's much better than you are." All you're doing when you point out a role model is saying, "Take a look — that's how it's done."

The only comparison you should make is "Look how much better you're doing this week than you were last week — all right!" Chart his string of successes. That's always good. Tracking how he's doing will surely help — that is, unless you say, "Wow, you were doing better weeks ago. Are you a moron?"

Avoiding the Pitfalls of Straying Off Message

You may be tempted to try something different and abandon the *Potty Training For Dummies* plan. Maybe your tiny tot just doesn't seem to get it. So you figure that you could try your mother-in-law's ideas this week, and if those fail, go with the potty plan that a work colleague told you about. Just mix it up a little.

Whoa, Nellie. Changing horses in midstream has pitfalls — so before you jump away, consider a few givens about toddlers that make switching plans a not-so-good-idea.

Young children thrive on consistency. A two-year-old would promise eternal good behavior if he could be guaranteed he'd get the same thing in the same situation every time. Mixed cues confuse a toddler more than they do an older kid; he has so little experience to fall back on that he's relying on you not to throw him curves. Messages that are a-changin' just don't help.

Sure, you may need loads of patience before the good stuff kicks in, but just know that your child is absorbing what you say — even though he acts out-to-lunch. He's taking it in, digesting it, and eventually, he'll put all the pieces together, and show you some grin-worthy potty action.

Respecting Your Child's Modesty Quirks

During potty-training period, your child may get a little weird about privacy — most kids do at some point. He may hide in his bedroom every time he changes his pants or clothes. And he may act offended if anyone tries to watch him or even go near his room. He definitely doesn't want anybody stalking him in the bathroom.

No telling where this brand-new modesty quirk came from. And who cares? Just go along with him, and let him keep you at a distance if he wants to.

Probably his ultra-modesty is just one more sign of growing independence — a new recognition on his part that he is a separate person from you, his parent or chief caregiver.

A right to privacy is a good thing to teach your child. He can be proud of his private parts — nakedness is fun for little kids (and big ones, too). But he also has to understand that people don't go out in public unclothed, and they don't fondle their genitals in public. To fit into society, he has to follow rules. He doesn't have to like it, but he does have to do it.

When you allow him his bathroom privacy, tell him that he can enjoy this at home — but at daycare, he will still have to pee-pee or poop around others. Most childcare centers don't allow total privacy for bathroom-goers.

Also, in public restrooms, your child must accept the idea of being chaperoned — no kid goes to a public restroom unescorted — ever. Allow no negotiation on that one!

Use your child's modesty phase as a chance to explain that you don't want him and his friends all to come in and watch you pee, or poo, or take a bath. "I'd like a little bit of privacy," you can tell him.

"Why?" he'll probably ask. Tell him, as simply as possible, that some things are right for family members only. And we do different things in different situations. He is beginning to learn about boundaries and respect for other people's requests.

And when he says, "I don't like rules," tell him that disliking rules is okay. But he still has to go by them. Life has rules. Obeying them helps everyone get along better.

Getting to the Bottom Line

The bottom line: You can't force your toddler to use the potty. (That's a really silly idea, anyway.) Push him and he may do a U-turn in a heartbeat and begin to loathe the entire potty premise. Potty forcing is (a) destined to failure, and (b) counter to helping him become a happy, self-motivated child.

In the business of growing up, you can definitely help your child when he faces developmental hurdles. Have a sense of humor, a ready smile, and a word of encouragement.

Yes, he will waver. Yes, he will totter. But with you behind him, he will not fall.

Chapter 11

Understanding Your Trainee

· ·

*W*ant a surefire guarantee that you're doing the right thing while potty training your two-year-old? Then make sure you relate to what she tells you about this whirlwind learning experience she's been swept up into. If she could share her feelings, she might tell you: "I went from a carefree little diaper-bum to realizing that the big people I like to please suddenly were wanting me to do some really hard stuff. I'm not sure I can pull off this potty thing, but I'm trying hard — really, I am. And, all I ask is that they try to stay patient with me, and understand that when I mess up my pants, it surprises me just like it does you. I'll get there, I promise!"

You, parent or caregiver, must stay positive and interested, ever ready to keep your toddler's spirits high by juggling her moods and clumsiness, as well as the occasional forgetfulness and the tiny body that doesn't always cooperate. Meanwhile, continue tossing out one-liners that motivate the youngster, no matter what's going on, and stay calm amid all manner of goofy behavior.

Getting Through to Busy Toddlers

"Hello!"

"Are you talking to me?"

So, you're probably not going to be training a mini Robert DeNiro, but you do have to penetrate the fog of a toddler's busy world. And, she may well be very preoccupied, considering all the exciting things she's got on her plate these days.

Just think of the wonderful avenues that have opened to her in the two years that she's been on earth. She's learned to wiggle, turn over, sit up, crawl, walk, and run. She cooed, then sampled real words, leading up to sentences, and finally, hit on her current toddler combo of yammering and laughing and whining and crying and teasing, and who-knows-what-else will be coming down the pike any minute.

And now that she's getting to the age of accountability, suddenly you and the others who take care of her are hinting that you want a consistency coup — both bowel and bladder control. She knows that you expect her to use the toilet, wipe, flush, wash up, and then even get her clothes arranged enough to walk out of the bathroom. That's one tall order for such a little person.

So, little wonder, considering how daunting it all seems, that she tends to spaz out from time to time. Her reasons are many and, to her, valid:

- ✔ "Don't bother me — I have coloring-book paperwork to do."
- ✔ "I have a million things on my sandbox calendar. Do we have to get to this right now?"
- ✔ "Sorry, I just can't go there at the moment — I'm obsessing over a missing crayon, and it's got me crazy!"
- ✔ "I'm up to here with this hygiene stuff. I can't talk to you right now."
- ✔ "Don't try to get me to perform. I'm totally blanking."

You get the picture. And now you're wondering exactly what you can do to get through to her — to pierce that bubble of "Leave me alone — I'm happy right now, and you're trying to make me do things. I can't handle the pressure."

While toddlers have gotten a bad rap due to the "Terrible Twos" nickname, every single day your child is becoming a bit less inclined to use the "No" card. Sure, she may still have her foot-stomping moments, but she is moving on down the road toward year number three, when cooperation becomes the gold standard, and stubbornness, a dim memory.

This is clearly hot-button time. You have an edge — you can play the familiarity card. After two years of hanging out with the kid, you know that certain things always get her attention. Whether she's a pushover for somersaults or dishwasher loading, the kid will listen up when you talk about something she likes. You may want to try some of the following ones, to get your imagination cranking:

- ✔ "You're going to the potty now, and after that, there's a really neat book I want to read to you. Let's go to the bathroom."
- ✔ "Guess what? Tonight, you get to stay up 15 minutes later than usual — and help me load the dishwasher. Please use the potty first, and then, come keep me company."
- ✔ "Go use the potty, and after that, I'll lie down with you for a few minutes and tell you a bedtime story and tickle your back."

> ✔ "I have some brand-new stickers for you to choose from (for your success chart), so go use the potty."

Don't bother with any next-day enticements because no toddler has the patience for that to be a good lure. At this age, she's all today-and-right-now. Give her instant gratification, and you'll snag her attention.

Motivating with Pizzazz

To use words that will motivate your child, you have to move her into a position that's praiseworthy. Don't throw out barrels of enthusiastic kudos unless she's doing something that she herself knows is somewhat cute. She won't be fooled.

Once again, you'll simply set up your toddler for success. (See Chapter 6 for more details on this.) One of the surest ways to get a small child's attention back onboard for potty training is to link a piece of praise to an actual task. The following are a few approaches that you may want to try with your toddler:

- ✔ Tell her to show you what a cooperative child does when a parent or caregiver asks her to go to the potty and sit and try to pee.

  Your one-line motivator: "What a good attitude — I love the way you do the things I ask, and cooperate with me."

- ✔ Ask your child to show you how she can sit on the potty and press her feet down hard on the floor, as if straining to do a BM.

  Your one-line motivator: "Great — you're really learning how to use your feet to help you start to poop."

- ✔ Have her show you how a child sits on the potty very quietly so that she can concentrate on peeing or pooping.

  Your one-line motivator: "I'm proud of my girl who really knows how to do an excellent potty-sit."

- ✔ Ask her to demonstrate how to empty the potty-chair bowl correctly.

  Your one-line motivator: "You're such a good learner, and I'm proud of that."

- ✔ Have her show you how a child sits on the potty very quietly so that she can concentrate on peeing or pooping.

  Your one-line motivator: "I'm proud of my girl who really knows how to do an excellent potty-sit."

- ✔ Ask your child to do the "ABC" or "Happy Birthday" song — words or humming — and wash her hands real well. Either song will lead to a just-long-enough-hand-washing session.

  Your one-line motivator: "Put an extra sticker on your chart for a good show — you did it!"

Expect to see your child's individual temperament and emotional tone come into play. These things affect the rate of many things she does, and reporting on her displeasure with wet diapers is one of them.

Some kids are very responsive to all kinds of stimuli, while others are withdrawn and passive. A child who has bonded in infancy with one main person is usually destined to enjoy skill mastery, so around age two or three, she will try to ape the enthusiasms that you show her — a fact that you can capitalize on in helping her grow more detached from her diapers. Soon, she will begin to sense, from your cues, that having a messy diaper is probably not the greatest way to live.

But don't try to bamboozle your toddler into caring about messy diapers if she's oblivious to them. Studies show that many preschoolers who have big problems with toileting had control-freak parents — or ones who were overly permissive. The best way to train is in the middle of these two extremes. Otherwise, you spawn confusion.

Fielding Odd Behaviors

Strange behavior just happens. You do it. Kids do it. Adolescents are known for over-the-top examples of it. So, try to take your toddler's zany escapades in stride. The less attention you pay to her attempts to get a rise out of you, the sooner the odd behaviors will fade away.

Some examples of odd reactions to potty training, and how you can handle them:

- **Potty King/Queen:** Your child uses the potty time after time, even when nothing comes out.

  No one has to tell you what this one's about — a ploy for attention. The best way to handle repetitious potty trips is to make her think you're not very interested in her making the Guinness Book of World Records. She gets no extra gold stars or stickers for time-after-time potty rushes.

  Praise the fact that she does pee or poop, and then quickly move the subject onto something else: coloring a picture, playing a game, building with blocks.

- **Flasher in the House:** When you introduced nudist potty-sits during Potty-Training Weekend, you had no idea that you were launching a freedom rider. Now, your toddler is making a habit of taking off her clothes and streaking through rooms.

  Just ignore this behavior, and it will go away. Her joy in shocking comes only when people act shocked.

- **Potty Terminator:** Your child suddenly develops a yen for roughing up the potty chair or its bowl. She tussles it, throws it around, and acts like she's got a vendetta against it.

While you want to roll your eyes at your mate (What's going on with this kid?), stay calm and nonplussed. *Whatever,* small fry!

Take the potty chair away, just like you would if she were wielding a chainsaw, and tell her you don't want her to get hurt or to hurt someone with it. No punishment. No discussion. Redirect her attention elsewhere: "Now, let's go outside and have fun playing ball."

✔ **Shocker Kid:** Only when someone visits does your child poop or pee in her pants, and then she presents you with the result, for the visitor's viewing pleasure.

One of two things may be happening here: Either your child is desperately trying to get your attention, or she's showing off what she can do.

Don't make a spectacle of your disapproval, because she shouldn't be ashamed of her little "show." Just explain matter-of-factly that some things are just for family, and potty exploits fall into that category. Some kids have a hard time understanding that folks from outside the home aren't as impressed with their body products as the immediate family circle.

REMEMBER

Your child doesn't yet know that her poop and pee aren't all that cute. You've been praising them a lot lately, so, on the contrary, she may be convinced these are some of her neatest tricks yet.

The cool head you develop (or have) during potty-training days will serve you well for the next 18 years or so. Let no form of quirky antics faze you — no matter how much of a shock jock your kid turns out to be. Remember, she walks with ease, she eats with efficiency, so why keep plucking worry-bubbles out of the air?

Trainee is dealing with many mind-boggling new demands. So, give her some space. The stalking thing is a turnoff. Just let her flourish in her own little way — and soon, it'll be, "Hey-nonnie-nonnie, she's trained!"

Chapter 12

Getting By with a Little Help

●●●

In This Chapter

▶ Potty training before and after work

▶ Helping relatives help your toddler

▶ Schlepping the training from dad's house to mom's

▶ Taking advantage of resource folks and Web sites

●●●

Thank goodness potty training isn't a solo effort. With the help of the many people who are interested in your child and in his potty-training prowess, you can lead the team in supporting your tiny tot's newest challenge — pulling off control of pee and poop functions.

Fond relatives and friends can be wonderfully supportive and helpful, especially when your child gets stalled and sputters. Of course, after all your well-laid plans, you'll feel a bit frustrated — even though you continue to remind yourself that the kid's bladder is the fly in the ointment. Your child is happy to go along with the game plan, but he has to wait for his organs to cooperate.

Meanwhile, stay focused. Enlist outside aid to help you stick with your plan, give you new ideas for motivation, and assist your child in hitting his goal. You'll find food-for-thought on Web sites and from medical sources, as well as from other parents and caregivers who can bolster your confidence on rough days. Ex-mates are usually up for contributing to the plan, too, because they love the little toddler, and also stand to benefit from a positive outcome!

Special Potty-Training Issues for Working Parents

One time when you may find yourself wishing you didn't work outside of the home is during the potty-training period. You may be sitting at your desk after your potty-training kickoff weekend (see Chapter 7) when the bizarre question, "Is Sammy peeing yet?" enters your mind. You may be in a meeting wondering, "What if he has an accident and someone yells at him?"

Remember, though, that kids are wonderfully flexible, so you should have no problem getting your child up for the idea of his daytime caregiver supporting his potty program. Thank goodness, he doesn't yet have that set-in-his-ways problem that hampers big people.

To ease your mind, satisfy yourself that you have adequately briefed daytime caregivers on your child's potty regimen, and that you're getting their staunch support and progress reports. (Get some tips in Chapter 9.)

If you have made your potty plan clear to day caregivers, you'll probably find that they comply with it, particularly when the things you've asked of them aren't overly demanding of their time or efforts.

Of course, when a working parent feels out of touch and out of control during potty-training days, it can be a bit unnerving. But, remember, you like your profession (or maybe you don't like it, but you need the paycheck), so figure out what you should obsess about — and what's better left alone.

Get over your sense of "only I can do it right": Truth is, lots of caregivers can take your kid through the drill just as well as you can. Most people who deal with children on a daily basis like kids and want to see them make progress — and this is especially true when it comes to learning to use the toilet.

Certainly, don't tell your child that you know he'd do better if only you didn't have to work and could hold his hand every day.

As a working parent, you can foster your child's daycare success by trying these tips:

- ✓ **Make sure your child has what he needs:** Do your part in providing that set of extra clothing (pullups, pants, and so on), so your toddler is well equipped for any daycare pee-or-poop accidents.

- ✓ **Accept whatever happens with style and grace:** When you pick up your child from daycare, be ready for whatever news awaits you. Your child may have had a nice dry, accident-free day — or he may have earned the daycare center's official bathroom hellion of the day award. Either way, he's yours. So, give him support whether he's toting a bag filled with wet or soiled clothing, or wearing a smile that says he had a super day.

  On the home front, you need to consider some special functions of reduced time slots for training. The following are tips for morning, after daycare pickup, and pre-bed potty time:

- ✓ **Get up earlier for a few months to provide some extra cuddling during potty times:** Though your days are undoubtedly hectic, try to factor in a few months of earlier-than-usual wake-ups so that you can let your child do his morning potty-sit peacefully before you race out the door. If you're shouting timelines ("we must leave this house in three minutes!") and he's whining and crying, the chances of good things happening on the potty chair are pretty remote.

✔ **Make end-of-day potty-sits unfrenzied:** Don't let your workday exhaustion spill over into a rush-rush attitude when your child is doing evening potty-sits. He doesn't understand why you're tired and rushing to cook dinner, and he shouldn't have to pay for it. Just let him sit there and do whatever he does, and pat him on the back for a fine try.

✔ **Don't have a big-time potty practice at bedtime:** If you postpone your child's really-good-and-important potty-sit until bedtime, you're just asking for delaying tactics. He knows by now that you're heavily invested in what happens in the bathroom; he doesn't like to go to bed; he's very likely, then, to use every trick in his stalling bag to linger on the potty chair forever.

✔ Set up your child's major potty try early in the evening — right after dinner, ideally — and make the one at bedtime short and sweet. This means you want to give him a last-chance shot at the potty, but you don't want to let it turn into a stay-up-late opportunity. ("Wait a minute — I need to pee-pee.") You know the drill.

Getting Support from Helpful Relatives

You've already sorted out the problem of different expectations concerning potty practices (see Chapters 2 and 9 for more). So, now you're very likely to benefit in a major way from calling on the help of relatives. They can take your child to the potty, of course, but they can also provide you with helpful advice and serve as a sounding board if you want to vent your potty-training frustrations (out of earshot of your child, of course).

Tapping into experience

Ask relatives (and friends) what they did about various potty-training hurdles: balking, accidents, and so on. Find out what worked for them and what didn't. When you ask for help from an in-law, listen carefully, and express your appreciation for the advice. Finish up with "I think I'll try some of those things." You want to make it clear that you're-still-in-charge and asking for advice doesn't mean you're asking for your mom to take over.

Getting away

Enjoying some time with your mate — or time to yourself — can be the very welcome end product of letting that "control freak" in you take a break for one evening. Just get away; drink a margarita and chomp on some tortilla chips. Lighten up, you big ol' parent, you.

To make it an easy getaway, plan well. You want these helpful relatives to be well equipped for your child's visit or sleepover, and here are some ideas:

- ✔ **Hand them written plans of the potty regimen:** You probably already did this (Chapter 9), but you can't expect other people to keep up with the list, so have another copy ready for them to reference.

- ✔ **Pack appropriate clothing and supplies:** Don't expect grandparents or aunts and uncles to run out and buy supplies just because your toddler is coming for a sleepover. They'll expect you to bring along the goodies, so be sure you try to think of all the things needed for training: the potty chair, potty chart (if you have one), potty prizes (if that's in your plan), and extra training pants, clothing, and so on.

  Even if you're used to being a fly-by-the-seat-of-your-pants parent, you should get your act together for outings. If you don't, your child will suffer from being "undersupplied," and he may falter, unsure what he's supposed to do about the potty.

- ✔ **Ease their fears:** Sometimes relatives don't like caring for a child-in-training, but not because they're worried about accidents. They're usually more afraid of doing something you won't like — or messing up the plan and turning the kid into a slacker.

  Tell relatives when you deliver your child to their house that you're not bringing him there so that they'll teach him how to use the toilet; what's important for your child is just some quality time with relatives. Explain to them: "I've packed plenty of extra training pants, so if he has trouble with his training — maybe from being out of his normal routine — just reassure him. You don't need to worry about it. Believe me, I won't."

- ✔ **Show your appreciation:** When you pick up your child from a relative's home, come bearing a gift. Bring a small plant or some chocolates or a box of stationery — anything to let that person know how much you appreciated her taking care of your child during a stage when most people wouldn't want the responsibility.

Potty training is tougher for those who aren't involved in it on a daily basis simply because that's not their norm. You need to be a coach for the substitute caregivers too. You have to arm them with information — let them know what you've been doing — and let them know that you expect accidents.

Potty Training with an Ex: Going from Mom's House to Dad's House

Assuming that visits to the other parent's home are a regular thing, you can probably count on support from your former mate.

Be sure you send the right stuff. Even though you may be rushing around to get a child packed for a visitation weekend, pack extra sets of clothing just in case of accidents. If your ex-mate doesn't have a mattress protector, send that, too.

Do whatever you can to make the weekends smooth and avoid the possibility of embarrassing situations. If the trip includes swimming, for example, send along the kind of pullups designed for use in the pool.

You can find many ways to keep this kind of arrangement healthy and comfortable for your child. The following are tips on how to reassure your trainee that the back-and-forth system will work:

- ✔ **Stress your belief in his potty skills:** Tell your child, "When you're at Dad's house, you can show him how much you've learned."

- ✔ **Plant the idea:** Ask him to post in his mind a little sticky note that says, "Remember to go to the potty!"

- ✔ **Don't shift blame:** When your child has accidents, you'll want to blame someone, and an ex-mate is always a handy target. But, don't play the he-did-she-did game.

Unless you know differently, assume that your ex is probably following the potty plan you set up for the very reason you told him: Success for your joint-venture child is a surer thing if everyone sticks with the plan.

You also want to do everything you can to de-stress the situation. Try some of the following ideas for keeping the dual-house potty deal fairly seamless:

- ✔ **Stay cool:** Remember, if you got along with this person, she probably wouldn't be your ex, so stay focused on what's good for your child when you're forced to resolve snags in caregiving. Don't get into an argument in front of your child even if your ex-mate meets you at the door with a grab bag of "your-fault" reasons the kid isn't potty trained yet.

   Being the cause of conflict between the two of you will definitely be a setback for a potty-training tyke, so just don't do it. If you can tell your ex is gunning for a squabble, ask her if you can give her a call later to discuss things privately. Keep your tone and words calm; little kids are amazing in their ability to pick up on discord.

✔ **Resolve problems:** When you do talk to your ex, if your child hears a fight, go to great lengths to reassure him that people do have arguments, but that doesn't mean they love their child any less — it just means they don't always agree. Hopefully, though, the conversation with your ex-mate will be conducted out of earshot of your child.

Try to keep the focus on the child's welfare. If you are accused of being "too soft" on training, reassert your belief in the *Potty Training For Dummies* approach, and tell your ex that changing plans in midstream would be a huge upset for kiddo.

Remind him that if your child has to do two different methods — going from one house to the other — he's likely to get confused and do neither.

✔ **Say thanks:** Exes are just like other people. They thrive on praise and wither from criticism. So, look for opportunities to thank your ex-mate for her efforts on your child's behalf: She's trying to help you rear the kid, and that's admirable — no matter how you cut it.

When tiny tot makes potty-training strides, share those successes with your ex and try to include him in the loop of those who contributed to the outcome.

Finding Outside Resources

In our multifaceted, multitasking lives, a number of resources are available for parents and caregivers who enjoy hearing what other parents are doing, and reading tips from doctors who are caregivers for children. Friends, too, are always ready to recount their experiences — failures, funny stories, and successes.

Web sites

Numerous Web sites offer advice on parenting issues, some of which are listed here.

Sites that offer parent/kid activities and parenting advice:

✔ Parenting.com: A one-stop resource for mom and dads, with tools, wisdom, and a database of solutions and answers from doctors, parents, and child-development experts.

✔ LocalMom.com: Cute site with 5,000+ question/answer essays that are easy to access; also has specific city info for several metropolitan areas nationwide.

✔ HipMama.com: A parenting magazine featuring art and info on mothering techniques and mystiques.

✔ KeepKidsHealthy.com: A pediatrician's guide to kids' health, this site is packed with terrific insight and information.

✔ Parents.com: This Parent Magazine–sponsored site features good information on toddlers by looking under the header "Ages and Stages."

✔ ParentCenter.com: This one covers health, fun, activities and parenting tips.

✔ Parentsoup: A part of the popular ivillage.com site, Parent Soup will send you its newsletter if you sign up for it. Look for plenty of parenting tips and fun items on rearing kids.

✔ ParentingMatters.com: This site is unique in that it not only offers tips for parents, but also a separate set of tips for grand-parents. You can read articles on aggressive behavior in kids, dyslexia, fatherhood, and more.

✔ Parenthood.com: A site that covers everything from financial issues of child rearing (saving money for college) to the basics, like breastfeeding. Offers scads of guidelines for effective parent-ing. Articles are from *Better Homes & Gardens.*

✔ Oxygen.com: A popular info site that covers numerous topics of interest to women and men, Oxygen has plenty for parents raising kids who want access to some of the latest/greatest tidbits.

✔ EarlyChildhood.com: Main features include activities, news, experts, sharing boards, and a newsletter. This includes a childcare-centered homepage for finding childcare providers and preschools.

✔ ParentNews.com: A potpourri of articles, family facts, resources, and tips.

✔ Zerotothree.com: This site is divided into a section of info for parents and another for child-care professionals.

✔ Dadmag.com: A cool-looking site that caters to dads who are raising kids. Covers a wide variety of man topics, from sex and fitness and sports, to the child-rearing areas: health, behavior, and activities.

Sites that feature product information:

✔ Thepottystore.com Here, you can shop for potty tools and chairs and other paraphernalia on-line. Look for support, articles, and products.

✔ ParentPicks.com: Product reviewers look at books, toys, and videos.

✔ PositiveParenting.com: This straightforward Web site has a Positive Parenting bookstore.

✔ WeBehave.com: Living up to its tagline "Where parents, teachers, and caregivers shop," We Behave features multiple potty-training products.

✔ Babiesonline: This site offers freebies for baby care, message boards, coupons, and a cute-baby contest. And, you can also shop at Baby Universe.

✔ ParentClicks.com: This site offers shopping, product recalls, newsworthy items, searches, and A-Z topics with great info.

✔ Growhome.com: Good Web site for parents shopping for nice, comfy clothing for potty training.

Sites with interactive advice/options:

✔ KinderStart.com: This search engine will lead you to all kinds of interesting kid stuff, but a big favorite is its Potty Board game. It also features lots of recipes, fun for tots, and a column called Ask the Doctor (seems like this multifaceted site covers a trillion subjects).

✔ Dir.groups.yahoo.com: Yahoo features online chat groups on parent/child topics.

✔ NationalParentingCenter.com: This site offers newsletter and resources for parents; has a dialog room so you can chat with other parents.

✔ ParentsPlace.com: Another part of ivillage.com, ParentsPlace is full of valuable information on babies, toddlers, family, and health. Also has message boards, chats, free stuff, and quizzes.

Medical professionals

Pediatricians and family practice docs are always ready to answer questions and offer tips on child-rearing issues of concern to parents. When you have a doctor's appointment for your child, take along a written list of things you want to ask about, so you don't forget in the flurry of getting in and out of the office.

Typically, most doctors today are proponents of child-centered potty training — the kind that starts up when the child is showing readiness signs (see Chapter 4) and thus, flourishes by the toddler's natural inclination to start using the toilet.

If you want to know about specifics of potty chairs and special trends (one-day training, for example), doctors will offer ideas, but they are also likely to advise you to read books and check the Internet for worlds of opinions.

When you're searching for more information on potty training in bookstores, look for books that were authored by an M.D. as main author or co-author. That way, you can feel more comfortable knowing that the ideas suggested are based on firm medical foundations. (You've heard enough old wives' tales by now to last you a lifetime.)

Support groups

Check community centers in your hometown for parenting support groups.

Parenting chat groups can give you advice on almost any aspect of potty training you want to hear about if you like to check on what other people do in certain situations.

The following is a listing of online support groups:

- ✔ Parenthood.com: If you click on "My Hometown," you'll find a list of local parenting support groups in various cities nationwide.

- ✔ dir.groups.yahoo.com: Groups online, some of which deal with potty training, such as pitterpatter and toilettraining.

- ✔ zerotothree.org: National resources on "Development Milestones."

- ✔ buddyscott.com/groups: Features parenting groups.

- ✔ supportgroupsgay/lesbian.com: Offers information on hundreds of support groups for gay and lesbian families nationwide. The national phone number is: (202) 583-8029.

- ✔ npin.org: The site for National Parent Information Network.

- ✔ ncfy.com/links.htm: National clearinghouse for the Administration for Children & Families — lists organizations that deal with family issues.

- ✔ ParentsPlace.com: Offers information on groups for parents.

- ✔ parentingresources.ncjrs.org: Covers various parenting topics.

- ✔ homeparents.about.com/CS/supportgroups: A site for stay-at-home parents that gives information on groups like Hearts-at-Home and MOPSHome.

If you're feeling shaky about any kind of decision-making in the realm of parenting, teaming up with more experienced and/or more confident parents may help you come to better, speedier conclusions.

No doubt about it, this country has a multitude of resources for parents who seek help. For names, addresses, and phone numbers, check with your town's city hall, government outreach programs, and churches.

Part V
Coping with Special Cases

"He's only partly potty trained. He can use the toilet but he still can't write his name in the snow yet."

In this part...

*P*art V tackles the parallel universe of true toughies: bed-wetting, mondo pee problems, hard core balking, and undie soiling. Then, we turn to making you feel comfy with the special issues of training disabled children. Just by making small adjustments to tweak the potty-training process to fit the individual, you can handle all of the above — and still stay perky and confident.

The hills are alive with the sound of music: your kiddo belting out "Me, me learned to wee-wee!"

Chapter 13

Managing Major-League Backsliding

- -

In This Chapter

▶ Getting through the setbacks

▶ Keeping a cool head and staying on message

▶ Handling your toddler's reaction — and your own!

▶ Knowing when to turn to your doctor

- -

*Y*our trained child has come undone, and that's a fact. Don't get flustered; just find a way to deal with it. What you once called "accidents" now seem more like trends. Not only are there slipups — and lots of them — but sometimes, your child appears unfazed, rolling along like she could stay half-trained forever and be very okay about it. Other times, she acts wracked with guilt and embarrassment, as if she's sure you're going to throw her out the door at any moment.

Though the situation may look dim (and strange) to you right now, actually, in a matter of weeks, you can have her back on track if you do a few specific things. Keep a cool head. Ask for her help in cleanup. And, when things don't improve, ask your doctor to aid in solution-seeking.

Expecting Setbacks

Many things can throw a child off course. Maybe she's so preoccupied with play that she forgets to go to the bathroom. Or, she's feeling shaky about discarding the routine of using diapers for pee and poop deposits.

At any rate, parents and caregivers should brace themselves for potty-training setbacks, which almost always happen.

Regression due to change

A child who's adjusting to something that feels big in her world (new home, new baby-sibling, family change) is not in a good place for polishing off potty tricks. Remember how confused you felt the first week of a new job (so much to learn, so little time)? You'd have hated also having to face a huge life stressor — moving from one house to another, suffering loss of a loved one, or experiencing a marriage disaster. One challenge a month is about as much as a person (especially a little one) can be expected to handle.

Typically, in a few days, a child adjusts to changes. Thus, her regression becomes a thing of the past, and she's back on track. (If you want, you can use disposable training pants for these transition days.)

When you notice that she seems less affected by the changes, with little ado, tell her you hope that she's now used to the new baby/new house/ whatever, because it's time to get back to using her potty chair.

A child can be reluctant to follow her usual routine because she has a new daytime caregiver with whom she still feels awkward. Fine-tuning her game may take time and patience, which also provides a good window of opportunity for you to see how well the new nanny or caregiver handles hitches in child rearing.

Recognizing your child's unique temperament

Don't forget that when it comes to accidents, a child's basic temperament inevitably comes into play, as it will throughout the process of potty training, and you can't heap guilt on someone who's just being natural.

Clearly, your child's general approach to life will affect her adjustment patterns greatly. So, if she's forgetful or spacey or head-in-the-clouds ditzy, she could well be a major-league backslider. And, you'll be tempted to preach: "If only you'd try to remember!"

A better way to handle the Airhead Syndrome is to aid and abet. Give your dreamy toddler a code word: "When I say P.C., it means potty chair, so you head for the potty chair. It's our new game." Think of a key word to help her snap to the action that the word should spur, and pull her back into the camp of the fully engaged.

Or, you may even get lucky — your child may be a neatnik who likes order. But, even neatness-driven toddlers can have lots of potty-training days when it seems they are flying by the seat of their pants — wet ones, at that. Again, you have to resist the urge to say "You know better than that!"

Oops! Maybe she has forgotten all the steps to the Potty Mambo (see Chapter 7 for a refresher). But don't worry — gently give her some reminders of what she's supposed to do, and she'll be dancing like a

pro again in no time — especially if you can keep from making her feel
bad about her slips.

One mom tells of a daughter whose shyness caused an embarrassing
incident three years after she was fully potty trained. The girl, who had
been easily potty trained at age two, came home from kindergarten one
day with her panties hanging low with a poop-load. When her mother
asked what happened, Kiki told of being afraid to ask to go to the bathroom. The child had a 140 I.Q., but she was extremely shy — thus, the
mistake.

Taking physical limitations into account

What looks like flaky behavior probably translates simply to physical
limitations. She may have trouble getting to the bathroom fast enough —
the result of being hampered by short legs and a lack of coordination.
Another good reason would be recuperation from an illness or getting
back to normal after being hospitalized.

But, what if you can find no logical explanation for the fact that your
child has suddenly forgotten her potty training altogether? Now, when
you refer to proper pottying procedure, she gives you a look of confusion, innocence, or guilt. Your first thought: She's doing this on purpose!
But, relax — that's hardly ever the case. Typically, the reason is a lack of
physical readiness, not deliberate willfulness.

Even a child brimming over with full-tilt potty-training excitement is
still very much hamstrung by her own little body and its rate of development. What's a little kid to do? Sometimes, pee just won't cooperate.

As your child gets closer to age three, her body is more likely to reach
the pivotal maturity peak it takes for bladder-and-bowel cooperation.
Some two-year-olds are already B&B mature — others, not quite yet.

Getting Back on Track

Ask any parent who has taught a child to use the toilet (one who is
truthful, anyway), and you'll hear that kids have lots of pee and poop
accidents. Just like when you were learning to drive and didn't get the
gist of parallel parking right away, these tots are total novices, and
should be treated with gentle understanding when they goof up. The
more lovingly you handle this phase, the better you will cement the
bond you're creating with your child.

Be patient with the greenhorn. Soothe yourself with the knowledge that
child development experts typically regard occasional bed-wetting as a
normal thing until age six! Don't view slips as bad behavior; keep

reminding yourself that your child's body and mind have to work together for potty training to be a total success.

If you think this is long and arduous and frustrating to you, just think how it feels to her — a tough learning curve that thrives best with unwavering support. Tell your child, "I know you'll be using the potty all the time very soon — you'll learn to remind yourself." So what should you do? Don't bring up potty training at all for a two-day break. Both of you take a breather. Change those training pants like a trooper and say nothing at all about pee or poop. You're the three monkeys of see no evil, speak no evil, hear no evil.

Practicing to avoid wet pants

Run back over the whole potty routine. You can do this right after a slipup — unless she seems upset by her mistake. In that case, wait to have your chat until the mistake is a few hours behind her.

Announce to her: "You're going to practice how to avoid wet pants. You'll remember — you were getting very good at it a few weeks ago, and I know you can do it again."

Take her through the steps, one by one. (Check out Chapter 7 for the complete potty-training routine.) Go slowly. Speak clearly and with pure patience.

If she resists ("I don't want to!") wait a few hours, then try again. Instead of taking a "you'll do as I say" tack, talk to your trainee like you're her best friend who just wants to help her learn something she needs to know. "This is what big kids do in school, so you need to know how to use the potty before then. I want you to feel comfortable in school someday."

Encourage her to role play what she could do the next time she feels a need to pee. The spirit should be "Hey, I know what you can do next time you need to pee." Keep it casual. "Show me what you'll do, the next time you feel an urge to go potty. I'll clap my hands when you get through. Let's pretend you need to go pee right now." Pause. "What I'd like to hear you say is 'I think I can do that.'"

Returning to training pants

If your child has already advanced to wearing regular underwear, you can put her back in training pants for a few days. Tell her that you're not doing this because you're mad at her — you just want to provide some backup for a few days, till she feels ready to go back to underpants. Be sure that you have no hint of scolding or sarcasm in your voice.

You'll know it's time to make this exception to the rule of never moving back to training pants when your child's embarrassment takes on scary proportions — she's crying and over-the-top upset. Tell her: "I know this is hard to do sometimes, and I can tell you get frustrated. But, don't worry — I'm with you all the way, and soon, you'll get to the potty on time — every time."

And, if your child is experiencing some major-league backsliding, a return to pullups is probably a very good idea to reduce the embarrassment factor. Make it clear, though, that this is just for a few days. "It's just taking your body some time to adjust, and that's okay."

Imagine her thoughts: "But what will we do? You gave the training pants away when I got my big panties!" "Sweetie, we'll buy some more. You probably will only need one package, and then you'll be back to using the potty again and wearing your big-kid underwear."

Staying positive

Say everything, do everything, feel everything. Use both words and actions to make her feel safe and secure, loved, and accepted.

During the initial backsliding, make no references to the potty chair at all for a few days. If she mentions it when she's with you in the bathroom, tell her that you're sure she will want to use it again. "You'll get back to it again, and that will be nice when you do. I'm sure you'll do well at using the potty again soon. You are a sweet, cooperative child, and I love you."

If you're just real darn lucky and she's suddenly inspired to use it right then, agree that she should go ahead. And, feel free to act delighted that she brought it up. "What a good attitude you have! You want to try again."

Stay low-key. Sometimes, when mom or dad or babysitter makes a huge, over-the-top deal of it, a child starts feeling weird or squeamish and decides that the issue is too heavily weighted, that she felt more comfortable when using the potty wasn't something that was expected.

Being practical

Try a brass-tacks approach to handling the practicalities of backsliding. In giving her tips, use a neutral here's-what-you-do tone that has absolutely no accusation in it. Just the facts, ma'am.

You may want to use the following tips, which will help your child to get past her backsliding hurdle with no bad memories:

- ✔ Limit her intake of fluids right before bedtime.
- ✔ Encourage her to get out of bed as soon as she notices that it's wet.
- ✔ Don't force potty-sits or cleanup.

Dealing with Your Toddler's Reactions to Accidents

The way you deal with your toddler's reactions to her accidents will have a huge impact on how few (or many) accidents still lie ahead of you. Each kind of response is natural, and should be dealt with as her reality.

Consider the following ideas for handling the various emotions she may show in reaction to her tinkle/poop troubles:

✔ **She may be upset by her accidents — she may look wracked with guilt.**

Give lots of reassurance: "I understand you feel upset when you have an accident, but you shouldn't feel bad about it. This happens when kids are learning to use the potty. It just takes time." If she feels guilty, tell her that she is just waiting for her body to catch up with what she wants to do. And that's normal. All kids have to wait for that.

✔ **She may act as if she doesn't notice them.**

Let her know that you notice: "Oh, well, you accidentally peed in your pants. That's okay, though — you're learning and you may need a few weeks to get used to the whole thing. Be patient with yourself." (Ignore the fact that she already seems very patient with herself — inside, she may be feeling sad about her performance.)

✔ **She may feel like you won't like her anymore, a common way for smart, perfectionist kids to react to potty accidents.**

You can spot this reaction by the shaky-insecurity in her body language: quivering lips, tear-filled eyes, as if she's saying "I know you won't like me." Reassure her that you love her regardless of how she pees or poops, or where, or when. Remember that some kids are just hard on themselves, no matter how gentle or undemanding the parents.

✔ **She acts like she isn't bothered at all.**

Talk about how nice it will be when she's clean and dry. Speak of that future time with enthusiasm, and tell her she'll be there soon.

One mom tells of her child's embarrassed reaction to returning to training pants: "Silly me. Silly diapers. Silly pants." Then the child began slapping her hands on her pullups. But the mom was quick to soften her toddler's self-image slump by being ready with a story on herself: "You know what, Marcy? Silly me, I spilled coffee on my new silk shirt yesterday. Silly shirt. Silly me. Mistakes happen. But I'm glad you still love me when I spill things on my shirt. Just like I still love you when you have a pee accident." Laugh about it with her. "We love each other even when we aren't perfect."

Giving reassurance

When your child has accidents, apply no pressure. No punishment. No force-feeding of skills. Give her reassurance in bucket loads.

As soon as possible, find a chance to give her some praise for staying dry. Check her pants often and say something positive to her about each instance of dryness you discover.

Remember, her accidents are occurring mainly because your child just doesn't have her act together. She's probably very embarrassed. So, stay calm and supportive: "You'll remember to pee in your potty next time, I'm sure." Fluff her hair, and remind your kiddo how lovable you think she is.

If your child's caregiver reports accidents to you at day's end, downplay the importance of the mistake by saying something like, "Missy wants to use the potty and she'll get the hang of it soon. Please give her lots of reassurance."

Ask your caregiver, kindly but firmly, to stick with your positive platform — the one you shared with her at the outset of training. "I know you'll help by cheering her on. Her body just hasn't quite gotten the message yet, but she's trying hard."

Clearing up any confusion

Believe it or not, your child still may be foggy on what's expected. So, one more time, talk about what you want in a clear and slow speech.

"To keep from having more accidents, let the feel of pressure remind you that your bladder is telling you it's pee time. If you listen to your body, you'll also hear it reminding you that poop is building up and wants to come out — in the potty, where it goes."

Dealing with Your Own Reactions

Another chance to get the derailed toddler back on track centers around that sticky issue of cleanup. The sheets are wet. The bedspread is soiled. Things really aren't cooking along the way they were just a few days ago — when you thought your child was potty trained.

Don't get nostalgic. Do remember that it's pointless to dwell on the past. Deal with today — and the reality that your child is in a slacker-stage of potty training. And, that's quite natural and all right.

Sure, you're feeling disappointed. But, an upbeat frame of mind will keep her in your camp. On that same note, you can try some of the following pointers on handling cleanups of your child's messes, with or without her help:

✔ **Get her help with messed-up clothes:** Your child can tote a pair of wet training pants and jeans to the bin where they are stashed. Then have her get fresh training pants and jeans and pull them on.

✔ **Ask her to help with wet bedding:** When you go to her room to change the sheets, ask for your child's help. Be calm and don't say things like "If you hadn't been such a mess, I wouldn't have all this extra work." That will only widen the gap between the two goals — your child's "I have no idea what you want" and your "I've got to get this kid potty trained or die trying."

What if your child refuses to help with bed cleanup? Don't force the issue and don't be poor-overworked-me. Say something like "I guess you're feeling a little embarrassed, so that's all right . . . Maybe next time you'll pitch in and help me. Or maybe next time you'll decide to use the potty instead, and we won't be changing sheets. That would be cool."

Keep your tone matter-of-fact. You're not being sarcastic — you're just giving one-more-of-a-jamboree of reminders.

✔ **Avoiding the poor-me ritual:** You may be tempted to tell her "I'm really disappointed that you don't want to clean up your mess. I work so hard, and no one around here helps me."

No way. Not appropriate. Don't make your child your weeping wall or your confidante. She lacks the proper maturity and frame of reference for processing your complaints. This is a little person, remember.

✔ **Keeping it real:** If your child asks why you're putting a rubber or plastic cover on her bed, tell the truth: "This makes it easier to clean up when you wet the bed." Then, add an upbeat comment: "But we'll be able to take it off your bed very soon, when you're using the potty chair again. I have faith in you. You're going to be very good at using the potty."

✔ **Coaching like a pro:** Keep good jive coming while you're cleaning up. Pummel her with encouragement. "You will get better at this. It's okay to have an accident. I'm not mad at you. I know you want to learn to go in the potty, and you will soon be doing that all the time."

✓ **Reminding her that all is well:** When you're finished with clean-up, give your child a hug and kiss and tell her you love her very much. You may well feel aggravated, but make sure she doesn't pick up on any of it. The message is this: "I love you even when you don't come through for me; I try to understand where you're coming from."

Doctor, Doctor, Give Me the News

Your child has reached a frightening stage — frightening to you, anyway. She, however, is totally relaxed because she's decided that wet diapers don't faze her. In fact, she seems totally okay with never, ever resuming using the potty chair. She's back in diaper mode and going strong — literally and figuratively. No muss, no fuss — not for her, anyway. So, it's time to turn to an expert, your pediatrician or family-practice physician.

Knowing when to seek medical advice

How do you know when you should seek medical advice? If your child is still not fully potty trained by the time she's four or five, you should talk to your pediatrician or family doctor about the matter.

When you go to the doctor, you can expect your physician to ask you for a rundown of what has happened thus far with your training efforts, how much fluid your child is getting before bedtime, and so on.

Wetting slipups night and day can point to a bladder or kidney problem or some other ailment (see Chapter 14 for more information).

If your doctor runs tests and discovers no physical problems, you have to deal with wetting as something that's natural. In most cases, bed-wetting after a child is toilet-trained does not point to other physical or emotional problems. Probably, the only problem is a bladder that is not yet large enough to hold a full night's urine.

She also may still lack the ability to awaken in response to the feeling of a full bladder. For day and night wetting, you can try several remedies that will help your child master bladder control (see the following section for more).

Translating the doctor's tips into action

Your doctor will probably want you to try some simple measures to see if these will resolve your child's problem.

To treat wetting after a child is toilet-trained, you can try some of the following, which your doctor may recommend:

✔ Limit your child's intake of liquids that contain caffeine.

✔ Take steps to make sure she doesn't get constipated. (See treatments for constipation in Chapter 16.)

✔ Encourage your child to try to hold back her pee a little longer before each urination. Explain: "If you can try to hold your pee a little bit longer, your bladder will soon be able to hold more pee, and that'll be good."

✔ Steer her to pee right before going to bed at night. Then, when you go to bed, wake her up and lead her to the bathroom.

If these measures don't do the trick after two months, you may want to try a bed-wetting alarm device. (See more on the alarm and other bed-wetting solutions in Chapter 14.)

Many doctors prescribe oral medication as a last resort.

While you're seeking solutions, keep reassuring your child that you understand that she wants to stay dry. "This is not your fault. Your body has to learn to get used to using the potty and getting to it in time."

Chapter 14

Dealing with Day-Slippers and Bed-Wetters

- -

In This Chapter

▶ Finessing day and night mistakes

▶ Keeping everyone on an even keel

▶ Knowing when to consult a physician

- -

Day-slipping. Bed-wetting. Accidents are nuisances, all right, but nothing that you can't handle — that is, until constant reminders from family and friends that "kids that age shouldn't have accidents" drive you round the bend. So you forget that your little tyke already has enough wetting anxiety and start pushing.

This chapter focuses on kids' pee slipups, most of which are bed-wetting. But, daytime accidents happen to wee lads, too, so here, we give you accident-busting tactics.

The most common developmental problem in childhood is bed-wetting. And, most kids who wet the bed are perfectly normal children. Tons of kids have wetting accidents occasionally. Doctors don't consider nighttime bed-wetting out of the ordinary for children who are younger than six, and in most cases, such incidents require no special treatment. Most kids resolve the problem themselves as they mature.

Truth is, doctors really don't know the exact cause of common bed-wetting because too many factors come into play. Often it's a simple matter of delayed maturing of bladder mechanisms that your child inherited via his gene pool. Nevertheless, your interest is in making accidental wetting a dim and distant memory. And, many solutions work well, from the highly successful bed-wetting alarms, to prescription drugs that either curb urine production or delay the bladder's filling-up rate.

So, keep your can-do attitude in place. Whether your child is in the rarely-wets-at-all group, or the daily-wetters club, we have tips and treatments that will improve the situation dramatically.

Understanding the Differences between Night and Day

Wetting at night and wetting in the daytime are two different problems. Most accidental peeing occurs at night. But about 20 percent of children wet during the day, too, and you have to handle kids who do both differently from those who do one or the other.

So what's the diff? If your three-year-old wets the bed, he either lacks the bladder development required to hold back urine all night long — or he hasn't learned to click in to the fact that a full bladder means it's time to wake up and scoot to the potty. Or both. On the other hand, daytime pee-slipups can also mean that your child just got busy playing or watching TV and wet himself. Typically, this kind of day wetting clears up in a week or two.

You'll find that most of the time, daytime wetting is harmless and easily resolved, compared to the much stickier challenge of figuring out bed-wetting.

 Wetting the bed runs in families. A child who has trouble with bed-wetting is very often the child of a parent who had the same kind of slipups when he was a kid. It's one of those puzzles that child development experts haven't figured out; no one is really sure why some kids don't wake up when they need to pee. Chances are, the child inherits a slow-maturing bladder that makes him a likely bed-wetting candidate. (An enuresis gene has actually been discovered.) No matter what the cause, though — the upshot (and what you're dealing with) is that unfortunate whammy-in-the-jammies.

On the other hand, managing daytime peeing appropriately requires a combo of skills — both mind and body have to be ready. When that's the case, though, this problem is usually fairly easy to solve.

Defining the terms

Normally, bladder capacity increases as your child's body develops. A bigger bladder helps him hold urine longer. And when he goes to the potty, he pees a bigger amount. If your child is three or four years old, he has probably already developed bladder control and adult-like peeing routines. Potty training helped him learn to hold urine for long periods of time and hold back the urge to pee. Unfortunately though, he may still have accidents after he starts school, and you have to be ready to help him solve his peeing troubles.

The problem for your child is this: His itty-bitty bladder isn't quite ready to hold pee long enough or to manage large amounts. Mostly, kids have trouble at night — bed-wetting is far more common than day troubles. But you also need to know about daytime wetting because it's something that about one in ten brand-new kindergartners experiences.

Here's the scoop. Wetting basically shows up two ways. Your child may suffer from one of the following conditions:

- ✔ **Primary enuresis** is when the child has wet his bed since toddler days and has never developed nighttime bladder control (no reflection, incidentally, on the way he was toilet trained).

- ✔ **Secondary enuresis** is when a child has stayed dry for several months, and then resumes having accidents. If your doctor investigates, looking for a significant stressor or physical problem — and turns up nothing — matters get even foggier. Most cases of secondary enuresis involve nighttime wetting.

Slipping up in daytime

Daytime wetting is unusual in kids older than five. Few children this age wet both day and night. When they do, a bladder or kidney problem is often the culprit, and that's fixable — your doctor will provide medication, and after your child has taken the required regimen of pills, the infection is gone, and so is the wetting, day and night.

Slipping styles and solutions

Daytime pee slipups come in many kinds and ways to handle, including the following:

- ✔ **Having a sudden need to go and frequent peeing:** When your child suffers these pee difficulties, offer support and reassurance. Typically, this will resolve itself (that's assuming your doctor has already ruled out a medical problem such as a urinary tract infection).

- ✔ **Wetting with giggling:** Some girls pee a little when they laugh. Treatment: forget about it — or ask your doctor about medication.

- ✔ **Peeing accidentally when running and jumping:** Oops! When your kid's running or jumping, he accidentally pees. Solution: Get him to go to the bathroom before he goes outside to play.

- ✔ **Having a hyper bladder:** The pee comes in small, frequent batches, and your child may dance around a bit, showing urgency. He needs to go, feels like he has to pee, but the grind of constantly having to race to the potty results in bad timing on his part — and thus, accidents. Too many urges, too little time — he gets so frustrated he loses his boyish enthusiasm for the potty-game.

Doctors may discover this child has a urinary tract infection or constipation. Certain medications can correct a child's antsy bladder, giving him time to make it to the potty. To retrain the bladder better, encourage him to pee every two hours.

✔ **Letting his bladder be a slacker:** The child with a lazy bladder urinates only every eight or nine hours and has pee accidents in between. Because he really doesn't sense a full bladder, his urine flows over, causing accidents. To get back on track, have him pee and then go back and pee again and then one more time.

In difficult cases, a doctor may suggest medication or catheterization. Typically, the lazy-bladder child will also have constipation and bladder infections now and then.

Solving slipping

Usually, parents and caregivers can benefit from trying some simple ways to handle daytime wetting at home or in a daycare facility. To address the nitty-gritty of wetting, try the following:

✔ **Devise a plan:** Create an every-two-hours peeing schedule for the child who has accidents because he pees too seldom. Let a timer signal him when he needs to go so you won't have to badger.

✔ **Simplify, simplify:** Irritants sometimes lead to urinary tract infections, so don't use any bubble bath products or harsh soaps. Switch to a very mild detergent. A urinary tract infection or urethral irritation can result from sensitivity to bubble bath, detergent, or other irritant.

✔ **Dump diet don'ts:** Restrict your child's consumption of caffeinated beverages, excessive water, and salty foods.

✔ **Promote complete emptying:** Have your little miss straddle the toilet so that she can empty her bladder completely. Sometimes, when she's in a hurry to get back to playing, or she's keeping her legs together to keep from slipping on the toilet seat, urine may get trapped in her vagina and leak out when she stands up.

✔ **Encourage free flow:** Prevent constipation by giving your child high-fiber foods: apricots, plums, prunes, raisins, vegetables, and whole-grain cereals and breads. For more on constipation, see Chapter 16.

Bed-wetting

Generally speaking, physicians consider the bed-wetting tag appropriate for children who have passed their fifth birthday but still wet the bed during the night. That amounts to about 20 percent of 5-year-olds — 1 in 5. Bed-wetting, yuck. But, don't forget that this involuntary kind of mistake is as much a shocker to the kid as it is to you. Imagine waking up to find yourself in wet jammies and lying on sopping sheets.

Embarrassed and chagrined, your child dreads facing you because he really, truly likes to please. Plus he has a sneaking suspicion that his unpredictable body is sabotaging him. Not a good feeling.

If your child is still having accidents during the night by the time he starts kindergarten (after age five), look to your doctor for help. He may want you to try a bed-wetting alarm (see the "Smart toys for tykes with bed-wetting blues" section in this chapter) — these cure many kids' bed-wetting. Or the doc may prescribe a drug that's good for clearing up pee slips.

Kids who wet — and ones who don't — show few behavior differences. Also, they are normal physically. Examinations of children who bed wet reveal that they are normal — physical defects are hardly ever the cause of wetting.

Nevertheless, bed-wetting creeps a child out because of the heavy-duty anxiety he experiences — so you, parent or caregiver, want to find out why he's wetting the bed and try some remedies ASAP.

Looking at reasons

You desperately want to figure out why your child is wetting the bed. You're sick of changing sheets. Your child is sick of being embarrassed and wet. So, it's time to hunker down and figure out what the problem is.

The lowdown on medical wetting lingo

So that you'll understand your doctor's urine-talk, read the "medical-ease" words often used in discussions of pee disturbances:

- ✔ **Urinalysis:** the common urine test that is part of your child's initial visit to the doctor to assess the wetting problem. It's used to check for a urine infection.

- ✔ **Enuresis:** loss of bladder control that results in urine being released — as in, peeing at times or places that are inappropriate for the child's age. (By the way, it's pronounced "n-your-e-sis.")

- ✔ **Diurnal enuresis:** accidental daytime wetting.

- ✔ **Nocturnal enuresis:** nighttime urine accidents or bed-wetting.

- ✔ **Behavior therapy:** treatment that doesn't involve medicine.

- ✔ **Antidiuretic hormone:** one that reduces the amount of urine the kidneys make. Some children benefit from using the nasal spray antidiuretic hormone DDAVP.

- ✔ **Developmental delay:** sometimes, the central nervous system matures slowly, resulting in the child's lack of arousal at night when he should feel an "urge" to pee. When this happens, he night-wets.

- ✔ **Spontaneous resolution:** the clearing of a medical condition without treatment. For example, many kids who bed-wet often just "grow out of it."

Some of the reasons your child may be wetting his bed at night are:

- **Maturing late:** Your child's bladder function is simply maturing at a slower rate than that of some children — a purely physical thing.

- **Experiencing the slowpoke syndrome:** Slow maturing of the central nervous system equals trouble holding nighttime urine. The child just doesn't sense that he has a full bladder — the message fails to reach his brain, and thus, the control of pee-muscle contraction is absent. Growing older is the answer in most cases, when the mind-body connection becomes more fine-tuned.

- **Having a pee-prone gene pool:** The reason bed-wetting runs in families is anyone's guess, but family history counts, as does a specific gene for bed-wetting that has been identified. So let that nix any notion you may have that bad behavior's the villain behind bed-wetting. Also, kids who will be very likely to wet the bed at night are those who have two parents who were bed-wetters.

- **Overproducing urine:** A child's body can fail to secrete enough of the hormone that normally would keep him from overproducing urine at night. Many studies point to low nighttime levels of antidiuretic hormone secretion in kids who wet their beds. The upshot: they produce too much pee, and meds may be needed to correct the problem. If this is the problem, ask your doctor about having your child use the nasal spray DDAVP, which supplies the hormone that limits nighttime urine production. Using this spray often results in dry nights — it just buys time while his body matures.

- **Responding to stress:** The child who has had dry nights and suddenly starts bed-wetting may be responding to his own fright and confusion about a new baby, a move, a divorce, or squabbles. This is common. You can get him back on track by reassuring him and, if possible, get rid of those gnarly stressors (except the baby).

Watch for signs of highstrung emotions that can accompany bed-wetting. A child who is suffering abuse often starts wetting the bed, and although difficult to think about, abuse does happen. If you have recently adopted a child, or you're a shelter caregiver or volunteer, watch for signs of emotional distress. Abused children and ones who live in shelters are often bed-wetters and daywetters. Their emotional turmoil, from living through hellish extremes of hunger, beatings, and sexual abuse, takes a toll and lives on in difficulty with normal toileting.

Taking hold of solutions

If you're the parent or caregiver of a child who has trouble with bed-wetting, be glad that today, most people are pretty philosophical about bed-wetting. It happens. At the same time, people who take care of children who wet the bed are more comfortable when they're equipped with knowledge. Learn all you can about bed-wetting.

Try some of the following cool ideas for things you can do to help your tot handle the physical aspect of wetting:

- ✔ **Plan a pre-bed potty trip:** Remind your child to tinkle before he goes to bed. Then before you go to bed, get him up to go once more.

- ✔ **Instruct him in careful peeing:** Your child can learn to use his muscles to put off peeing. He develops a waking-up-at-night routine. In the daytime, he pees on a schedule (every two hours, perhaps). He works on using his muscles, taking his time.

- ✔ **Go slow on the H$_2$O:** Try limiting amounts of liquid that he drinks right before bed. And make sure he avoids drinks with caffeine and aspartame. Fluid limitation may not do the trick, but it's still worth a try, many parents contend.

- ✔ **Try timed wakeups:** Many parents think that their heavy-sleeper kids have trouble getting out of deep Zs enough to snap to the fact that they need to pee. You can try a wakeup at about the same night every evening, which sometimes works. Go along with your tot but let him show the way to the potty, and hope that this leads to his own automatic waking up — perhaps his body will start reminding him, "Hey, we pee at 1 a.m.!"

    Most doctors don't think a child really learns anything from urinating while basically comatose. But some parents report that it works and leads to dry nights.

Don't resort to any of the quick fixes sold to "cure" bed-wetting. These often turn out to be exercises in futility and just ramp up your child's frustration — one more "answer" that isn't! You don't want your child to feel as if you'll sign up for absolutely anything to get him to stop. Label him a winner, and he will become one.

Other things you can do to help? You can make sure his sleep setting is conducive to getting up to go to the bathroom during the night. Try the following ideas:

- ✔ **Tweak the environment:** Children sleeping in very cold rooms are more likely to wet their beds. Keep his bedroom at about 70 degrees and the hall and bathroom about the same.

- ✔ **Provide sleep-spot protection:** Have a mattress protector, bedcover of rubber or plastic, and a ready supply of fresh sheets handy.

- ✔ **Light up his life:** Bathroom and hall nightlights can eliminate the spooky factor.

As for rules of engagement, remember the simple (but important) rule on potty training's easy up/easy down clothing. Nightclothes should be simple to undo and pull down in the night. You can guess what will happen if your toddler decides that his pajamas require too much work — stretch, yawn, snooze. The rest, as they say, is bed-wetting history.

Create a bubble, ensuring that your toddler's family is a safe haven from teasing about bed-wetting. You can't control outside hecklers, but you can make sure your child is treated respectfully at home. Making a big deal of bed-wetting is wrong, and you can make that clear to all who surround him.

Ask siblings to help. Your toddler may tell you his big brother is bugging him about being a bed-wetter. So get with the child who's making fun of the family toddler and ask for cooperation. "Frederick needs our support while he's trying to work this out. He sure could use your help. What do you say?"

Also, ask your child why he thinks he's bed-wetting. If you're incredibly lucky, the answer may be a simple one: "It's too scary — the hall's dark." So you give him a nightlight and a flashlight or a night escort (you). On the other hand, if he has no answer, don't press.

Don't forget to explore the possibility that nighttime "monsters" are keeping your child glued to his bed. Kids get spooked easily. If he thinks dangers are lurking in the shadows, you can be sure that wetting the bed will seem like a small inconvenience compared to the risk of being eaten by a hall-monster.

If he seems upset, investigate the possibility that his concerns are leading to bed-wetting. Ask him: Is anyone at daycare scaring you? Is there something new that's frightening you? Is it hard getting used to having your grandmother living with us? Is your new nanny nice to you?

What if nothing you've tried so far solves the bed-wetting? In that case, you summon up every atom of patience in you — and just assume that growing up will eventually resolve the problem. Get lots of good cleaning materials. In the meantime, every day of the week, give your bed-wetting child hugs a-plenty and keep the home solutions coming.

Avoiding a return to diapers

You're probably sorely tempted to pop the diapers back on his little booty. That way, the small whippersnapper will be good-to-go, and your crazy stress level gets knocked down a few pegs, right? Well, wrong. The poor kid is confused enough by his pee accidents, so wave a big red flag that he's a potty-training flop, and you may turn a small problem (wetting now and then) into a big one (accidents all the livelong day).

Don't feel bad that you practically drool when you pass disposable diapers in the grocery store. Sure, you could grab a pack and put a diaper on him and manage to justify the setback. But a better idea is sticking to your global plan for potty success, which continues to march forward if you keep him in training pants and turn excess energy to helping him polish his Potty-Mambo steps.

 Busy working parents want to know the norm in bed-wetting frequency, partly because getting up to change bedding takes its toll on their rest and their time. Health professionals find that most children who suffer from this problem wet their beds seven nights a week. And some even urinate several times during a given night.

No wonder the idea of shuffling the kid back into diapers sounds awfully good! But while lapses can be a pain — especially when you've just finished celebrating having a potty-trained kid — you shouldn't overreact and immediately slip him back into diapers. This signals surrender. Your child figures you are giving up on him — not the message you want to send. He may follow suit and give up, too.

Tough problem, granted, especially when your child wets the bed frequently and shows no signs of stopping. But remember, some kids just have itty-bitty bladders that can't hold much urine. Even a year or so after being potty trained, they may have trouble making it through the night without a trip to the bathroom. Others have to work really hard on developing an ability to respond to the full-bladder pressure.

Instead of putting him back in diapers, play up the angle of how neat you think it will be when he wakes up dry all the time. Pleasing mom or dad looms large in most little kids' minds. Right now, he definitely cares what you think is cool. (Enjoy that while it lasts!)

Handling the Emotional Aspects

You're naturally going to feel surprise and disappointment when your child has accidents — especially if you thought he was fully trained months ago. But overreacting will only pump up the problem. Keeping your cool can go a long way toward helping your accident-prone loved one on an even keel.

The following sections give you tips to help everybody come through these accidents none the worse for wear.

Reassuring your trainee

You can keep wetting accidents in perspective by calling on your sense of humor. Remember, in the great scheme of things, pee dribbles are no reason to call in the U.N. peacekeepers. And the Discovery Channel won't be covering your child's backsliding, either.

Just focus on giving-trainee-a-happy-life even during this period when he's accidentally sprinkling pee droplets here and there. If mistakes crop up, reassure him often and warmly. Let him know you believe in his potty future. Put the issue on the back burner of his young life, where it belongs. No tension in the air that's thick as the burrito you ate for dinner.

Gently and lovingly, minimize the importance of your child's bed-wetting and daytime slips. Keep reminding yourself and other caregivers that he's not wetting on purpose or with malice aforethought.

Your child definitely may feel sheepish about having accidents that he doesn't understand. Try some of the following pointers for handling the mental anguish of daytime wetting:

- ✔ **Dry those tears:** When your child gets upset, reassure him that his bladder will get better as soon as his body learns to cooperate. No fault-finding or punishment. Truth is, your child just can't control his bladder yet.

- ✔ **Lay it on thick:** Each time your child does pee in the potty, talk up the advantages of being a "big kid" — getting to make a few decisions, having privileges, wearing grownup outfits, getting praise from relatives. Remember, most children are dazzled by the notion of what may lie ahead in the kingdom of cool kids. His motivation can help lead him to solutions that may work for him.

Your child is not rebelling or wetting the bed just to cause you grief. So downplay the "shame" that he's feeling. Tell your child: "This happens to lots of children, so don't feel bad. You'll soon be having dry nights all the time. I'm sure of it."

The child who wets the bed has a big-time burden, so you should stay as lighthearted about this problem as you would be about a downsized appetite. Children have phases and learning curves — normal behaviors for them. But bed-wetting puts a considerable crimp in your child's social life. He won't be eager for sleepovers as long as he needs to keep his "secret" under wraps. And being isolated isn't good for anyone.

Your child feels as if he's the only kid in the world who's a bed-wetter. His sad yearning: "Why can't I be like all the other kids in my class?" That's your cue to jump in and soundly reassure him: "Sweet child of mine, this country has four million toddlers who are potty training this year, and lots of them wet their beds." If he says, "But nobody at my school does." Tell him, "Yes, they do — they just don't talk about it. And all of you will grow out of it, I promise. And I'm going to be right beside you all the way."

When your child gets down on himself, tell him a tale of another child (maybe a family member) who had trouble with bed-wetting. This provides an amazing amount of comfort.

Just as important as handling the physical part of accidental wetting is knowing how to keep your child's self-image intact during this period when he's somewhat in a slump from feeling like he's disappointing you (and himself). Try some of the following ideas for helping your child keep the matter of accidental wetting in perspective:

- ✔ **Sample motivational peeing:** Ask him to visualize himself getting up during the night and going to the bathroom to pee. Make it fun. "Pretend right before you go to sleep that you see yourself getting up and walking into the bathroom. . . ."

- ✔ **Be war buddies:** Invite your child to pitch in when you're changing wet sheets and covers; this helps him "cover his tracks" and reduces the embarrassment of having the whole family clued in on news of every single accident.

- ✔ **Teach him how to do self-talk:** Say to him, "Sebastian, tell yourself that you really, truly want to wake up clean and dry. You can do this. And it will feel great!"

- ✔ **Soothe his frazzled nerves:** The wet sheets and bedspreads and blankets will survive these months or years, but the guilt can hang around and ditch confidence in a big way. Make a major point of soothing your child so that he doesn't feel guilty.

- ✔ **Cheer him up:** Just wander by and give your child a kiss and tell him that you know he's going to learn to stay dry. "I can just see you waking up in the morning, all nice and dry and happy. Won't that be neat?"

- ✔ **Play let's pretend:** If your child does better having dry nights when sleeping at the homes of other people (friends and relatives), this probably means that he can't reach the level of deep sleep as easily during sleepovers. So when you tuck him in at night, ask him to pretend he's spending the night at Nana's house — and imagine that he will be dry in the morning. Eventually, your child will be able to have dry nights at home when his mind/body connection matures.

- ✔ **Chat up the joy of all-dry-nights:** Most doctors agree that the child's motivation to resolve bed-wetting can be a huge plus — not because he's wetting the bed purposefully, but because he hasn't hit on the right solution to changing his peeing-while-he-sleeps. If you both keep thrashing around for answers, something may click. Either that or the problem will correct itself as the child matures.

Staying positive yourself

As your child encounters yet another obstacle in his ongoing discovery of what the world is all about, he needs your loving support and encouragement that he'll be able to get past this roadblock.

On the other hand, if you punish your tiny tyke for his mistakes, you will only add to the stress-load he's bearing, and that's really, really counterproductive. To an amazing degree, your warmth and kindness will cement that ever-increasing bond with your child. Facing this and other challenges, he will feel comforted by knowing that he has a strong and devoted ally, who makes all tough times easier to endure.

So don't fall into bad patterns. For parents and caregivers, the no-no list goes like this:

- ✔ **Don't nag your child about wetting.**

- ✔ **Don't sentence him to sheet changing (unless he's up for it).**

- ✔ **Don't punish.** Treat wetting as NBD (no big deal). Don't scold or ground him from fun things. Kids do outgrow this problem. Meanwhile, you must stay on his you-can-do-it team.

Smart toys for tykes with bed-wetting blues

Many childcare experts swear by audio moisture alarms, which work especially well for school-age kids who have some degree of bladder control.

You follow the directions provided with the device, but basically, the alarm has a water-sensitive pad that is worn in the child's pajamas, a wire connecting to the battery-driven control, and an alarm that goes off when moisture is first detected. If the sound doesn't wake your child, someone sleeping in the same room can give him a nudge when the alarm sounds.

Most children are fairly easily conditioned, which is why child developmental experts and physicians are very high on bed-wetting buzzers. See `http://store.yahoo.com/the pottyshop/bed-wetting.html`. Although these alarms do help most bed-wetters shed their troubles, the process takes several months — and the child has to want to work it.

Another kiddie-tech device is the PC Potty Timer — software designed to aid kids in potty training. Featuring soothing sounds to sleep to, the timer lets you also generate your own alarms, or add music files. You decide when you want the Potty Timer to sound a friendly alarm that wakes your child or reminds him to use the potty. Kids like the timer's theme sounds, with characters who encourage your child to get up and go potty. `http://pottytrainingsolutions.com`.)

Remember that many things, including sexual abuse, can cause a potty-trained child to start bed-wetting. Sometimes, a very domineering parent or caregiver can paralyze a child emotionally, resulting in wetting problems. Intolerant of failure, this kind of individual can intimidate your child because he sees wetting as defiance, and metes out severe punishment.

 Even though you have limited amounts of time with your child, stay on top of his mood changes. With bed-wetting, you are searching for stressors that may be causing the little kid's troubles.

Seeing a Doctor

Certainly, don't be afraid to seek help from a specialist. If the bed-wetting just won't quit — and you see no signs of progress, take your child to see a primary care doctor or a pediatric urologist. The latter is usually the doc you see when your child has a problem that requires surgery (or if the cause of his random-pee-patterns remains a question mark). Although disease usually isn't behind bed-wetting, a child can have diabetes, or infections and urinary-system defects.

If day wetting isn't resolved readily, consult with your doctor so that your child can be tested for a urinary tract infection or some other problem that's causing daytime dribbles.

Seeing the signs

Expect normal "accidents," but watch for trouble signs. Even kids whose toilet training is far behind them can have an occasional wet night, as often as twice a week for several months after potty training. This slacks off for most, but some still tinkle accidentally at night when they're four and five years old. About school-starting time, the problem is usually gone.

But oops! What if your child is still wetting the bed after his fifth birthday? How unusual is this?

One of ten children older than five has trouble with nocturnal enuresis, and about two-thirds of these are boys. Remember though, these kids who wet the bed after age five rarely have any other physical or emotional problems. As mentioned earlier, the problem is almost always due to slow development of a child's control over the full-bladder sensation and his lack of heads-up reaction to that.

Give him time. Give him love. Soon, he will learn to make it to the potty in time.

If your child reports that peeing "burns" or "hurts," he definitely needs medical attention as soon as possible.

Consider seeking help in the following cases, whether you witness these firsthand or these are the results of reports from your child's caregiver:

- ✓ **Your child uses the potty regularly, but often has wet pants, too.**

- ✓ **He appears to be fully potty-trained and then begins peeing and having BMs on the floor all the time.**

- ✓ **He has painful BMs even though you have increased dietary fiber and reduced his dairy intake.**

- ✓ **Your child is six and still bed-wetting.**

- ✓ **He experiences unusual straining or burning when trying to use the potty.**

- ✓ **He hides away the evidence of mistakes.** (You find wet pants in his toy chest, drawers, or under the bed).

- ✓ **His urine is cloudy or pink or you see blood on his undies.**

- ✓ **He often has genital rashes.**

- ✓ **He tells you that he has "funny-feeling" (tingling) legs, or you notice unusual clumsiness.**

- ✓ **You see signs of underwear soiling.** (See Chapter 16 for more.)

Preparing to go

When you decide to consult your doctor, present the idea with good cheer: "Hey Jack, let's go see what Dr. Shoquist can tell us about how to help you learn to pee in the potty. I know she'll be able to help us."

If he asks if a doctor visit means he's in trouble or has "been bad," say "absolutely not." Give him a hug and kiss and reassurance. "No, you're wonderful. It's just that you're having trouble holding your pee long enough to get to the potty, and I'm pretty sure our doctor knows some ways to help you. We have to solve this and get you back to the fun parts of being a kid."

Downplay the scary aspect of the clinic visit by telling your toddler honestly that the two of you are going there to ask for some tips. No one is going to hurt him.

The more information you can provide the doctor, the better equipped she will be to find an answer. Ideally, take your doctor a sheet of information on your child's fluid intake, daytime voiding frequency and volume, number and time of bed-wetting episodes, sleep patterns (restless, snoring, sleepwalking, nightmares), and his typical food-and-beverage from the time he gets home from school or daycare until bedtime.

At the doctor's office, you will probably be asked these questions:

- ✔ **Does any other member of the family have a history of bed-wetting?**

  Go figure! If you wet the bed as a kid, your child will probably stop his dribbling problem at the same age you became dry.

- ✔ **How much liquid does your child drink most evenings before going to bed?**

- ✔ **Are the accidents happening when he's playing and way too busy to want to stop?**

- ✔ **How often does he urinate and when?**

- ✔ **Does your child usually have an accident when he's crying or agitated?**

- ✔ **Is there anything unusual about his method of urinating or the way the urine looks?**

- ✔ **How easy (or hard) was potty training your child, and how old was he when he was fully potty trained?**

- ✔ **Is the child under any major stress right now?**

As part of the evaluation, your doctor will want to know the child's health history, so take along that information.

Later, if your child is still having problems (perhaps on a follow-up visit), you'll need to take into the doctor's office 24 hours' worth of the tot's urine that you have collected.

Expecting tests and treatments

If your child continues to wet the bed, even though he used to have dry nights, your doctor will want to do a workup — the bed-wetting could indicate that something is amiss in his body. Usually though, anatomic abnormalities and psychological problems are unlikely causes.

If you seek a doctor's help, she can certainly assess the problem and come up with a treatment plan. As a rule, the best results in treating bed-wetting come from a team effort, involving patient and family in an approach that fits the child.

First job for the doc is ruling out causes of bed-wetting such as urinary tract infections and the presence of posterior urethral valves in a boy or an ectopic ureter in a girl. A child with posterior urethral valves will probably look like he's straining when he pees, and often his stream of urine is very small. The hallmark sign of urethral obstruction is a weak or interrupted stream of urine, or having trouble urinating at all. As for ectopic ureter, that also has a classic sign — the child who has an ectopic ureter wets all the time. Although these problems sound scary, they're easily taken care of with medicine, catheterization, or minor surgery.

Daytime accidents may point to an unstable bladder — that means your child may need bladder-relaxing medication. But usually your doctor will try several treatment options before resorting to meds for a young child. A big drawback is that many kids simply relapse when taken off the drugs.

In general, doctors dislike the idea of long-term drug use for daytime wetting, compared to letting a child just outgrow the problem. On the other hand, a doctor probably won't mind writing a prescription for a day-and-night-wetting seven-year-old who wants to enjoy a weekend field trip or a summer camp. A commonly used medication for nighttime wetting is *desmopressin* (DDAVP tablets or nasal spray), which works especially well in children who produce such large volumes of urine at night that overflow results — the drug reduces the amount of urine produced and works quickly. In children older than six who have enuresis, *imipramine* is sometimes used.

Diagnosing your child's enuresis may be no more complicated than the first two steps in the chart — assessing a urine sample and feeling the stomach. But if your doctor suspects disease, obstruction, or some other problem, he may perform more tests. Fortunately, only about 1 percent of enuresis cases are spawned by something serious. In Table 14-1 chart below, you'll also find the treatments that are typically used to solve various conditions.

The ABCs of UTIs

Urinary tract infections (UTIs) are common in young children, particularly females. Bacteria enters the urethra or is carried to the kidneys from another part of the body through the bloodstream. UTIs include: *cystitis* (bladder); *urethritis* (urethra); *pyelonephritis* (renal pelvis and kidney). The first of these is the most common, caused by bacteria in the urinary tract when the stool contaminates the urethra. Symptoms of cystitis are: pain in the lower abdomen; pain while urinating; frequent urination; and blood in the urine. A kidney infection spurs more general abdominal-area pain and fever. Kids who have bed-wetting and day wetting often have UTIs.

Table 14-1	Possible Problems and Solutions	
Diagnosis method	*Possible condition*	*Possible treatment or procedure*
Urine sample	Urinary tract infection	Antibiotics
Stomach palpation	Constipation	See Chapter 16 for treatments.
X-rays or ultrasound	Neurogenic bladder and urethral obstruction, ectopic ureter, spine abnormalities	Medication, catheterization, or surgery
Tests for various diseases	Diabetes, epilepsy	Treatment of the disease usually resolves bed-wetting

In the event that your doctor uncovers a physical explanation for your child's leakiness, she will then initiate treatment.

Working parents want answers and solutions — yesterday. For that reason, you may beg your doctor to prescribe some kind of medication to solve your child's wetting problems. But not so fast there. Your doc may view medication for bed-wetting as the court of last resort, and if that's what she's telling you, listen.

To dance on past those gnarly daytime pee accidents, your child must get his bladder-and-brain in gear, and the upshot will be dry pants. The nighttime wetter must find a way to wake up so that he can pee in the potty. Although theories abound on how to accomplish these feats, it's a good idea to try simple remedies first and postpone resorting to medication. However, when early measures don't resolve the problem, one surefire method is the combination of a bed-wetting alarm and medication.

Just be patient, and reassuring. The lad's day will come.

Over-the-top tinkle troubles

Most pee problems can be easily resolved, but *Hinman syndrome, Ochoa syndrome,* and *myogenic detrusor failure* are tougher. Doctors believe that kids, mostly boys, get Hinman when they develop odd habits during potty training; the child learns to contract his pee muscle while urinating and then loses the ability to know when he's peeing accidentally and when he's peeing purposely. This can spin off into all manner of problems, from urinary tract infections to bladder failure. Clearly, your doctor will want to treat Hinman early and aggressively.

Evaluation of a child who might have Hinman syndrome includes a thorough history, physical exam, x-rays, and urodynamic assessment. Sometimes, just observing the child as he urinates will provide clues. For example, if a child strains and produces an intermittent stream, an anatomic or functional obstruction may be the problem. What doctors usually discover is a large-capacity bladder with a large residual of urine.

Ochoa syndrome — also called *urofacial syndrome* — resembles Hinman but also causes an odd expression. The child tries to smile but grimaces instead.

Myogenic detrusor failure, which results in numerous urinary tract infections, is treated with medication or catheterization.

Enuresis can also be an early sign of diabetes mellitus. Other diabetes symptoms in a child are

✔ Failure to grow or gain weight

✔ Increased thirst

✔ Dehydration

✔ Severe diaper rash that fails to respond to treatment

✔ Persistent vomiting accompanied by weakness or sleepiness

✔ Increased urination

Sickle cell anemia is another illness that can cause bed-wetting as can certain spinal cord problems. If your child tells you that his legs feel "weird" or you notice that he's unusually clumsy, have your doctor check out your child's spine.

Chapter 15

Handling a Hardcore Balker

● ●

In This Chapter

▶ Figuring out what's going on

▶ Exploring ways to deal with it

▶ Coping with two (or more!) balkers

▶ Cheering her to success

▶ Enjoying your relationship no matter what

● ●

Sometimes, a toddler just digs in her heels and refuses to use the potty. Her words or actions make it clear that she's not going to do it. So, parents and caregivers thrash around for reasons. The child is a challenge. Or she has a mind of her own. Or she is just flat-out stubborn. No matter how you choose to label hardcore balking, the bottom line remains the same: Your toddler is making potty training a universe of her own, filled with dragons and drawbacks.

Your challenge is unraveling the maze she has created. You'll bolster her way to success despite assorted roadblocks — and you'll be there to share in celebrating her eventual victory over that unruly potty chair. But first you must decide if something physical is causing the balking — or if your child's just going through a brief bad time — or if she's really and truly a genuine balker.

Psychologists call persistent defiance in a child *oppositional defiant disorder,* but a rose by any other name still spells trouble in potty-training city. Refusing to use the potty equals defiance, even if you can find something that's making your child balk. At any rate, you can try some simple solutions that usually work. Or, if those fail, you can encourage her to take responsibility for her potty progress while you, literally, back off. Stay cheerful and optimistic through the ups and downs. And, reward good efforts with positives aplenty.

Scoping Out the Problem

The length of time it takes for kids to master using the potty varies greatly — the learning curve for normal children is 16 to 60 months.

On average, kids attain bowel control by the time they reach about 30 months old, and they have bladder-deeds down pat by 33 months.

So if your three-year-old isn't making progress and seems to be resisting every attempt to train her, you need to dig a little to figure out what's going on in her pint-sized psyche.

To figure out what kind of problem you're dealing with, check for the following indications of a potty-balking stage. If more than three fit your child, you're probably looking at a full-fledged balking situation:

- ✔ You saw clear-cut readiness signs in place at the kickoff of potty training. (Remember, very important to gauging whether your child is really balking or just not ready is the certainty that you started training her at the right time.)

- ✔ You've been trying to train your child for more than six months, and she still isn't using the potty regularly.

- ✔ Your child goes to use the potty only when you take her there.

- ✔ Sometimes your toddler soils her underpants. She tends to hold back BMs and gets constipated.

- ✔ Your strong-willed child acts like she's taking a stand against giving up diapers.

- ✔ She's dry after naptime.

- ✔ Your child argues — a lot — and acts flat-out mad.

If your child's tightly wired temperament sets her up for arguing — defiantly and aggressively shouting "no" — you must keep searching for management techniques that fit. They exist — you just have to find them. Many times, a child's negative behavior during potty training is a result of her basic temperament (difficult), plus a glitch in a parent's handling methods. To get an objective opinion, talk to your physician, who can help you analyze the situation.

Sometimes, a child has tantrums to get attention when parents or caregivers seem too busy or preoccupied to respond to her needs. Sometimes, an adult's own irritability spills over and affects the child. Either way, the child who dabbles in stubborn behaviors may entrench this as a habit, and then a pattern develops of snagging her parent's attention by being a pill. To ease your child's insecurities and improve the level of trust, set aside a special week for extra-strength closeness. Make extra time for reading, playing, cuddling, and talking. After that, you may see the balking disintegrate before your very eyes. If not, proceed with the suggestions in the following sections for handing over the potty-training reins to tiny tot herself.

Checking for physical causes

Before you go ahead with the hands-off route, review some possible physical causes for your child's dislike of potty training. One of the following problems may be the culprit behind her balking:

- ✔ **Check for rectum woes:** If using the potty hurts, your child will avoid it. A child who's constipated can hold on to her BMs with a vengeance. Try the simple solution of starting her days with plenty of fluids and a fibery cereal, and see if that solves her problem. (For more on constipation, see Chapter 16.)

- ✔ **Look for citrus-burn:** Some children gets rawness of the backside that makes them not want to potty. Often a food allergy is the problem. Frequent culprits are citrus foods and drinks.

- ✔ **Watch for signs of pain:** You may see signs that suggest she's experiencing pain with peeing or pooping (see Chapters 14 and 16 for some possible causes). That means you need to take her to the doctor for an assessment of the problem.

Digging for emotional causes

After you eliminate physical causes as reasons for your child's reluctance to use the toilet (see the previous section), try to determine whether your child is actually a hardcore potty-balker. Perhaps that's harsh labeling, but consider it a term meant only for your head and our book (shh, no one else has to know).

Patience isn't a virtue to a two-year-old

One grandmother tells of helping her two-year-old granddaughter make a Christmas gift; she glued a measuring tape around the outside of a small can, and stuck a pincushion on top. All was fun-and-games until Nana told little Maggie that she could wrap it for her mommy and put it away for Christmas, three days later. In protest, Maggie cried, then escalated into a tantrum. Clearly, she wanted to give her gift to her mommy right away. The magical gift-making moment had evaporated.

Nana was reminded of a lesson from her own busy years of child rearing. Two-year-olds don't understand postponing fun, so adults shouldn't set up disaster scenarios. The same goes for potty training: Don't make things so complicated that your child spirals out of control, frustrated by expectations she finds impossible to meet.

Could it be ODD?

You could be wondering, considering the way she has balked at all your potty-training efforts, whether your child has full-blown oppositional defiant disorder. So, ask yourself the following questions:

- ✔ Does she disobey much of the time?
- ✔ Has this been going on for six months or more?
- ✔ Is your child more cooperative at school than at home?
- ✔ Does she blow her top often?
- ✔ Does your child seem to be doing mean things on purpose?
- ✔ Does your child shift blame to other people or other objects?
- ✔ Does she seem moody and short-fused?

If you answered yes to three or more, your child may have ODD. Typically, this disorder is diagnosed when parents and caregivers face that their child isn't growing more cooperative like other kids do, when she is five or so.

View this as a problem your child has — not some kind of willful acting out. But don't expect a quick fix. Counseling, not pills, will be prescribed. Most healthcare experts theorize that ODD comes from a combination of a child's temperament and the way parents handle her — plus her perception of their attitudes. The combination isn't productive, so the child gets more and more difficult.

Good starters for you — at home — are the following:

- ✔ Try to give a minimum number of orders.

- ✔ Outline your expectations, reasons for them, and consequences when these are not met.

- ✔ Help your child know what to do when her anger starts spinning out of control.

- ✔ Encourage your child to try a skill or hobby and become good at it.

- ✔ Show her how to rephrase sentences to get better results: "You know, I'd like to hear you say, 'Could I please play with those blocks?' instead of 'I want those blocks right now!'" Explain that the way she talks to people has a lot to do with whether they respond in a good way.

- ✔ Discourage whining and yelling: Go to her, kneel down and look at her. Take her hands and describe a better way to express what she wants. "I'd like to hear you say, 'Daddy, play ball with me like this, please' instead of 'I'm mad! You didn't do it right!'"

- ✔ Give frequent reminders of your love: Write her little notes. Give her unexpected hugs and kisses. Tell her: "When I see you, I feel so happy."

The following can help you figure out if your child's reluctance to use the potty may be a reaction to a home or daycare problem. That will help you determine if your child is truly a potty-balker or is just having a few bad days. Check out the following sections for reasons your trainee may be balking.

Mixed messages

You may want to look at the messages your child gets. Often, a child who repeatedly and openly defies her parents is one who lives in a household fueled by family chaos and parenting inconsistency. You must set up rules and stick to them. You need to enforce your potty-training rules (and others) in an atmosphere of clear expectations and instructions, and make sure they're not emotionally fueled. Calm, cool, and helpful are the operative words.

Common sense will tell you that no one calls a kid names and gets good potty results as a payoff. Obviously, refrain from fiery outbursts — "You little balker!"

Kiddie stress

If you think your child is balking because she's reeling from emotional turmoil, reduce the stress in your home. A child who is angry won't function well when trying to learn a new skill. So you may have to wait to recharge her bowel-and-bladder batteries when she's past the troublesome issue — whether that's a new baby home from the hospital, a grandparent who just moved in, or a parent who returned to work (the separation has upset her). See Chapter 5 for more on stressors.

Reaction to feeling too regimented

Double-check the tightness of your parenting reins. Sometimes a child who balks at toilet training is doing so because all other areas of her life are so restricted and controlled. Do you choose what she wears all of the time? Do you insist on perfect manners? Do you make the call on how she spends her free time? If you answer, "yes" to these questions, you probably need to loosen up a bit.

Some tots are delicately calibrated instruments. Not all of them, mind you, but some. When your child opposes you, don't take it personally. In most kids, the ability to tolerate frustration is small-small-small. Handle her with the right combo of patience and love, and she will grow up wonderfully well, curbing frustration tornados and becoming the love of your life.

Trying a Few Options Before Handing Off the Baton

So, after weighing the evidence, you decide that you may indeed have a little madcap balker on your hands. (If your child is three and still doesn't have her bowel and bladder acts well under way, start looking for answers.) You wonder what to do. You're not ready to give up on her, but you don't know what should come next.

First, quit wringing your hands. Yes, your method worked with your other kids, but it doesn't seem to be working with this one. Time to consider another way to get the job done.

Just because some method turned out to be a real winner with your first child, who's easygoing, that doesn't mean squat if you're now working with a more high-spirited child.

Someone — friend or coworker or relative — is going to ask you "So how's Mia's potty training going?" But keep the truth ("It's pretty sucky right now") close to your vest. Instead, say a little speech that you've planned for such occasions: "She's pacing herself right now. But Mia will be trained soon. Late bloomers always come around." You are still Mia's promoter and biggest fan — you don't want to be negative about her lest it get back to her or she gets well-meaning but unwanted advice.

Potty training even may have gotten stalled because you were getting on your child's nerves. Maybe — just maybe — your personality clashes with your toddler kept her from succeeding in potty adjustment.

Try gaining some insight by brainstorming with your child's daytime caregiver. Being with your child during the day gives her a different perspective, and perhaps the two of you can come up with an idea that may work for your tot.

At any rate, the following are some techniques that you can use to get a potty-training balker to cooperate:

- **Test the water:** "You didn't want to use the potty yesterday, so I guess we should pack some pullups for our trip to the store, right?" She may surprise you and say, "No, I want to try the potty before we leave."

- **Point her in the right direction:** Some parents report enormous success simply by putting a guiding hand on the balker-kid's shoulder and directing her to the bathroom. But don't let this slide into roughness or force.

✔ **Act unfazed by her antics:** Show your balker that her tantrums and grandstanding roll right off your back. Stay calm. Don't show annoyance even though you may well be feeling it.

✔ **Promise fun times ahead:** Hold out the fascinating lure of what big kids get to do. They can go more and better places because they're potty trained. They get more privileges because they are more grown up. They get to do special things around the house that are reserved for older kids.

✔ **Praise good choices:** When she does the right thing in other areas, leap on the chance to praise her. For example, if she puts her toys up, make a big deal of it. "Good girl! You're really learning to make good choices. Hip-hip-hooray for you!" Toy retrieval may seem unrelated to potty training, but you'll find that the excitement from good feedback overflows into other parts of her life — if you're lucky, one of them may be the bathroom.

Hopefully, after you give these ideas a few weeks to work, toilet-training resistance will clear up. Six weeks would be about right.

When you get a chance to work it into a conversation, mention to your tot how nice being clean and dry feels. Talk it up, never even mentioning the potty. Put the emphasis on how nice clean hands are, fragrant aromas, and so on. You may even want to take a photo of her in a cute outfit, looking all fresh and spiffy, and admire it with her. "See how sweet it looks to be nice and clean. I like it when I'm freshly showered and in clean clothes, don't you?"

Putting your child in the driver's seat

From your child's perspective, learning to use the toilet has become your thing, and that's not good. So, just alter the dynamics. Encourage your toddler to accept that her body control is what's in question here — not yours. She has to figure this out. Soon, she'll get the hang of the idea. Peeing and pooping in the right place (as in the potty!) will have a lot to do with her acceptability in most social circles, and that will dawn on your child at some point.

If simple solutions fail to work, proceed to Plan B — giving your child total responsibility for potty training. You're no longer her keeper. You are putting her totally in charge. So step back and wish her well. "I think I'll let you decide when you want to go to the potty. You're a good girl — I know you can figure it out." Caution outside caregivers and relatives — "no reminders or pressure." To carry out your new plan of putting your child in control of her potty progress, follow the steps outlined below ("Working the program") for two months.

Expect to feel very, very antsy when it's time to put your small fry on her own. And, don't think you'll be able to do this without a few qualms.

Responsible parents won't find it easy to let go and give the child responsibility for herself and her potty practices. Stepping back from a child who's having difficulties is tough. Guilt and duty will pelt your brain with all the reasons you shouldn't abandon your child in this tortured time. So, you have to rename it. "Abandon" is not what you're doing when you choose to hand off the learning-potty-stuff to your child. The only thing you're shrugging off is the role of keeper. Basically, you're butting out.

Meanwhile, you can use the coping mechanism of doing things for yourself, without your child. Take walks. Go to the gym. Get out with friends. Don't spend all your time worrying about your child and talking about her lagging behind in potty training. Tell yourself: "Her balking isn't third-degree burns over 90 percent of my body, but I'm acting like it is."

Distancing yourself from the process

How do you distance yourself from the your toddler and her potty training? Following are some tips that will help you make it clear to the trainee that this is their thing.

Get down on your child's level for the backing-off chat. Look into her eyes and speak with kindness. Hold her hands. Make a clear-cut exit by telling your child this: "I think you can learn to use the potty all by yourself. I have faith in you, so I'm going to back off and give you the space to learn. You'll do better that way. You know where the potty chair is, and you know how it feels when you need to pee or poop." Ask if she understands what you said: "Do you understand what I mean?" Of course, she'll shake her head yes. But, the truth is, you'll see as time goes by if she actually gets it.

Pretty panties perpetuate potty training

One mother tells of giving up after two years of trying to potty train her child. "She just wasn't interested in it, and wouldn't even try. She acted like I was speaking a foreign language. Her balking looked more like boredom. Then, a friend of ours gave Alana some panties and she loved them." The next thing that happened was Alana's daytime caregiver reported to Mom that the four-year-old was doing really well using the potty during the day. "She's close to being trained."

Mom realized that two fortunate happenings had converged to give the child a reason to use the potty: Alana was wowed by pretty panties that she was dying to wear, and the caregivers at daycare took a matter-of-fact approach that just happened to suit her.

Don't expect to find it easy, or natural, or fun, to distance yourself from the process that your child is struggling with daily. She wants to do the right thing and learn to use the potty — but she also seems to take a certain mischievous delight in defying authority, in digging in and saying, "no way." This kid's a pint of TNT. But, by distancing yourself from her defiance, her learning curve, and her reluctance to get on the potty chair, you can absolutely defuse the spiral of balking.

Working the program

You have a plan. Knowing what you're going to do will pump up your confidence in the letting-go process. The following are good ways to let your child know she's now the one in charge of her potty progress:

- ✔ **Have your lines ready for slip-ups:** The first time she poops or pees in her undies and lets you know about it, stay cool: "Okay, I see that you went in your underwear, and that's your choice. You don't have to go in the potty, but someday I know you will. Everyone who grows up learns to go in the potty. For now, you get to choose whether you pee in your underpants or in the potty chair, which is made for peeing and pooping. You'll eventually be doing it that way, I'm sure. Also, I'm going to be nearby to cheer you on. You're a good child who always learns things, so I know you'll make this work."

- ✔ **Address the mess:** The first few incidents, help change your child's messy underpants. Take a neutral attitude. Don't discuss potty training or accidents or punishment. Don't discuss anything. Move quickly ahead to doing something totally unrelated with your child, or steering her to play with a toy.

  By all means, don't ignore messes: You can't let her walk around in messy pants, so take a firm stand on the cleanup part.

- ✔ **Up the ante:** If her act doesn't improve at all after three days of this, take your child through a demo of how to clean up her pants after she messes in them. Show her how to empty them in the big toilet, and then where she should put the dirty outfit. Tell her to let you know when she has gotten messy and needs to get in the tub to clean up, so that you can turn on the warm water to a proper temperature. After she's in the tub, it's her responsibility to clean herself.

  Act as if you're ready to go through this for years, if necessary. Expect some whining, crying, or an out-and-out tantrum. To this, your response is: "I know this is hard. And I know you're upset, but soon you won't have to do this because you'll learn to stay clean."

Sticking with the program

Following are tips for handling this change-of-behavior curve:

- ✔ **Don't remind her to go to the potty:** Stay out of it — her thing, remember.

- ✔ **Praise her attempts:** If she comes and tells you, "I'm going to sit on the potty," say, "that's good." But don't go into the bathroom with her.

- ✔ **Applaud poop or pee:** Any instance of her being clean and dry should merit a hug and smile from you. Give recognition for successes and no sign of anything for screw-ups. For successes, she gets pennies to put in her bank to save for something special or whatever other reward you're working with.

If your child wants to sit on her potty chair beside you when you're on the toilet, cheer that idea. You still didn't lead her there, or make her potty-sit — so she remains in charge of her potty actions.

With your new hands-off program, your child may ask you about going to the bathroom before bedtime. "I go potty for night-night?" Keep your response consistent with the New Deal: "That's up to you. If you want to pee or poo, you can. Remember, now you get to decide."

Don't forget that your child knows the drill; she has been through the hourly potty-sits of Potty Mambo Weekend. She has done post-nap, post-meal, and pre-bed visits to the loo. So if she turns to you for guidance, and you can't resist giving a mini-boost, keep it low-key and minimalist — nod your head or give her a thumbs-up.

Be careful! Don't give your toddler the notion that you like her when she does good stuff but not the rest of the time. Conditional love isn't comforting. Stay happy with your child and have fun with her no matter what's happening in the bathroom. Don't let your relationship shift into low mode just because she's a no-show on the potty chair.

Looking for the results

Typically, the natural course of this dog-and-pony-show is that she'll try to get your attention in a brand-new way — by cooperating and showing you her new peeing-on-the-potty trick. When this does occur, tell her how happy you are for her. "Wow, now you won't have to clean up in the tub so often. Good for you."

So that you won't inspire another spiral of balking, stay low-key and just hope that her own interest in getting rid of the cleanup and the mess will set her straight permanently. But don't throw a celebration — that's too much ado over cooperation that she knows she should have given you long ago.

Sometimes in the parenting or caregiving game, you help the most by giving your kid wide berth. To hover is human; to get out of the way, divine.

Distancing yourself doesn't mean being disinterested. You still respond when she asks a question about potty-training procedures, inclination, cleanup, and the rest. Don't zone out completely.

When you're working on letting go, be sure to get your daytime caregiver aside and let her know what's going on. Tell her: "Please let Matilda go to the potty any time she asks. She's having trouble with potty training, as you know, and I want to jump on any opportunity for her to go in the potty. But let it be her idea — don't push because I've put her in charge now. Thanks so much for your help."

One mom tells of a balking program that took a bizarre detour when her daughter got in charge, all right — she started flushing away her dirty pants each time she pooped in them. The toilet would overflow, but the instigator stayed blissfully out of the fray. The way she saw it, she had gotten rid of her mistake, and now it was her mom's problem.

So, what's a parent to do if her kid goes bonkers like this? Just take care of it: "We can't flush anything down the toilet but toilet paper and poop and pee. Others things stop it up, and we'll have overflow messes every time. If you do this again, you will have to clean it up yourself because flushing your pants is not allowed." Show her where the dirty pants actually go, and tell her that's what you expect from now on. Simple. Truthful. And effective.

Letting her change her own clothes

Stick your hands in your pockets the next time you feel compelled to jump in and change your child's clothes.

She wet them; she changes them. If you continue with the fix-'em-up-tuck-'em-in trend you have going, your child will passively allow it. But, by the same token, she'll continue to believe that potty-training skills are your thing. So your toddler will want you to make it work from your end. Somehow.

Good luck on that one.

Dealing with More Than One Trainee

If the balking blues come in multiple doses (you have twins, triplets, or more), don't fall into the trap of comparing the balker with a more cooperative sibling. You know, in your gut, that's a bad idea. But do take advantage of the handy role model. Putting the success story nearby to do her pottying biz sure won't hurt your slacker.

Typically, in multiples, one's a trailblazer (the sibling who does most things first, or the one who's just more daring). So let the other(s) observe the smarty-pants kid as she uses the potty. All comparisons will be hers, as she watches the little role model and decides maybe that could be pretty cool.

By the way, each kid should have a decorated potty chair of her own if your budget allows. Again, the goal is to have your child (each one of them) view potty learning as her own individual thing — her bladder, her bowels, not yours, and not her sibling's.

Responding When She Finally Gets It

When that little hardcore balker finally gets a handle on her potty program — and she will! — be the first in line to congratulate her.

Check out those dry pants as often as possible right after she is trained, and let her know how proud you are of her efforts.

Keeping those rewards coming

But don't dare heave a heavy sigh and assume you can slack off on the rewards. Not so fast. Hedge your bets by supplying a steady stream of good feedback: kudos from relatives, you're-such-a-big-kid acknowledgments from lead caregivers.

A child who is newly trained is still shaky, at best. So you have to reinforce the good stuff and make sure she stays trained.

Also, don't be too fast in proclaiming "great — you've done it!" Why? Simple. That may signal a second-wave protest; your toddler gets her back up and takes a new slant, like withholding bowel movements. (See information on holding onto BMs in Chapter 16.)

Saying, "I knew you could do it!"

Just because you feel like the weight of the world has been lifted from your shoulders — thanks to her finally using the toilet — don't assume that your child knows that you appreciate her efforts. What probably still looms large in your toddler's mind is how frustrated you seemed when she balked at using the potty — and then you switched gears and suddenly relinquished the reins entirely.

Clearly, she may be a bit confused by all of it. And, no doubt, she definitely needs you to jump in and shower her with hugs and kisses and love declarations.

Naturally, if you try the ideas listed here and your child continues to oppose potty training altogether, the see-your-doctor rule definitely applies.

Do look forward to the completion of her potty training. But, don't make it your life. Then, one fine day, she will come to you and smilingly say, "Oui-oui, me wee!"

A quiet celebration is in order. You don't need to break out the champagne; a simple spread of cookies and juice, served tea-party style, will do. Maybe an ice-cream drink.

Anyway, as you've surely guessed by now, most hardcore balker-kids are just channeling Frank Sinatra. Their mantra is — and always will be — "I did it my way."

Keeping Your Relationship Fun and Healthy

Keep in mind the old saying "Make hay while the sun shines." You have limited time with your child, so make lots of it enjoyable. Because you mainly see your child mornings, evenings, and weekends, you may want to search out chances to have positive experiences: Try to find ways to brag on your child that have nothing to do with the potty.

For example, lots of toddlers like to try to sweep, so let her do that. Laugh together, and have fun with it! Another example: Take a walk and talk about things she sees: Kids have an uncanny way of opening our eyes to the joys of nature. The message: Positive behaviors get more attention around this house!

Until your child is on strong footing with her potty, listen carefully for things she says that may be clues to the snags. And, keep talking to her, encouraging her, reminding her that she is a smart, super kid.

Parents who have the most trouble with their children are usually ones who constantly remind their kids of their faults. Thinking that they're doomed to be losers, these kids turn the gloomy predictions into realities. (Kids are like a box of chocolates; you never know what kind you're going to get — but all of 'em are good.)

Chapter 16

Soiling Beyond Toddler Years

● ●

In This Chapter

▶ Curbing constipation

▶ Seeking medical help

▶ Dealing with stool-soiling of other origins

▶ Making sure that daycare is caring

▶ Sidestepping future problems

● ●

*B*ack behind the potty chair, you find a little pair of superhero underpants stained with poop. So, what the heck's going on here? You may well suffer a mini panic attack when you suddenly spot soiled underwear that suggests that your little potty-trained darling isn't really potty trained, after all. (We're talking every poop remnant, from skid marks to full-tilt logs in the undies.) You wonder, has the kid gotten lost in a baby-time-warp or something?

The good news is, stool-soiling — medically termed *encopresis* — isn't as scary as it seems. Most kids who do this are just over-the-top constipated, so they unconsciously hold in BMs because it's painful to poop. Constipation is a vicious circle that starts when a toddler tries to keep from passing hard stool, and then the longer he waits, the more it hurts when the BM finally occurs. The other kind of stool-soiling is a bit tougher — kids who aren't constipated, but still soil their undies because they get comfy with the habit of holding onto their product — usually from constipation, originally, and then they lose the "feel" of needing to go. And, some children even get into a cycle of withholding and constipation after illness (medication left them constipated).

At any rate, many parents and caregivers — squeamish about stool-soiling — just put off having to deal with it. So, tiny tot's left all alone and sad, sitting in his messed-up Spiderman underpants. He didn't poop in his undies on purpose — hey, he can't even figure out when or how it happened! And if you think a bed-wetter feels like an oddball, imagine being a kid who has accidents that are conspicuous and smelly. He's embarrassed; you're embarrassed; so is everyone within a 40-foot radius. So, go on a rampage for answers and soon, you'll be able to eliminate the inappropriate poop problem, and save Buster from becoming an outcast in his little social circle.

Tackling the Issue

Mostly seen in kids ages three to seven, stool-soiling affects about 2 percent of children. But many cases go undocumented because parents don't want to talk to a doctor about trouble that's this embarrassing.

Surprisingly, the problem often slinks around undetected for months. The kid isn't fully aware he's messing up his underpants, nor is the parent or caregiver. And that's too bad because early on, you can solve this simply. But let a few months pass and your child will develop an unconscious habit of gritting his teeth and holding BMs inside.

Encopresis is accidental BM-soiling in an inappropriate place for the child's age, usually resulting from constipation. It starts when your child first has a BM that hurts due to hard stool, so he says "whoa," and begins avoiding bowel movements altogether, which leads to chronic constipation. If this goes untreated, his sense of having a full rectum gets muted, and when he doesn't click to that fact anymore, liquid stool overflows. Encopresis comes in two types:

- ✔ **Primary:** The child has always soiled, and has never had a period when he successfully used the potty for BMs.

- ✔ **Secondary:** The child was potty trained and started soiling later — when he started school, encountered a stressful situation or just began withholding poop because he feared a painful BM episode.

  Problem is, if he used to be trained, you may even scold your child because you assume that he knew what he was doing and just got lazy. But he probably didn't even realize what was happening and thus, could not have prevented it.

Certainly, soiling episodes stump parents and caregivers. You see scads of articles on bed-wetters, but you don't find any tips for pants-poopers. So, you may have a hard time figuring out what you're supposed to do.

Fortunately, simple constipation is the usual culprit behind stool-soiling, and that's easily resolved — typically, in a couple of months. But if your child proves to be a tougher nut to crack, just keep offering encouragement and repeating the remedies that have been somewhat successful. The longer he sticks with the pattern of holding in and ignoring BM cues, the more trouble he'll have getting back to using the bathroom normally.

Do find a resolution. Being ridiculed by his peers for being Poopie Boy can haunt your child for the rest of his life.

If he's still soiling when he starts kindergarten, have a private talk with the teacher about your child's situation. Ask her to handle this gently because you know she's going to be a key figure in his life. Explain that your child is already undergoing medical treatment, and share any pertinent doctor tips. Don't be surprised if she's less than eager to take on this responsibility — yet another reason for you to find a speedy resolution.

Consider home schooling until your child shakes his stool-soiling ways. Otherwise, you're submitting him to the taunts of peers in a regular public or private school setting. That can't be good.

Keep in mind that short stuff isn't soiling his underwear just to give you trouble — rest assured, he has a physical or psychological problem.

Eventually, your little kid will be squeaky clean, and the problem will be history. Meanwhile, you hone your coping skills and never doubt the bottom line: Your child is lovable. Always, every day, cherish him to pieces.

Looking at the roots

As gnarly as the problem sometimes gets, its roots are often innocent. A potty-trained tyke starts going to daycare or kindergarten and finds it hard to get to a bathroom. Potty trips are more regimented and less frequent than he's used to. So a pattern emerges. From not eating enough stool-softening foods and not drinking enough water, or from holding back his stool, he gets constipated, and soon figures out that rock-hard BMs are difficult to push out. So he just chooses not to have a BM. In most cases, a child gets constipated when he begins to associate pain with bowel movements.

Pretty soon, he's so constipated that his *rectum* (the final part of the large intestine is where stool is stored) gets *impacted* — stool has built up and made his rectum widen. Plus, his rectal muscles are stretched out. As a consequence, he loses most of his ability to feel the presence of poop. What was once the kid's unmistakable signal to have a BM has faded away.

Now he has no sensation. Poop keeps on building up because none of it gets out. Basically, the longer that fecal matter remains in the large intestine, the more water is absorbed by the surrounding tissues and the harder and drier the stool becomes, which makes having a BM more difficult and more painful. This, in turn, allows liquid poo to leak out. Previously, this liquid stool surrounded the mass of stool lodged in the lower bowel.

This liquid poop makes a sneak attack on your child — he's surprised to find poop has leaked into his underpants. The walls of his rectum have been *distended* (widened) for so long that he has lost sensitivity in his rectum, which leads to no urge feeling. The upshot is encopresis.

Usually, the child stool-soils his underwear at least once a month for several months — and, typically, this occurs in kids four or older.

Checking for constipation

Constipation, as the stinker behind the stool-soiling troubles, can be treated with home remedies, or you can take your child to see a physician. If you try three days of home remedies and nothing helps, you need to take your child to a doctor for treatment and, if necessary, for removal of the stool that has collected in the lower bowel. That way, you give the tot a fresh slate.

Clearly, your child is too young to have a clue what constipation means, but if you see his pants smeared with poop, check for signs of constipation. See the following list of constipation signals:

- **Fewer than three BMs a week (in a child two to five years old)**
- **Emptying stool incompletely**
- **Very small BMs (as compared to the size of his normal output)**
- **Infrequent, large BMs**
- **Small amounts of hard, small, pellet-like stool**

Specific health indicators that point to constipation are

- **Tummy aches and bloating**
- **Loss of appetite**
- **Wetting day and/or night (poop buildup makes the colon swell and press on the bladder)**
- **Straining hard**
- **Bleeding from a cut or crack in the skin around the anus or in the rectum**
- **Being unwilling to potty**
- **Odd body language, such as:**
  - **Clinging**
  - **Hiding**
  - **Crossing ankles**
  - **Squatting**

Basically, constipation just means your child is not getting rid of his entire load of poop because he's having trouble getting it out — it's too hard, too backed up, or stuck inside his rectum.

Don't panic if you detect a trace of blood once or twice on your child's stool or tissue; this points to a crack or tear in his anus, which is simply a common and non-threatening condition that can accompany constipation. If this continues, though, see a doctor to get it checked out.

Maybe he just gets too busy to have a good BM, and this results in erratic patterns and frequent soiling. Soon, the child's trying to avoid having a BM come out at all. He's no fool — he knows it will hurt.

Correcting constipation at home

If you can tell that your child is constipated (see the preceding "Checking for constipation" section), steer him back to soft, normal stools. In most young kids, diet's the cause of constipation, so attack food-and-beverage first thing by following these tips:

- ✔ **Make sure your tot is drinking lots of liquids.** Give him juice, milk, and water. A dehydrated child often has hard stools. Don't overdo the milk, however — too much whole milk contributes to constipation. (Try peach and pear nectar–these juices by Kearn's contain *sorbitol,* a good natural laxative.)

  Ever wonder whether your kid gets enough fluids? If he's peeing at least every three hours while awake, he's probably well hydrated.

- ✔ **Increase the amount of fiber your child takes in.** A preschooler or kindergartner should eat about two servings of fruit and three servings of veggies daily. If he isn't a fan of vegetables or prunes or raisins, hand out fiber breakfast bars, fiber cereals, grainy breads, bananas, apples, or peanut butter. Your child's fiber intake should be about five grams plus the age he is in years — for example, if he's four, he needs nine grams of fiber per day.

- ✔ **Cut out snacks right before bedtime if your child has trouble with nighttime soiling.** That way, his bowels won't get loaded up right before he's inactive (asleep).

- ✔ **Give him a warm beverage shortly after a meal.**

You can also try some constipation solutions that aren't related to food or drink. Consider the following:

- ✔ **Have him bathe.** Warm water may act as a subtle bowel stimulant.

- ✔ **Give him a tummy rub.**

✔ **Give your child some boundaries for placement of bowel movements.** Tell him that when he needs to have a BM, he can put it in the big-people's toilet, in the bowl of his little potty chair, or he can do it in a paper box that's in the bathroom. "You decide," you tell him. "What if I use the toilet?" he asks, looking for a reward. Tough times call for drastic measures. "I think you deserve a prize if you can remember to use the toilet for your BMs for a week. That would be great."

But suppose he asks you what happens if he poops in the cardboard box. Your answer: "Then it will be your job to take the box out in the yard, dig a hole, and bury it — each time." Too over the top? Given the situation, maybe not. Do anything you can to find a way to eliminate a problem that makes people shun your child everywhere, from Grandma's house to daycare. You're not punishing him by giving him three places for poop placement; you're telling him that he has choices.

And what if he responds to your plan by pulling down his pants and dumping his load in the corner of a room? Lead him to the spot and ask him to help you clean up the poop. Then have him accompany you to the potty, and watch you dispose of it. "See, it's easier if you just do it in the potty," you tell him. Calm. Nonjudgmental. No "bad boy, bad boy" stuff.

Encourage your tyke to sit on the toilet after his meals. Don't be surprised if he seems hesitant, thanks to painful past experiences. But promote the idea of trying to have BMs or the problem will only compact itself (literally). Natural reflexes will stimulate a BM about 15 minutes after a meal.

Definitely don't give enemas, suppositories, mineral oil, or laxatives without your doctor's advice and approval. You can't treat constipation in a child the way you would if you were constipated — just pop a laxative pill or two. Laxatives aren't used often in children. Don't put him back in diapers and send the message that you expect accidents. Instead, show compassion: "Let's put our heads together and find a way to solve this. I know we can! You and I are so good together, as a team."

Your child may try to make you think he can stop soiling if you'll give him a reward. Don't buy it. He says "give me a toy and I'll stop," only with serious misgivings about whether he can deliver. Remember, if it were easy for him to resolve the soiling, he would have found a way already.

Seeing a Doctor

Fast problem-solving for your child is key because many children have these accidents unknowingly several times a day. When loose, watery stool continually dribbles out due to hard-stool backup, this is clearly a recipe for disaster for any child who ventures outside the safety of his home. You and your doctor need to find a way to clear up the problem before your child starts kindergarten. Otherwise, your five-year-old is in for a heap of trouble at school.

So, here's the drill: You need to know what signals should send you to the doctor, what you can expect when you get there, and some of the treatments a physician will recommend.

Recognizing when to see a doctor

You may want to skip entirely the home remedies for constipation and go straight to a doctor, who can recommend treatments and help you determine what's wrong. If your child seems extremely constipated, a doctor visit is the best idea, anyway, because small fry probably needs a clean-out/tune-up with an *enema* (forcing liquid into the colon to clean it out) or a *suppository* (a small medicated capsule inserted into the rectum where body heat causes it to melt). If your child was toilet-trained and is now soiling, it's very likely his bowels are impacted, which means he probably needs an enema to dislodge the backed-up stool. Also, a child who's five and still having soiling incidents needs a doctor's help whether he's constipated or not.

Seeing a doctor is an absolute must if your child has blood in his stool, black stool, or if he's in obvious distress — vomiting, hurting when he tries to use the potty, feverish — or the constipation comes on very quickly. In these cases, promptly take him to the doctor's office. (The exception, as mentioned earlier, would be a trace of blood on toilet tissue once or twice.)

You may think your child should just stop it — but he can't do that. Just saying, "I'm telling you to use the bathroom, not go in your underwear" isn't helpful. Remember, until you find a solution, your child is incapable of controlling his soiling.

If you know your child is into poop-withholding, your doctor can assist you in teaching your child self-regulation. You'll probably need a professional's help to unravel this mind-body barrier. Your goal: The tot must learn to listen to his body and what it tells him about poop needing to come out.

Unloading the poop problem on your doctor

During your doctor visit, don't feel timid about laying out soiling details for a doctor. Clearly, society has several subjects that aren't talked about — and encopresis is one of them — that's why 1,000 of 1,000 people on the street don't know the meaning of the word, unless one of them went to medical school. And don't feel guilty — the fact that your child is having trouble holding his poop doesn't mean that you're a bad parent. You just need answers to help get your child's problem solved.

Take to the doctor visit a written record of your child's BMs (size, type, frequency), soiling episodes, medications he takes, and a list of the treatments you've tried. This information will help your physician figure out how to solve the problem.

Poop-withholding in a school-age child can result from his busy new life, so your doctor may ask your child whether it's hard to get to a bathroom at school. Maybe your kid hates the regimen: bathroom trips only at certain times; having to ask to go; the look of the school bathroom; or just the idea of having to take time out to go. He could feel shy about the whole thing. So, his stool gets impacted, it hurts to go, and he swears off BMs altogether.

The doctor will take a medical history and do a physical examination. If the child doesn't respond to more conservative measures, your physician will evaluate further for long-shot causes, such as cerebral palsy, spinal cord disorders, a pelvic mass, hypothyroidism, urinary tract infection, or trauma.

Looking at treatments

To make sure your child is primed for treatment, a doctor will want to know up front if he's disruptive — successful treatment can be tough with such kids. Thus, he may want to try to help you smooth out the behavior snags while also addressing the stool problem.

If it turns out that your child has an *impacted rectum* (overload of poop in his rectum), the doctor will want to remove this — enema or suppository time — and get him back on an even keel. Often, this is the case.

Treatment options include the following:

- ✔ Softening the BM with a stool softener or laxative is the first, and often best, try. Unless your child has an impacted rectum, your doctor will want you to see if this conservative route resolves your child's constipation.

- ✔ Removing backed-up poop with an enema or suppository in the office will take the load off if a laxative or softener fails to help. Then, after the child has a fresh slate, the doctor will have you give him a stool softener or laxative temporarily to get him cranking (on the potty) again.

✔ Using biofeedback for kids who are having trouble resuming normal bowel habits. Though biofeedback is pricey and time-consuming, some children are able to put soiling behind them permanently after treatment.

After your child is back to normal — having regular BMs and the soiling has stopped — you'll wean him off the medications per your doctor's instructions and get his potty training back on track.

Start potty training with the same gusto you did when you first launched it (in another lifetime!), but remind your child that you know he already knows all about it — and that this is just a refresher course. "I'm sure you'll be using the potty just like a big boy in a week or two! We got your poop problem all fixed up, so you're set to go."

To avoid future bouts of constipation, try these ideas:

✔ **Cut down on foods that tend to constipate:** excess of whole milk (more than 32 ounces a day in a child three to five years old), cheese, pasta, and potatoes. Basically, dairy products and bananas tend to constipate. Think of light/white foods as problems for constipated kids.

✔ **Have him potty-sit several times a day, five minutes per sit.** Encourage him to try to poop after each meal.

✔ **Use daily laxatives for the time recommended by your doctor.** You physician most likely will suggest milk of magnesia, *senna* (a natural laxative), or mineral oil. Mix it into a beverage your child likes. A combination of milk and molasses is another option.

The laxative will result in daily BMs and little or no soiling. But if your child has trouble with bloating, pain, soiling, or large, hard BMs, call your doctor — she'll modify the treatment.

✔ **Praise and reward your child's efforts at toilet-sits.**

Treating Other Physical and Psychological Problems

Often, a child who doesn't want to do a BM in the potty just has a very stubborn temperament. Along the way, he also develops problems with constipation and painful bowel movements. Things pile up and spin off into an all-new level of resistance: "I won't use the potty!" He digs in his heels because he fears having a BM that hurts; and he has already fine-tuned his ability to refuse. Straddling comforting babyhood and big-kid expectations, and displeasing everybody in sight, this kid is not a happy camper.

Just like with kids who soil because they're constipated, square one is getting that problem resolved, which may call for unloading the impacted stool. Your doctor will set up a treatment program so that you and other caregivers will know what to do about poop-on-the-potty refusals. Top of the agenda is normalizing BMs, which need to be regular, with soft, comfortable-to-expel stool.

Speculating about causes

Disease or birth defects rarely cause soiling. And, generally speaking, holding back poop becomes a physical habit. If your child was already potty trained and then started soiling, a backup of stool results in skid marks. But what if you got the constipation resolved, and your child is still withholding his stool? This means he has become accustomed to avoiding BMs — so, essentially, now he's psychologically constipated. Being psychologically constipated can turn into a big problem with serious repercussions if it isn't nipped in the bud.

These stool-soiling kids, who make up about 20 percent of all those with this problem, have daily BMs that are normally shaped and sized, and the youngsters are healthy and well adjusted outside the bathroom realm.

In some cases, a child's stool-soiling can be traced back to tough potty training; he was pushed or punished or coerced. As a result, the child learned that holding on to stool was one way he could control his environment.

Your youngster may also have come to feel possessive about his BMs. So he holds back his BM until he can escape from the vicinity of the toilet. He suspects that giving up a BM to the potty means giving in to a parent or caregiver's master plan. For some reason, he doesn't want that "control" and seeks to sidestep it. Similar to the child who refuses to open his mouth to eat certain foods, the BM withholder can try your patience.

In studies, these kids don't have more behavior problems than other children their age. The only common denominator for stool-withholding kids is that most of them have rather difficult temperaments. In a word, he's a pistol.

A psychological form of withholding, however, can go hand in hand with constipation, and but which came first: Did the constipation cause the child to shut down and stop having regular BMs? Or was he already withholding poop, and the constipation only came along coincidentally, thus reinforcing the behavior?

Signs of a psychological origin of stool-soiling:

- ✔ **Showing no medical problems**
- ✔ **Soiling to draw attention or to control a situation**
- ✔ **Acting fearful of having BMs**
- ✔ **Soiling pants almost every day**
- ✔ **Having bowel movements of normal consistency (soft)**
- ✔ **Having huge BMs only once every four to five days**
- ✔ **Acting disinterested in using the toilet for BMs even though he pees in the potty**
- ✔ **Appearing unaware of the odor of his poop when he poops in his pants**
- ✔ **Soiling in bed (at night or naptime)**

Having a big BM only once every four days suggests big-time that your child is withholding his BMs — and not just because they are hard and painful to pass.

Knowing what you can and can't do

Try to stay patient — and take a matter-of-fact approach to stool-soiling. Assume that this, like other problems you have in parenting, will pass. So, you do what you can to decrease the humiliation that he's experiencing with these accidents — and you get him involved in the day-to-day tending to poop overflow.

Consider these your goals:

- ✔ **Getting BMs back to normal**
- ✔ **Weaning your child away from poop-withholding ways**
- ✔ **Helping him learn to control his bowels normally**
- ✔ **Eliminating the family's over-scrutiny of the soiling child**

Meanwhile, during poop-attitude-adjustment period, try these ways of coping with day-to-day soiling issues:

- ✔ **Delegate dirty-clothes detail:** Having a child wash out his own smeared/stained underpants is a subject of controversy. Some think it reeks of punishment, but not if you just ask your child to help — you don't force him to. Some kids hate having messed up their underwear, and are glad to get involved in washing it. Then, when he starts wanting to get rid of the job entirely, he's motivated to work to stop soiling and will cooperate with your ideas on how to accomplish this.

If he complains about having to fool with "yucky, smelly" clothes, just agree with him that it's indeed tough to have to do that. You know; you've done it.

✔ **Shift dump duty:** Leave his soiled underpants by the toilet and casually ask him to dump the contents. "Sweetie, I'm busy cooking our dinner so would you help me out?" In two seconds, your child has a new role; you just put him in charge of body-product disposal.

Point out that big kids have their bowel movements in the toilet while you're toting his underwear to dump the stool into the potty bowl. Tell him you're sure that's what he wants to do as soon as possible. Let him watch or help, ideally.

If he shows a desire for you not to flush it, leave it in the toilet water a few minutes. "You come back and flush it in a little while," you can tell your child, putting him in charge of sending the poop away to the pipes below.

✔ **Anoint Mr. Clean Jeans:** Don't ignore his soiled jeans. Definitely tell your child to clean himself up as soon as possible (but don't sound impatient or irritated). Be matter of fact. For obvious reasons, you can't let him walk around with a mess in his pants. Some parents believe that making a child wear his dirty pants is a good punishment. Not so — bad idea.

✔ **Endorse his "never having to say he's sorry" privilege:** Don't expect your child to apologize or admit his mistake — neither one is important — but he does need to change clothes.

✔ **Downplay freaky-geek stigma:** Keep your response simple when he mentions to you, "At school, all the kids make fun of me for stinking." Your heart will be breaking, but just hug him and respond sympathetically: "Well, they won't do that anymore after you use the toilet for your BMs." You now tack on a positive: "Soon, you'll love how good it feels to have clean underwear when you can help your body tell you when it's time to go."

Because stool-soiling is a huge taboo in our society, almost anyone — teachers to nuns, friends to in-laws — will respond with a shudder and a look of disgust at the mere thought that a child could be leaving deposits in his underwear. So your "big kid" (school-age) is plagued by the problem he has — and the fact that people want to avoid him. Don't let him feel alone with his soiled pants.

Dealing at Daycare

Pants-soiling children in daycare have an extra burden — the embarrassment factor shoots up about 300 percent. So try to enlist the help of your outside caregiver in maintaining a low-key attitude during the time when the two of you are working this issue.

Your caregiver's job description calls for taking care of your child's needs during daytime hours, so you can reasonably expect these things:

- ✔ **She'll clean him and help change his clothes as needed.** (Ask the caregiver to encourage your child to do as much of this on his own as possible.)

- ✔ **She'll keep his pants-soiling confidential, not sharing it with the other kids.** If they do pick up on the odor, she'll downplay the situation.

- ✔ **She'll keep you informed as to his progress.**

- ✔ **She'll give him any medication that you authorize.**

- ✔ **She'll keep him away from "white/light" foods that constipate.** You can ask your provider to do this, but it's far better to send a lunch that has the foods you prefer.

- ✔ **She'll encourage him to drink a lot of water.**

If your daytime caregiver seems irritated by having to deal with this problem, start shopping for a new daycare center or nanny. A person who can't (or won't) deal with a problem like stool-soiling sympathetically definitely isn't someone you want taking care of your child. What should arouse more compassion than the poor child who's dripping poop? He certainly doesn't need a daytime caregiver giving him grief, in addition to the misery he's giving himself, and that other kids are heaping on him.

And, the following are the things you don't want any caregiver to do:

- ✔ **Give up on him**
- ✔ **Punish your child for soiling**
- ✔ **Make fun of his dirty pants**

Preventing Future Bouts

After your child leaves constipation and stool-soiling behind, avoid future bouts with proactive measures:

- ✔ **Have a heart-to-heart talk with your child.** Explain how the body works — the way his muscles warn him that it's time to go to the toilet. Tell him he can have his muscles release the poop, or alert them, "Hey, don't let it go yet." Your kid has to learn the cause-effect thing — if he doesn't go to the potty, he's likely to get some surprise poopie in his underwear.

- ✔ **Take moves to ease stress.** Some children get constipated when they're upset. If you think that's the case, try to reduce the stressor as soon as possible. Also, explore the possibility that an outside caregiver may be too rigid in his potty-training approach.

✔ **Set aside special times for your child to potty-sit in a calm, unstressed manner.** Hectic households aren't good for potty troubles. If your child complains that there's "never time" to get in the bathroom for a BM — perhaps, it's pure gridlock — fix this.

✔ **Make sure your child gets exercise.** Movement stimulates digestion and facilitates regular BMs.

With other caregivers, relatives, and the family doctor, you're partnering in a plan to help your child put poop-withholding behind him for good. Try some of these easy finishing-touches:

✔ **Give him big doses of tender loving care:** You want him to act grownup and do grownup things like using the toilet. He's most likely to do this if you're willing to baby him at times when the going gets rough.

✔ **Reward daily potty-sits:** Try daily toilet sits, and offer him incentives — something small like M&Ms — to reinforce successes. (As we've mentioned previously, though, using food for incentives is your last-ditch method — far better to deal in stars or stickers or itty-bitty toys.)

In the back of your mind, though, be realistic. With encopresis, relapses are common, especially at times when your child is under a great deal of stress or his routine is changed. He may need laxatives off and on for years, but always check with your physician first.

Your goal is to eliminate entirely your child's negative association — that BMs bring pain — and sometimes, changing that perception is no quickie. Plus, you don't want to turn him into a laxative junkie.

Chapter 17

Training Children with Disabilities

• •

In This Chapter

▶ Handling special physical issues

▶ Working with emotional disabilities

▶ Incorporating coaching techniques

• •

*C*learly, potty training a child with a disability can take the difficulty level up a few notches. In some kids, emotional and physical drawbacks are built into the equation. Also, you have to consider your child's developmental age. A developmentally delayed child who is chronologically four years old but who functions at an 18-month-old level is not ready for potty training. If a child functions at around a two-and-a-half-year-old level, chances are, she's ready for toilet training. The good news is that many — in fact, most — children with handicaps can be potty trained.

But you can ease a tough assignment by using the right coaching approaches. Pass out extra doses of patience and assistance when you're potty training children with disabilities. Expect frustration to overwhelm your child at times, making her learning curve a bit herky-jerky. Overall, you probably face a slower learning process because your child may get bogged down by difficulties in understanding what she's supposed to do or by the hardness of making her body move as needed — or both.

But don't let the size of the challenge scare you. Simply think of this as a mastery you will help your child accomplish — but one that will take time. To start with, your child will feel disappointed — she tries to deliver what you want, and it's hard to do. So the key in teaching a child with disabilities potty skills is using manageable doses — and applauding the baby steps your child does take.

Physical Issues

Handling the physical aspect of training a child with a disability is wildly different with individual kids, depending on the disability. You may need to provide high-tech props that facilitate movement from walker or wheelchair to the toilet (see the "Working with Special Gear" section in this chapter.) Or, your child may need nothing more than some bars to grab onto when she's sitting down — and your friendly assistance.

One of the hurdles that parents and caregivers face is that kids with physical disabilities sometimes are so hamstrung by their limitations that even the idea of pleasing adults doesn't motivate them, the way it does other children. Also, some aren't moved by the idea of being a big kid or wearing big-kid underwear because they're happy being "little" and "dependent" — it feels safer, considering the physical mountains they must move every day, when they're trying to move around successfully.

Obviously, different disabilities have special problems built in. To discover the best way to potty train your child, try some of the following ways of obtaining advice on potty training a child with a disability:

- ✔ Study up on your child's disability. A good resource for info is the Parent Training and Information Center in your state (check out the directory of these on http://taaliance.org on the Web).

- ✔ Seek insight from other parents of children with disabilities. Your community will probably have support groups, or you can join one of the many on the Internet. Check www.egroups.com.

- ✔ Ask an occupational therapist or psychologist for advice on potty training a child with a disability.

Understanding muscle control issues

While most children can control their bowels and bladders by about age three, kids who have disabilities may take much longer. Their medical problems can delay the development of the muscle control a child needs to regulate herself. In some cases, a physical problem can even prevent a child from developing this ability. Check with your doctor to find out whether you can expect eventual potty use — or not. Remember, however, that a doctor is not a prophet. (We've all seen enough tear-jerkers to know that kids often surprise even their doctors.)

You have the advantage of knowing this particular cupcake better than anyone. So, if you're pretty sure that she can be trained, you have nothing to lose by trying — as long as you're not pushy or critical.

Coming to grips with your child's muscle control issues is key to helping her become potty-proficient. You'll discover, as you investigate, lots of strategies that work in training special-needs kids.

Sometimes, a child's motor difficulties will make her use the potty only if you take her. Escorted, she will do it. Otherwise, she's a no-show. The good news is that eventually she'll decide to go on her own, but that may take time.

 Get your physician to be your ally. She should provide you with information on understanding your child's limitations and boundaries insofar as muscle control. You don't want to try to get your child to perform actions that are beyond her capacity, but you do want to be there with encouragement.

Enhancing physical progress

One of the best ways to enhance your child's physical progress is to potty train her like you would any child: "You can do this — I know you can. We'll find ways to work around your brace." (The chapters in Part III run through the whole Potty-Training Mambo.)

To promote physical adjustment to potty training, you can forge mind/body links in the following ways:

✔ **Help her connect bathroom with body functions:** Move into the bathroom for diaper changes and emptying diapers — you want her to associate poop and pee with the place where the toilet is.

✔ **Brag on tiny successes:** Make sure your child gets huge bravos for the baby steps she makes, whether that's making a tiny dribble in the potty bowl or saying "I potty" after she has done it in her diaper.

✔ **Help her handle nighttime frustration:** For a child with disabilities, staying dry at night is hard. You can expect a child who lacks mobility to have trouble making it through the night dry, and she'll need special handling and empathy. You may need to transfer her from wheelchair to toilet many times before she's able to handle it by holding on to grab bars (see the "Working with Special Gear" section later in this chapter).

 Before you kick off her program, make sure she's eating and drinking a nutritionally sound diet. You don't want constipation to get in the way of progress. (See Chapter 16 for ways to prevent and treat constipation.)

Next, talk to her about the body signals that tell your child she needs to go potty. (See Chapter 7 for more on this.) Unfortunately, certain physical disabilities tone down that urge feeling. Remember, too, that a child with a disability may have a muted sense of body in general, so being messy may not bother her.

Your child may miss the potty sometimes, so you should tell her not to worry about accidents. She may also be pretty bad at cleaning herself and walk away a mess. All toddlers are fairly messy at this stuff, but the disability may take your child's messiness quotient up a tad. If handling toilet paper is out of her league, just do the task for her. She may eventually learn how by mimicking your moves — but for now, you remove the possible frustration involved in her desire to be clean but lacking the coordination to accomplish that.

After addressing diet, body signals, and messiness, try these ways of enhancing your child's potty progress physically:

✔ **Set up a success-oriented environment.** Get removable obstacles and stressors out of the way. Install handrails or other physical supports so that she can feel safe and sturdy when she sits on the potty. (See the "Working with Special Gear" section later in this chapter.)

✔ **Pad the potty seat with foam (from a crafts store) or buy a softer, padded toilet seat if your child thinks the seat is too hard or cold.** (See the "Working with Special Gear" section in this chapter.)

✔ **Use waterproof sheeting on surfaces where your child sits so that she can hang out clothed in just underpants or diapers.** That way, she can be wet long enough for the feeling to bother her. The waterproof stuff is there just to make cleanup easier.

Working with special gear

You can train a child with a disability on a specialized potty chair (custom-made for the child); or build steps up to the potty; or mount a set of grab bars on the walls on each side of the adults' toilet. You can also purchase some terrific wheelchair-conversions that make potty use easier for a wheelchair-using child.

A tot with motor developmental problems is often potty trained on an adaptive toilet seat or extra-high toilet, which you can shop for at a medical supply store, or online at Websites such as www.ataccess.org, www.abledata.com, www.columbiamedical.com, or www.invacare.com. Another possibility is checking with your occupational therapist for availability. Some state agencies provide equipment for families whose incomes make these pricey toilet options out of the question.

Some of the aids and options that are good for potty training a child with a disability are the following:

✔ A custom potty chair, or one that's modified from an existing chair, is available from Able Generation (www.ablegeneration.com) — they work with kids and their parents to get the product just right.

✔ A wheelchair with a hinged center-section padded seat that lowers to become a commode chair.

✔ A manual wheelchair that lowers to convert to a commode chair that fits a standard toilet.

✔ A cushion that self-inflates to assist a child in going from wheelchair (the getting-up part) and moving onto the toilet.

✔ Grab bars on each side of the toilet for leverage in moving from a wheelchair or walker to the toilet.

✔ Padded toilet seat reducer ring (this provides secure and soft seating for a child who's very slender, or who needs lengthy potty-sits).

✔ Toilet supports that come with chest strap, safety belt, padded cushion, armrests, and footrest.

✔ Safety rails for extra support, and a swing-away bar to mount by the toilet.

✔ Child commode chair, which has adjustable-height legs, swing-away safety bars, commode pail, padded headrest, adjustable foot rest, seat reducer, and seat belt.

By the way, special equipment may be covered by your health plan. Your doctor will be the one to indicate why certain equipment is "medically necessary" — important buzzwords in today's managed-care world of health insurance.

Emotional Differences

In the same way that every child is different, each separate disability has its own set of limitations that may affect the potty-training process. For example:

✔ An autistic child may have trouble understanding what you expect. As far as prompts for potty use, parents and caregivers can get creative, keying in to what would fit the child. For example, a tyke who is autistic can benefit from the talking picture frames that are widely available in drugstores and departments stores. You can record messages that remind her of various potty steps and place these so that she can touch and listen to a message — both practical and fun.

✔ A child who is mentally challenged can be stumped by the sequencing of the actions and the cause-effect of linking her body with its products. Try using a chart that has drawings or photos of each part of the process. You can even draw funny little stick pictures of a child going through the steps, and put these on a piece of poster board. That way, you're helping her remember what she's supposed to do — and what comes next.

Show these actions with symbols or drawings to illustrate each:

- •Lisa pulls down her clothes.

- •Lisa sits on the potty.

- •Lisa pees and poops in the potty.

- •Lisa wipes her bottom, front to back, with toilet paper.

- •Lisa pulls up her undies and her shorts or pants.

- •Lisa pushes on the toilet handle to flush it. (Leave this one out if she's using a potty chair.)

- •Lisa washes her hands.

- •Lisa sees Mommy (or Daddy or Miss Marple) smiling, happy with what she did. Clap your hands!

✔ A child who has a physical disability and normal intelligence may not want to move from a sheltered, cared-for existence to one in which she is taking greater responsibility for her body's movements. To her, that sounds unfun. Deal with this by frequent explanation of the potty steps, consistency, and lots of praise-giving and potty opportunities. Your job is to hit on exactly what turns your child on. Is she jazzed by charts-with-stickers? Would she be thrilled with the idea of wearing pretty panties?

In dealing with your child's emotional issues concerning the potty, keep reminding yourself that most kids without disabilities find potty skills tough to master. So, if your tot acts like she's conflicted, that's not a bad sign — she's just reacting normally.

Accept that change is a hard-to-swallow concept for many children with disabilities. So, if you can get her past the change-is-scary moments, you will be warming up to progress.

When you think it could be time to potty train your child, review the critical readiness signs outlined in Chapter 4 and synopsized on the Cheat Sheet at the front of the book. The following are strong indications that a child with a disability is ready for potty training:

✔ **She has dry pants for long blocks of time.**

✔ **She shows signs that she knows when a bowel movement is coming.**

- ✔ If playing with a toy, she stops when having a BM and perhaps looks around, or makes expressions or sounds.

- ✔ Your child responds as if she understands when you ask her to go get something or hand you a toy.

- ✔ She tries to help with undressing and dressing.

- ✔ She listens when you read a book to her, and her attention span is growing.

- ✔ She shows a certain pattern to her poop/pee cycle.

If your child attends a daycare facility, ask her caregiver: "Does Annabelle pay attention when other kids use the potty? Does she ever ask you about it?" This can also be an indicator that she's warming to the idea.

Another idea for making it fun: Give her a little bell or Halloween noise-maker to shake or ring. Act like the signal device is a cool gift and tell her, "I want you to use this when you want to tell us you need to potty. That way, I can come and help you get there." If she gets carried away with this noisy signal, tell her the story of the boy who cried wolf. She'll understand that you'll stop responding if she just uses it aimlessly. And, if she just can't restrain herself, let the noisemaker morph into new use as a toy. Tell her: "That didn't work very well for us as a potty-signal, so you can just play with this."

However, if the shaker system does work well, send it along with your child to daycare and to grandparents' homes and fill them in on its purpose.

Coaching Techniques

Coaching that really clicks, though critical to success, can vary widely from child to child. But in children with disabilities, nothing takes the place of consistency, repetition, patience, and encouragement.

Houston mom Martha Steele tells of her frustrations in trying to train her adopted child — four-year-old Alexis, who has cerebral palsy. "I'd just given up and decided she was never going to be potty trained," says Steele, "but then she got interested in using the potty at the day-care center where she stays while I'm at work. . . . And, about the same time, a friend of ours gave her a pair of frilly pink panties, and she loved the idea of getting to wear those. Now, Alexis is potty trained and happy about it!"

People who work with children with disabilities believe that potty training them differs from training other kids only in that it takes a great deal of patience, extreme consistency, and a longer learning period.

It's helpful to try a few weeks of just visiting the potty, and then add some peer role modeling: Pair a potty-trained sibling or daycare friend with your child with a disability, and let them take buddy trips to the bathroom (you go along for the ride, of course). Pretty soon, potty skills become familiar because watching other children is a big motivator.

To make her feel like a natural in the bathroom, teach your child potty-lingo basics. Coach her in the meanings of wet, dry, poop, and potty. (See more on potty words in Chapter 6.)

Aiding and abetting her efforts

Potty visits, singing, and fun attitudes are ways you can aid and abet the training of a child with disabilities.

You can use one of many potty songs to help your little chickadee warm to the idea. This works for children with Down's syndrome, developmental delays, cerebral palsy, and kids without disabilities. If you use a potty-training video (see Chapter 3), you can pick up the song that's repeated a zillion times there, or you can just make up one of your own: "Emma's going to the potty. Emma likes to use the potty. Here we go to the potty!"

Suddenly potty training becomes a razzle-dazzle, amusement-park moment. Kids are so pliable when they're getting into the spirit of fun outings. If your child wants to continue her crooning while she's potty sitting, that's fine, too. Whatever works for her, works. A songbird trainee is a happy little lass.

When you're training a child with a disability, you basically use the same routine you would with any child — but just expect a lengthier learning curve. Just as with other kids, there's no certain age for startup — it depends on when they're ready.

Try the following steps to make a potty-training success of your child:

- ✔ **Be very consistent:** Take your child to the potty every two or three hours.

- ✔ **Sing:** This gets your child in an upbeat frame of mind for making visits to the potty.

- ✔ **Give plenty of reinforcement:** With every success and good try, give her enthusiastic praise.

- ✔ **Be extremely patient:** Expect this to take time, and be very patient.

Another key to getting your child potty trained is making this a priority. At the same time, though, don't rush the process.

Also, keep the tiny trainee in the right underpants. It's smart to use off-brand cheaper training-pant diapers instead of the more expensive ones that are so padded the child can't really tell when she's wet. Just as with any other kid, you want a child with a disability to feel that she's wet. The youngster who's having trouble understanding the point of the potty needs to know — clear and uncomfortably — when she's wet and soiled. Also, switch to real underwear as soon as possible. Many children are inspired by the idea of wearing big-kid underwear.

By the way, don't be surprised if you find that your child with a disability responds better to the potty-training efforts of daycare workers. The different nature of the relationship may make a child listen more closely. She's used to taking instructions from her outside caregiver as a normal part of her day. Besides, some children think Dad or Mom's a pushover, so they don't always listen.

If your child has trouble with bed-wetting, you can try using a bed-wetting alarm. (See Chapter 14 for more on bed-wetting aids.) Though a moisture alarm often solves the problem, it usually takes any child months before she finally catches on. But if your small fry is basically kind of anxious or jumpy, this probably isn't a good option — a bed-wetting alarm may make her even more nervous.

If your child is soiling her underwear, see Chapter 16 for ideas on solving this problem. A kid can be chronically constipated for many reasons.

Handling a lack of interest

In the disabled arena, some kids just aren't interested in using the potty. And some act as if they aren't interested because it seems so tough to try. Obviously, just like when you're training a kid without a disability, you'll see a wide range of funky behaviors that stem from this apparent lack of interest — real or imitation. The following are some off-the-wall moments and difficulties you may encounter and ways to handle them:

- ✔ **Peeing on the floor:** Ask your child to help you clean up the mess and tell her that you'll take her to the potty when she needs help. If that doesn't work, watch for signs of an upcoming BM or pee moment and scoot in and swoop her off to the potty.

    If this problem persists, take your child to see a psychologist for help in resolving the random peeing.

- ✔ **Crying when you take her to the potty:** Some kids are super sensitive. She could be afraid of the toilet and needs reassurance that nothing will hurt her. Show how the toilet works when you use it; illustrate that you walk away undamaged.

    The other possibility is fear of disappointing you. Let her know that you just want her to try sitting there — and just see what happens.

✔ **Peeing on her wheelchair without saying a word:** Sometimes kids in wheelchairs don't want to go through all the hassles involved in using the potty, so they hang onto the good old diaper days because they're easier. So be firm in reminding her that the potty is the proper place to pee or poop. Stay patient, but make expectations clear.

✔ **Smearing poop on the wall and floor:** Don't assume that she knows this is wrong. Young kids often don't have negative associations with the smell or sight of feces, and autistic children often smear their feces, as if touching it appeals to them. You can motivate your child to quit being a poop-smearer two ways: Have her help clean the floor and walls. And show her that your poop falls into the potty and gets flushed away — and that you don't play with it. Then, get out some paper and finger paints and show your toddler what she can use to make pictures.

✔ **Saying she doesn't know what to do on the potty:** That's your cue to re-explain — one more time — the steps involved in the potty process. You need to keep teaching over and over the right things to do. Be consistent with your message "You can do this — I know you can." (Try the potty-poster idea in this chapter under "Emotional Differences.")

✔ **Having tantrums when asked to potty-sit:** Make the process different by having her doll sit on the potty. Talk about what the doll is trying to do on the potty, and read a potty book.

✔ **Playing in the toilet water:** Keep the potty covered until time to use it. Then, when she is sitting on the potty, give her something to play with on her lap while she waits to pee or poop.

✔ **Getting off the potty and walking away, or acting bored when she potty-sits:** Show a potty video to this child (see Chapter 3), and talk up the excitement of "getting it right." Also, you may want to try tiny rewards for her successes.

Find a way to make your child think of potty-trips as good things — enjoyable times spent with parent or caregiver. Keep field trips to the potty short and laid-back. Give help when needed, and otherwise, let your child propel herself. Set a timer to go off to signal when she can get up. Tell her: "That's the end of your potty-trip fun!"

Don't be surprised if your child with a disability chooses the end of the day — when both of you are dead tired — to insist on a diaper. Sometimes, children get themselves into a baby-mode when they see parents who work, and that sends them spiraling into Babyland, when things were simpler. Your response? Do give her a close encounter — but not of the diaper kind. Hold her. Dance with her. Sing to her. Read to her. Your response to the diaper request? "You wear panties now, and hey, you're doing just fine with them. Let's keep them on."

Part VI
The Part of Tens

The 5th Wave   By Rich Tennant

And now, I'd like to share some of my day with you.

In this part...

Part VI, just to make sure we've tied up all the loose
ends for info-junkies, we bring you some oh-by-the-
way lists.

You get ten ways to pump up potty prowess (go, kid, go!).
We give you ten reasons to let little Bucko lead the way.
You get ten woulda-coulda-shouldas that parents who've
potty trained (and screwed up) wish they'd known in
advance. And the Poopbah of Potty Training addresses
some of the usual problems trainers face.

We figure you've got your mantra going. And, everything
else you'll need is packed into this last part, making
Potty Training For Dummies a virtual potty lovefest.
Schweee, babee!

Chapter 18

Ten Answers from the Expert

• •

In This Chapter

▶ Listing common problems

▶ Giving easy solutions

• •

*Y*ou've listened to old wives' tales (interesting and amusing). And you read magazine articles (also interesting and amusing). And your relatives wind up telling you what you really need to do (very interesting and amusing). Now we add a little more input to the mix. Check out the common problems and some simple solutions the Poopbah of Potty Training presents in this chapter.

Marking Territory

Dear Poopbah of Potty Training,

My son is three-and-a-half, and he pees in corners of rooms, on various household items, and even in his toy box. What should I do?

Territorial Terror's Mom

Dear T-T Mom,

Chances are, he's just making the same point that dogs make: "My space, my place, check it out!" Or, he could just be making a bid for more attention.

So, have a chat. Don't be heavy, but make your message clear: "Listen, honey, I can see that you know how to mark your spots, just like a little puppy, but that's not going to work. You know how to aim your penis — I can see you have that down really well! But please aim your pee into the potty."

If he complains that he likes to do it the way he's doing it, and that yes, indeed, it does work, you repeat: "I really want you to use your potty chair for all your peeing and pooping. I know you can do it like a big boy, and big boys get to do special things, like go to baseball games and Disney World." Also, look for times when you can brag on him for putting on his shoes, or stacking his blocks, and so on.

If he continues to spread his pee randomly, give each instance a frown and tell him, "I don't like it when you do that. Please pee in the potty." If that has no effect, give him the paper towels to clean up his mess each time. After several episodes of this, most children will fall in line with the original plan. By the way, if he refuses to wipe up his puddles, you do it, but let him know how you feel: "I sure hope this is the last time you pee in the corner of your bedroom — this takes away from time we could spend doing fun things."

Sending Him to School Untrained

Dear Poopbah of Potty Training,

My child isn't trained yet, and school starts in three months! What can I do?

Panicky Pop

Dear Panicky Pop,

Many kids who start kindergarten still wet the bed at night, and others have trouble with the niceties — straightening their clothes, flushing the toilet, washing their hands thoroughly. But, most are daytime trained, so if your child is still day-wetting, consult your doctor.

Brainstorm with a professional to come up with ways to make the most of the months you have before school starts. Your child may have a simple problem that has been holding him back, and perhaps you can find out how to "fix" it. (See Chapters 14 and 15 for solutions to some common problems.)

If nothing really helps before school starts, have a conference with the teacher or principal — or consider alternative schooling ideas.

Ask for their ideas — you can bet that educators have encountered this in the past. And tell them your child may need frequent trips to the bathroom (without anyone making a big deal of it), or he may need a stash of extra clothes. Also, explore the idea of home schooling or Internet schooling.

Handling a Potty-Mouth

Dear Poopbah of Potty Training,

My son is so into potty words that he's driving us crazy with "you're a big poop" and "I wee-wee with my pee-pee on you!" How should I handle this?

Word-Warrior's Mom

Dear Word-Warrior's Mom,

Don't overreact, and you may find the habit disappears when he doesn't get shocked responses. Basically, you don't want him to think his words pack dynamite-power.

But you can tell him that you don't like to hear that kind of talk — and lots of other people don't enjoy it, either.

Micro-Managing the Process Comes Naturally for Me

Dear Poopbah of Potty Training,

I'm using Potty Training For Dummies, but being strict. My son's not responding well — where do I go from here?

My-Way-or-the-Highway Mom

Dear My-Way Mom,

An overbearing parent or caregiver is what's often behind the child who doesn't complete potty training until he's four or five. That's not to say your plan is doomed — just think about giving up your tendency to over-control situations, and at least experiment with letting your child lead. (Chapter 20 has some reasons to follow your child's lead.)

Micro-managing the potty process is putting too much of the potty-deed-doing in your hands and too little in your child's. The problem with that is, he's the one who has to get in the groove. No amount of prodding will make his body or mind cooperate better. And probably, too much heavy-handedness will give him a good reason to be a slug. His train of thought will golike this: "I should just give up now, 'cause I'll never get it perfect!"

He Wants to Go Back to Diapers

Dear Poopbah of Potty Training,

My child was excited when I put him in big-kid underwear, but now he wants his diapers back on. What next?

Conflicted Caregiver

Dear Conflicted,

Help him role-play putting away the diapers — make a ceremony of it — for someone else's baby or the next family infant. Perhaps, attach a small gift like taking him somewhere special as a symbol of the "growing-up" moment. You want him to get the idea that ditching diapers will take him to a better, more fun place. If he has accidents in his pullups, just be patient and reassure him that kids who are newly trained often have that happen.

My Son Still Wets the Bed

Dear Poopbah of Potty Training,

My son is a happy five-year-old who has a calm temperament. But he wets the bed every single night. What should I do?

Mom of a Soppy Sleeper

Dear Mom of Soppy,

Many children his age — especially boys — are still wetting the bed at night. Most of the time, they spontaneously outgrow nighttime bed-wetting .

Sometime before he's eight, he'll learn to wake himself up at night. But, if he's upset by his bed-wetting, or you find you can't handle it very well, try some of the solutions suggested in Chapter 14.

First, though, check with your doctor so she can rule out a physical problem as the cause.

Is Putting Him in Cool Undies a Good Incentive?

Dear Poopbah of Potty Training,

My boy Bart just doesn't get the potty thing. So I want to go ahead and put him in the little superhero underpants, so he'll get moving. Good idea or not?

Terminator Mom

Dear Terminator Mom,

Racking up zeros in the bladder or bowel department probably means his body isn't quite ready to deliver. So if you get him all outfitted and he doesn't use the potty correctly, he's all dressed up with nowhere to go! Next thing you know, he'll be feeling like a failure. The pants were bought to reward success that hasn't yet happened — the "gift" of cool pants would probably just make matters worse.

He's Peeing and Pooping During the Night

Dear Poopbah of Potty Training,

I kept my son in pullups at night because he still pees at night sometimes. Then, a month ago, he started having BMs at night, and because he feels embarrassed about it, he tries to dump out the diaper before I see it. What comes next?

Mother of a Covert Agent

Dear Mother of a Covert Agent,

Be glad that he knows pooping in his pullups isn't what he's supposed to do. That's good news. So, try these ideas to solve the problem:

- Talk about what you're going to try to do with him. Assure him: "I know you can do it — we'll just arrange things to make it easier for you."

- Feed him dinner by 6 p.m. and make sure he goes to the bathroom shortly afterward and again at bedtime. Remind him to listen for his body's signals that tell him he has to poop.

- Tell the diapers goodbye. Explain that you think he'll remember better at night if he's wearing big-boy underwear. Outfitting him in "low expectation" padded trainers has probably encouraged him to relax and go in them.

- Tell him that he can come get you for a star-chart reward during the night if he gets up and has to poop.

Refusing to Sit on the Potty Chair

Dear Poopbah of Potty Training,

When his potty chair was new, my child liked it. Now he's bored with it and has a fit every time I try to get him to sit down on it. He's doing pretty much all his stuff in his pants now.

Potty Pistolero's Pop

Dear Pistolero's Pop,

He's rebelling against your plan — but you can turn this around by agreeing that he has a "prize" in his body products, and you want him to choose to put it in the right place. But wait a few weeks before taking up the potty training again. He'll probably forget why he didn't want to go and the push-pull of giving in to your wishes will be a vague memory. If this doesn't work, see Chapter 15 for more ideas.

One Twin is Dragging the Other One Down

Dear Poopbah of Potty Training,

One of my twins adapted perfectly to using the potty. Rocco, at 18 months, would take off his diaper and climb on the potty before I even introduced the idea. But Scout's a bad influence. He'll romp around naked and pee on the floor. So, now Rocco is following his lead. I have a real mess on my hands. Neither is trained, and neither seems to care.

Dynamic Duo's Dad

Dear Dynamic Dad,

You're thinking of twins as a duo, but that's not the case when it comes to potty training — and lots of other things. Get rid of the mindset that's evolving here — "if little Scout could just be more like smart little Rocco." Gear up for glorying in each kid's individuality. One may sing; the other may dance — that's what makes twins so much fun — the differences!

So let each child show you when his readiness clicks in. Each separate child. Remember, internal clocks and bladder and bowel development aren't necessarily identical twins.

In training two-of-a-kind, avoid asking, "Why can't you be good like your brother?" If one wants to train sooner than the other, which sounds like the case with your Rocco, go ahead and work with him. But don't impose the plan on the un-ready Scout.

Chapter 19

Ten Ways to Pump Up Potty Prowess

· ·

In This Chapter

▶ Framing the challenge for your child

▶ Prepping in a way that delights a toddler

▶ Getting past temperament

· ·

*P*umping up potty prowess is a win-win for you and your child. So going full tilt into the wonderful world of new-skill-learning has to be a bonding bonanza.

You get to spend time with the little toddler. You get to help her experience positive self-image vibes. You have the privilege of assisting her in mastering potty use so that she can move right on up to her next developmental opportunity.

Softening the Setting

Set up a toddler-friendly environment where she'll feel safe and secure. Make sure that the potty area and the bathroom surroundings are cheerful and comfy and welcoming. Surround her with brightly colored towels, posters, and her success chart. Supply cheerful props and pleasant fragrances.

Properly Framing the Speed Bumps

She's strutting around in cool big-kid pants — clearly, a fashion risk-taker. Then, oops! She hits a speed bump — feeling shy at a friend's house, or being with a new nanny, or going on a plane for the first time. The result? Accidental tinkles.

So, you'll pump up potty prowess by giving your child a frame of reference when she makes mistakes. She wants to know: Is it awful to dribble in your panties? Am I bad or dumb or silly?

She'll turn to you when she pees in her pants at a movie. And when she walks away from the potty chair and has a bowel movement in her undies the day after her potty-training celebration party. Your little darlin' has no idea what's going on, other than the fact that everyone is looking very disappointed.

As the caregiver, you must jump in and offer warm words of calm: "All little kids have accidents when they're getting used to the potty. No biggie! Don't worry." Of course, don't warn of accidents unless she has one — give no up-front warning that plants an idea. Keep her churning out a string of successes as long as possible. But when she slips up, be ready to say "don't worry — you'll get it soon, you cool potty-girl, you!"

Jazzing Up the Challenge

Any time you see her interest flagging — and those glazed-over eyes tell you that she's dreaming fondly of diaper dependency — get creative.

Jazz up the potty challenge with some new theatrics. If you have to tap-dance around the potty or play Britney Spears for background ambiance, do whatever it takes to get her elimination juices cranking again.

Mix things up a bit — get her an "I'm a Potty-Training Pro" T-shirt, or a lei and a cute aloha shirt that match her bright red undies. Flavor potty-sits with bigger and better rewards: a new video, a movie, a book. Or put a few drops of food coloring in the potty water, so she can enjoy the color change she creates when she pees.

Be braggy: Play down mistakes and super-size potty-product praise.

Using Your Insider Knowledge

You know this little toddler through and through. So put that insider knowledge to use.

For example, if she's a natural-born chatterer, sit with her while she's on the potty and talk about things. That way, she'll look forward to those times and make them bigger parts of her repertoire. If she concentrates best in total silence, provide that. If she's always eager to get up and leave the potty behind so she can go back outside and play, use that as leverage: "We'll go play ball in the yard when you're through using the potty."

Taking the High Road

Don't get caught up in "you said, I said" battles. That will halt progress every time. If you and your toddler tend to lock horns simply because your personalities don't mesh, put differences aside so that they don't interfere with potty progress. Being right won't help you help her, and both of you want to get the job done.

Applying Pottying Skills to Real Life

Pump up potty prowess by making it carry over to other areas that call for taking a task to the finish line: She learns what to do. She does it. Then she has to try to take it to completion — the plateau of using the potty skills regularly and dependably.

Reinforce this process by telling her: "You're good at remembering how to use the potty, so I think you can learn the steps to turning on the TV."

Make it clear what you expect by presenting it numerous times in a help-ful tone — don't let impatience creep into your voice; "I've told you this 50 million times!" is counterproductive.

Focus on the long-range value of what she's learning. Imagine her in high school: She learns how to do an equation in algebra. She does many of them correctly. She takes the newfound knowledge to comple-tion by becoming good at it.

Putting the Ball in Her Court

Keep your child keenly aware that the ball is in her court. Those are her little undies she's trying to keep clean. She's the one sitting on the potty and trying to produce something in the right place, instead of flinging it willy-nilly into a diaper. This is "her thing."

A kid this age finds incredible joy in trying-her-wings. Chat up the con-cept that she's getting kinda-sorta independent: "You're learning to do so many things all by yourself. I'm proud of the way you pull your clothes up and down when you use the potty. Good going!"

Letting Her Know She'll Succeed

You can enhance her potty prowess by being a loudmouth. Tell her you know that she'll soon be using the potty all the time and wearing big-kid panties. Make it clear that you know she'll succeed — in potty training and many, many other things. Talk it up around the house — let siblings, spouse, in-laws know that she's getting the drift of the potty, and all of you will soon have a toddler who's trained replacing a one-time diaper-babe.

Cheering Her Slam Dunks

Cheer her on to a whoop-and-whammy slam dunk — as in, the defining moment when all parts are in place: She gets it! Smart, savvy, and swift-on-the-potty. She won't walk away from potty training just knowing how to use the potty — oh, no — much more. She will walk away feeling like she's a super-smart little superstar tot because she has mastered several new things: clothes-wrangling, hand-washing, potty-handling, and pee-and-poop placement. Only one way to interpret that coup: "Mucho grande!"

Crowning Her a Potty Princess

Ah, her day has come. You knew it would!

She's using the potty regularly. And, having no more accidents. It's coronation time, clearly.

Make an aluminum-foil crown and scepter and declare her royalty. Ask family members to join in celebrating her successful potty-deeds! Invite her grandparents for the party.

The celebration is an excellent motivator. You've touted it in advance — played it up big time — and now, the moment is here at last. Your child has been looking forward to her crowning (even if she didn't exactly understand what it would be).

Looking back at the coronation also helps cut down on accidents because she feels proud of herself. And rightfully so!

Chapter 20

Ten Reasons to Let Your Child Lead

. . . .

In This Chapter
▶ Responding to his instincts
▶ Taking the ball and running with it
▶ Wanting you on the sidelines

. . . .

*F*ollow the leader doesn't usually come to mind when you try to push or pull or pivot your child into place during potty-training days. That's why you must keep telling yourself all the good reasons for letting your kiddo take the reins this time.

He definitely will do better in the long run if he learns to handle his own challenges. And learning to pee on the potty is only the first of many challenges to come. He will listen to his body and find his own potty approach. And, he'll let you know what he needs from you.

Hearing His Body Talk

Your child will show you by his actions that he's ready to learn potty skills. (See readiness signs on the Cheat Sheet or in Chapter 4.) You want him to learn how to respond to his body's cues. Parents and caregivers should always encourage a child to respond in positive ways to his body. That sets a good precedent for all health issues, such as eating only when you need fuel and not just out of boredom, for example.

So you send the kid running into the game. Let him make mistakes. Dry his tears when he's disappointed. And when he hits the potty target, praise him to the skies.

Setting the Pace

Your child needs to set the pace. If he wants to soar, he'll find a way. If he tends to shuffle his feet and plod, he will.

If his bladder and bowel control are slow in coming around because his body is a late-bloomer, he may take longer to get where he's going. At any rate, your role in the process is as support staff. Let him know that he gets to lead the way and that you're right behind him if he needs help, advice, pointers, or tissue.

Finding His Motivation

He needs to find his motivation and hit his mark. He's best equipped to lead this parade because the inclinations of his mind and body are the chief players in the potty game.

You're a helper who, from the time you saw the first signs of toilet-training readiness (staying dry longer, wanting diaper changes), made it your job to check for patterns that enable you to steer him gently in the right direction (toward the potty) at prime times. But you like letting him lead because these are his biorhythms — not yours.

Trailblazing via Temperament

Your child's temperament will help him get used to the potty by growing accustomed to it in his own way — if you're not blurring his view by getting in his face. Blazing his trail can set the stage for potty-training success. Discover what he needs from you, and help him whack through the high brush.

Learning Pee and Poop Signals

He's learning a new skill. So he needs a coach who knows when to move forward and when to step back. Sometimes, you may just need to get out of the way so that he can concentrate on pee and poop signals — and what they're like.

Making It Up as He Goes

Another reason your child should lead? You may think he's acting ornery when he's just showing you an alternate way of approaching potty training — one that may work better for him. He wants to venture out and sample his own method of getting used to the potty. That's okay — even if that means diverging from your well-charted plan.

Such behavior reminds you that your child is an individual, separate person, with his own preferences and his own good ideas.

Learning How to Self-Propel

He needs to be out front in order to develop self-control.

You know — and we know that you know — *way more* than your toddler about the potty and way more about pretty much everything else in the world. You'd be in big trouble if you didn't.

But in the potty game, you want to make your kid feel in charge of his fate. So carefully water down your words of wisdom so that you don't come off sounding like a know-it-all. If you whack him repeatedly with how big and wise and experienced you are, his confidence and motivation may wither away.

Right now, he wants to discover that he can do something all on his own . . . without too much handholding.

Signaling When He Needs Help

Your toddler can let you know when he needs sagging spirits bolstered.

If you've clued into what makes him tick, you can jump in with encouragement when you see that little face fall.

Sure, he'll get confused and bummed when he misses the potty altogether, or can't make his mind cue his body, or feels like he's "too dumb" to get his act together. But all the while, he's got you standing by, never doubting for one minute that he's going to succeed. And telling him that over and over and over.

Be a great coach. Pat him on the back. Tell him you have faith in him. Then send him back out onto the field with his peers with cheery words of well-wishing: "You can do this!"

Knowing When to Sit a Game Out

Your child may need to step back and review progress.

A good reason for him to be in charge of his potty progress is that he may occasionally need a little hiatus. Potty deeds come to a complete halt, and that means small fry is telling you "I'm a little tired of trying this right now — it's not working for me." Are you listening?

Don't prod. Just follow the leader: He knows what he's doing!

Getting to Know Himself

If you're back there warming the bench during potty training, your toddler, whirling and swinging on the field, will learn some valuable things about himself.

Certainly, no parent or caregiver has an easy time of handcuffing himself when the child he loves is having trouble fine-tuning a new task. But sometimes, loving means no meddling. Very often, potty training can be like that.

Let him lead.

Chapter 21

Ten Woulda-Couldas If You Got Do-Overs

. . . .

In This Chapter

▶ Offering hindsight nuggets

▶ Wishing you had done that one thing differently

▶ Seeing your child thrive even when you screw up

. . . .

A h, the value of hindsight. All of us become absolutely brilliant when we get a chance to look back and reflect on those woulda-coulda-shouldas.

Parenting is one pursuit that really, truly makes you wish you got do-overs. But, alas, you don't. So, you have to realize that even though you fully expect your child to be virtually paralyzed unless you're hovering nearby, that's probably not the case. One of your most important jobs is working toward just the opposite — rearing your child so that some fine day, that little whippersnapper will soar marvelously well on her own. All the wonderful support and tutoring and love from you and others will catapult her on to independence and success. That's one goal of parenting and caregiving. Right now, you're learning your role, just as your tiny tyke learns hers.

Here you'll discover a few potty-training traps some parents fell into and later wished they hadn't. The headings tell you what you *should* do.

Zipping Your Lips

Enough already. Some of us have trouble with our mouths. We think we have to have the last word — with friends, mates, and kids.

But potty training is one time when you have to give up the process to your child. Her body. Her bowels. Her bladder. She has to get her act together, and your nagging will not help matters one bit.

Positive comments, on the other hand, are always welcome!

Knowing When Enough is Enough

Looking back on your child's potty-training days, you spot your big mistake: You never gave the matter a rest! You made every single blooming moment of the day a learning opportunity because you, working parent or caregiver, had little time for child-rearing and worried that your child would suffer from enrichment deprivation as a result. Your motives were good — your relentless attitude, not so good.

Lesson learned: Give the potty subject some breathing room, and your child will be much less likely to get sick to death of the toilet issue.

Curbing Your Tidying Tendencies

Douse that burning desire to straighten things up.

It doesn't matter if your toddler's pants are crooked, or she has toilet paper trailing out of her pull-ups, or she managed to upend the potty chair with her clumsiness. If you always hop in to set things right, you make your child feel not so bright and pretty clumsy. Resist the temptation. Don't set yourself up as the Goddess of Clean and Order. Kids are better off hearing much less in the way of tidying advice during potty training. So they look a little messy, or they make things topsy-turvy. The house won't fall down. You won't lose your parenting badge. Life will go on.

Stifling the Urge to Go Back to Diapers

The *Potty Training For Dummies* book told you it wasn't a good idea — that a return to baby diapers would signal failure to your child. But you didn't listen, did you?

It's easy to see how it happens: You have a long day at work and come home to a mega-accident. You're tired and frustrated and thinking that potty training on top of everything else is just too much. So you put your accident-prone princess back in diapers.

Big mistake. She loses confidence, you send mixed messages, and the process takes longer and has more setbacks.

Try to handle things one accident at a time. Don't let a single little slip ruin the progress you've made.

Resisting the Desire to Compare Kids

You knew the minute you started doing the comparison bit that you were probably crossing the line. "Your sister was trained in two weeks, honey pie." From that day forward, two-year-old Britta hit the wall. Thanks to your pointing out that she didn't measure up, she had fewer and fewer successes. And fewer. Damage assessment: She was four years old before she could be called fully potty trained.

Lesson learned: Don't compare your little sweetheart to anyone. Don't talk about her potty-training screw-ups around other people as if she didn't have ears to hear your comments. She is her own special self, and you should honor her individuality as the precious gift it is.

Stopping the Steady Barrage of Bribes

As a kid, you always envied the children who got a wad of money for good report cards. And how about those candy bars just for picking up their clothes? But your parents didn't believe in bribes, and in compensation, when your turn came for parenting, you went to the toy store and stocked up.

You bribe your child to eat his veggies. You hold out a toy to make him walk to it (first steps). And right next to his singing/dancing potty chair, you stashed a wealth of treats and prizes and expensive gifts. But soon, what seemed like a good idea at the time turned monstrous. You wound up with a child who won't cross the room unless you hold out a prize. Not his fault. Yours. So stop the madness!

Zapping the Noise-Maker Potty Chair

"I should have paid attention when I read in *Potty Training For Dummies* that people with nervous temperaments shouldn't buy singing potty chairs. What was I thinking?" By the time your child got the hang of potty deeds, you were ready for the loony bin. You never liked "Old McDonald Had a Farm," so why in the world did you buy a chair that blasted that song out every single time your toddler tinkled or pooped? That's a lot of choruses, if you think about it.

Taking a Laid-Back Approach

Looking back, you realize you were a real jerk. Your kid would flub up and pee on the floor and you'd go ballistic. You kept charts of her screw-ups in your Palm Pilot. You were, clearly, a total psycho during potty-training days.

Lesson learned: A parent or caregiver shouldn't take potty training to heart. No matter what, your child will end up using the potty just brilliantly. And she will thrive no matter how "unskillful" you are at helping the process along. Now you know it would have been better not to look at her potty success as your own personal triumph.

Laughing More, Frowning Less

One high-achiever dad tells of being so intense in his potty-training approach that he even showed his daughter a video of her making potty mistakes — tearing off the wrong amount of toilet paper, for example. After that, Grimsville was the tone for the whole potty-training process. "I should have had a sense of humor. Lots of things were funny. But I'm a control freak! Still, I found out the bottom line: Sasha's potty habits were something I couldn't predict or control, no matter how strict I was. That was true growth for me."

Laying Off the Guilt-Tripping

Parenting may not come with a manual, as people are fond of saying. But you do get a natural bent for guilt tripping. Let a big person get in front of a little kid, and guilt trips just seem to flow from his lips. One mom tells of accidentally falling into this mindset during potty training her daughter Leah. "I absolutely told myself that there was no way I would be one of those goofy mothers who make their kids feel bad. But I did give Leah little 'looks' when she had accidents. And I sighed. And I did the crossed-eyes thing. I have to admit I was a major pain. That's what I'd do differently if I got to do it over again."

Going with Your Gut

"My husband insisted that he knew all about potty training since he'd had kids from a previous marriage, so he was sure we should 'punish' my Isabel — his stepdaughter — when she had accidents."

This mom gave in to her husband's insistence on making Isabel wear wet panties around the house to make her feel ashamed. "I still remember her sad little face, and how she kept tugging on me to let her put on dry underwear," this mother recalls. "It was a really bad idea, especially when I realize now that she was doing the best she could — her body just wasn't cooperating very well at first."

Lesson learned: Follow your good instincts.

Index

• S •